THE ROAD TO PERSIA

DARIUS VASSELL

First published by Inama Enterprise Ltd, 2017

Twitter: @vasselldotnet
www.inamagroup.com

For the avoidance of doubt, everything I have recalled in this book is from memory and since no one owns history, one is theoretically free to recount actual events. The problem is always going to be that memories are flawed and indisputably selective things, so no two people are likely to remember the same event the same way. Every attempt has been made to remember the content, but I take no responsibility or liability for any inaccuracies that others concerned may identify, no matter how big or small. These are my opinions solely, and do not form the basis of any universal fact. I am happy to adjust the text in future print if I am persuaded that events or conversations were different and that my version has led to any negativity, concern or upset.

Darius Vassell on behalf of Inama Enterprise Limited.

Printed by Bell & Bain, Glasgow, Scotland.

Cover design and typesetting by Gary Webster, Oporto Sports.

Cover photography by SM2 Studio.

All other images © Darius Vassell
and Inama Enterprise Limited unless otherwise stated.

Every effort has been made to trace the copyright, any oversight will be rectified in future editions at the earliest opportunity by the publisher.

CONTENTS

ACKNOWLEDGEMENTS

There are so many people to thank, and I hope I don't forget anyone, so here goes. I'd like to thank all of the clubs and teams I played for; Romulus Boys, Aston Villa, Manchester City, MKE Ankaragücü, Leicester City and England. The thanks extend to all staff, supporters, managers and teammates for their help and faith in me.

The Aston Villa youth coaches that helped me gain my chance in the professional game, including the likes of Dave Richardson, Tony McAndrew, Kevin MacDonald, and Steve Burns. All associated club doctors and physiotherapists that helped to get me fit, showing great patience when things became challenging, and looking after my general well-being. Jim Walker and Alan Smith especially, for toughening me up and helping me to understand the importance of taking care of my physical wellbeing.

Thanks also to Stan James, who discovered me for Aston Villa, may he rest in peace. Thanks to the staff at my schools Yenton, Maney Hill and John Willmott for helping me with my education and the role they played in preparing me for life. Thanks to my housekeeper turned family friend Jo for always being there and I'm forever appreciative to those that assisted my wife and I during the pregnancy and birth of our daughter.

For the book itself, and their help, thank you to Volkan Demir, a true friend who I met in Turkey and helped me through the difficult times there and was invaluable for the chapter on my time in Ankara. Thank you to my co-author, Dean Eldredge for his time and for helping to make this project a reality and to his Oporto Sports business partner Gary Webster for the creative cover artwork and all design and typesetting within the book.

I'd like to thank all of the photographers, Press Association Images, Simon Mooney and The FA, Anadolu Images, Manchester City Football Club, TRS Wedding Photography, Antony William Knight and especially

SM2 Studio for the cover image and for the lovely photos they took of my family. Thanks also to the printers, Bell & Bain, for their guidance throughout and to the distributors Data Mailing Solutions.

Thank you to all of the media outlets who have spoken to me and have supported me during my career, and also during the promotion of this book, and thank you to the PFA who do a great job supporting current and ex-footballers.

Thank you to the FA for making sure the 'Dream within a dream' went smoothly off the field and for continuing to be genuinely friendly, professional and supportive, years after my involvement with the team.

Thanks to my motorcycling affiliates Ducati Wolverhampton, NWB and the Bikesafe project all for providing the guidance to further understand safety on both the road and track.

Thanks to Neil Fewings and WMG for all the efforts in getting my life sorted during some of the best years of my career.

To all the friends that have come and gone, to those that are distant and to those that remain close by, I'm truly thankful for all the joy that we've shared and grateful for the loyalty you've shown. I'll never be too far away.

In memory of my former manager at Aston Villa, Graham Taylor, I would also like to make reference to the fact that the majority of this book was written before he passed away. I hope I have offered a true and honest reflection of our time working together and what a good man he was.

Last, but certainly not least, thanks to my family for always believing in me; especially Vanessa and Jamie for always being there, to my auntie Marion and uncle Steven, whose company I really enjoy and lifts to training I'm forever thankful for, to my dad for sharing experiences and for always fighting my corner as a dad should do, to my beautiful wife Amani for completing me as a person and bringing us Persia and finally to my mum, for raising our family, as a single mother. Those long walks home from the child-minders' turned out to be great training for me.

I couldn't be prouder to be releasing this book, and to be telling my footballing life story, but I simply couldn't have done it without the help of all of these people.

Darius Vassell

For my family;
past, present and future.
This book is for
all of you.

FOREWORD
BY DION DUBLIN

When I first met Darius at Bodymoor Heath, Aston Villa's training ground, one thing was clear; he was incredibly quiet. That was until he was surrounded by his crew, including the likes of Jlloyd Samuel, Darren Byfield, Gareth Barry and Lee Hendrie, among others. Then he came out of his shell and from never disturbing anyone, he was suddenly pretty vocal.

D was lightning quick on the field, one of the fastest I've played with; he's up there with Darren Huckerby. He was so strong; he was the only player I knew who could do one-arm pull-ups in the gym and had more tricks and skills on the field than I think even he could manage.

Although we didn't play hundreds of games together, we knew each other's game inside out; I would talk him through a match, a role I think he enjoyed me taking on, and our understanding grew over time. Looking back, I don't think he believed in himself enough, or rather he didn't believe in the player he could become, and there was so much more to come from him. If he ever got in a bad mood, or got angry just before taking the field, defenders would see a side of him that they weren't expecting; a rampant Darius Vassell would mean a nightmare for defenders. No one could touch him.

I was so proud of D when he played for England and he never let his country down, but I just feel that if he'd have played more at club level and if his club managers had shown more faith in him, he could have earned forty or fifty caps for England. He was that good, they just couldn't live with him.

Away from the game, he's a loyal character. When he's around those he trusts he can be chirpy, funny and has lots to say, without ever being loud or arrogant. D is an intelligent boy, who has always spoken sense; it's just that people never really saw that side to him as the media part of football wasn't really his thing. He just came in, did his job and went home. In fact, on occasions he'd ring me and ask me to speak to the media for him, which I didn't mind doing. Maybe the fact that he wasn't confident enough to speak to the press cost him a little at times? Perhaps the managers he played for didn't give him enough of a chance as they didn't have the confidence in him to deliver? He just tried to let his football do the talking.

When he was younger and I was one of the senior players in the Aston Villa squad, alongside Gareth Southgate, I was very hands-on with the guys. If I did see one of the young lads stepping out of line, I would feel it was my place to have a quiet chat with them. If they continued and if they weren't pulling their weight they would know about it, and on occasion I would send them in, off the pitches, and D would see what was happening and would come over and apologise for them. We'd then go in for lunch and talk about it. Darius was a good judge of body language and he could tell if I was angry very quickly and would show respect to the senior players. He would always listen and was always prepared to work and learn.

One year we were on a trip to Dubai and we had time to go for a couple of beers in the bar. Me, D, Jlloyd, Lee and Mark Delaney were there and all of a sudden we were engrossed in a competition to show who was the strongest, led by none other than Mr Darius Vassell, one of the most competitive people I've ever come across. For over half an hour we were all trying to lift a tall and heavy bar stool with one arm from the very bottom of a leg. Not easy to do at all. It was obvious that Darius was the strongest, but he was so desperate to prove it and just kept going. His competitive edge really showed there. That edge came up again when Olof Mellberg joined the club, and Olof was very quick, but there was no way that Darius was going to let him take his mantle of being number one sprinter at the club, so Olof had to settle for second place.

Underneath his persona, D is a determined winner. He didn't allow that attitude to come through enough in his career though, as he was only confident in what he knew he could achieve and I think part of that was due to his sensitive side. I think we saw, at most, perhaps 80% of his talent; there was 20%, maybe more, left to give. I would have loved to have seen him at full capacity.

I've played with hundreds of footballers throughout my career, and due to the nature of the game, trust is a big factor for me, and probably for most footballers. I trust Darius completely and I know that he always had my back and still does. He is an unassuming, quiet lad, who in my opinion with the talent he had, should have achieved more, but most importantly now, I am proud to say that D is a very good friend.

I've got to tell you this, recently at my housewarming party, Darius and Amani both fell asleep in a car outside the front door of the marquee while the party was in full swing with music blaring. Five minutes later they woke up, slightly embarrassed and red-faced, even though you couldn't see it on Darius. I don't know if it was tiredness from their daughter Persia keeping them awake, or maybe it was something else (wink, wink) but they were just shattered.

You've always been a rubbish drinker though D, so I'm going to say you had one too many shandies. Oh and by the way, you still owe me a fiver mate.

1

GRAVITY

I was nervous, but then I've always been nervous when it came to football, and this was England. There was an incredible level of noise in the stadium, but I knew exactly what I was going to do with my penalty; exactly where I was going to place it. I shut out all of the noise and calmed my nerves. Whenever I get nervous I have to simplify things, as that's the only way I can stay focused. I had a job to do and I simply had to hit the back of the net. If I'm honest, I didn't even know what the score was when it came to my penalty, which I guess people may find hard to believe, but I just needed to block any distractions out completely. I had to score.

I visualised that I would strike the ball hard and low in to the corner. I was never a regular penalty taker, but low and hard was what I'd been taught and I backed myself to score. I believe that all footballers taking a penalty should approach it with that one focus of scoring, and ignore everything else. It isn't easy to do, but if you allow distractions to creep in then it makes your job more difficult. I didn't change my mind either. Whatever happened in the next second or two was meant to be. That was the way I looked at things.

In focusing on striking the ball cleanly, and not looking up at the goal or at the Portuguese goalkeeper, Ricardo, I saw the sand around the penalty spot lift up as I hit the ball. There was nothing we could have done to change the sand issue. We'd watched as David Beckham missed our first penalty of the shootout as this had affected him, causing a slight slip and then Rui Costa had blazed over for Portugal, but we could hardly get the spot replaced at that stage. It was the same for both sides but I hadn't wanted to allow the issue in to my mind. I paid attention to how I placed the ball down ok, with the ball sat up, but I was in my own little zone by then. Players had been talking about the sand from the previous penalties but I knew that I had to block all of that out.

As I struck the ball I lost some power from the sand issue though. It didn't feel like a crisp connection to me and the next thing I saw was that he'd parried my penalty – and then there was just noise. My head went down immediately. Emile Heskey was the first person over to me. He'd experienced difficult times with England himself, so I think he could empathise with what I was going through at that moment. I don't remember looking up again for a while. I just couldn't look at anyone. I mean, I didn't even know there was another penalty to be taken, I just thought it was all over and we were out of the Euros.

My mind turned to the build-up to this; we'd been together for so long and it had all come down to a penalty. We had trained together for weeks, living with each other in a hotel, and it all ended with me. I suddenly felt very emotional. I didn't like the feeling that all eyes and focus would be on me, and I felt as if I had let everyone down; that I'd let my nation down.

I tend to be very hard on myself and I let my feelings linger, but the players were amazing. They didn't want me to feel like that. There were some really senior players in that side, and a great captain in David Beckham, where as I was relatively inexperienced compared to them so they supported me through it.

Then there was a glimmer of hope. Portugal had their penalty to take, so there was still a chance of a reprieve; still a chance that this journey we were on could be extended. It all happened so fast though and Ricardo, who had previously whipped his gloves off to save my penalty, ended the hope. It was such a blur to me. My mind was probably elsewhere by then. He hit the ball hard and low, to the opposite corner where he saved my penalty and that was it. We were out.

My emotions were all over the place at this stage. I was just crying my eyes out; in fact most of us were. My abiding memory of the moments after the game was of David Beckham taking the responsibility for the result, and taking the blame on his shoulders. I felt like it was my fault. I'd missed our final penalty and seconds later we were out of the tournament, yet the way he conducted himself after that in terms of the look on his face and his interactions with the rest of the team showed just what it meant to him.

The team had practiced penalties throughout the tournament, after every training session. Personally, I opted out of practicing. I didn't believe that it would help me; I didn't believe that you could replicate the situation of taking one in a pressured match environment, let alone in a European Championship quarter-final. I knew I could score penalties so I didn't need the extra buffer of knowing that I could score in training. That just wasn't going to help me. Each to their own though. I know that people have debated England taking penalties after friendly matches, to attempt to recreate the atmosphere of a knockout situation, with the crowd staying behind to watch but each player would know in their heart that it wasn't the same. For me, if you are taking bad penalties then you should practice them, but if you can take them and you believe you can score then there is no point. Also, more importantly than all of that, I didn't want the game to go to penalties. I was thinking about how I could help England to win the game in normal time, not penalties. Anything but penalties.

There's always been a fascination with penalties in our country. I suppose that seeing as we've been knocked out of so many tournaments that way, it is going to be a common topic of discussion. I do think that on the whole, they are a fair way of deciding games, but at the top level in a game like that, it just seemed so cruel.

I had actually visualised my potential involvement in the Portugal game. If called upon, I imagined that it would be towards the end of the game, with the scores tight, with me needed to come on and score an equaliser or a winner. I certainly didn't imagine coming on so early in the first-half, after Wayne Rooney departed with an injury. It wasn't the way I'd seen it in my head. Normally, when I was on the bench for England, I could gain a feeling for how the game was going, and then Sven would bring me on towards the end with the aim of using my pace to create havoc for the opposition defence. I would do exactly what he asked me to do; getting in behind them and creating opportunities for others. In this game, I had to take a breather and really adjust to the pace of the game. It was almost as if I was starting the match as I was on so early. I wasn't making any mistakes before we reached penalties, but the game just wouldn't settle down and I can't remember getting that magic moment in open play that every attacking player hopes for. I felt as if I played my part in the game, and there was a strong belief throughout the side that we would win it, even though we no longer had Wayne.

As I've said, after my penalty miss I didn't want to look up and I didn't want people to see me after the game. If there was ever a hint of sympathy towards me I'd try to avoid it. I hated all of that. I was gutted and I felt hands on my shoulders at different times, but my head was in my hands. Sven, the coaches and the rest of the squad were great. I just didn't want people to feel sorry for me. I didn't like being that person and I certainly didn't want any of the attention. My tears came from the shock of it all. I don't normally cry, but I had to let it out in some way.

I guess that there was an air of inevitability about the game though. At least that's how I felt anyway. As the match went on, certainly after Portugal's late equaliser and after Sol Campbell's header was disallowed, it seemed as if there was only one way this match was heading. It seemed like one minute I was sat on the bench waiting for my chance and in the blink of an eye I was stepping up to take the decisive penalty in a shootout. I didn't even know if I'd be taking a penalty; despite all the practice and planning that everyone had gone through, there were injuries and substitutions and of course I ended up taking our seventh penalty, but you can never be certain that a shootout would go past the initial five penalties. Gary Neville stepped up to ask everyone if they wanted to take one, and then they became the first five. I put my hand up, honestly, and said that I didn't want to take one of the first five. I wasn't scared of taking penalties, it just wasn't something that I was a specialist in, so I wanted the best penalty takers to go first to give us the best chance of winning. Those who had started the game and were confident, senior players, were the ones I felt were best equipped to score. Gary was talking to me as if I was a senior player though. That was a change, as I was normally a substitute playing a cameo role at the end of the game, whereas I'd played since the 27th minute and throughout extra time. Mentally, I felt like we were in a good position at this stage. As a team we were being organised by Gary and by our captain, and people seemed ready for the challenge. I, however, remember feeling as if there was a big finger pointing down at me from the sky. I can't really explain that feeling; it was like whatever was going on around me was irrelevant and that regardless of what I'd said I was destined to end up at the centre of everything, taking a penalty. Before any penalties were taken, I took a moment and asked myself, 'how did I get here?'

Today, with hindsight, I can honestly say that playing for England wasn't something I ever expected to do. It wasn't a burning ambition from day one; it was something that happened very suddenly. Again, that same hindsight left me wondering what if? If I'd have scored and we'd have won, we could have faced the Netherlands in the semi-final and with Rooney injured I would have stood a great chance of starting the game as well. That's football I guess.

We were all gutted as a team, and I've never been part of a group of people like that. Teams tend to have different sections and dynamics, like young, older, northerners and southerners and they choose to keep themselves to themselves. We were together. I remember Frank Lampard being distraught. He is football through and through, and he seemed to take the exit harder. He'd dragged us back to 2-2 with his goal in extra time and he was in bits. Owen Hargreaves, who'd replaced Steven Gerrard in the last ten minutes of normal time, was with me afterwards consoling me as we were good friends. I was scared to go in the changing rooms, for the fear of the looks I'd get, but it wasn't like that at all.

Sven spoke at great length to everyone in the room and the staff were very supportive. Sven is such a gentleman; the kind of manager that players enjoy playing for. Despite hearing noise though, I didn't take anything in. I couldn't tell you a word of what Sven said, or anyone else for that matter. I was just looking at my boots, it was a complete blur. I know that Sven believes that was the year that we should have won a major tournament. He's had an unbelievable career as a manager, so he shouldn't have any regrets really, but I know that if he could make one change then it would have been to win something for England. Sven wasn't a complicated person, he was always straightforward with his players, but I think the way we lost that game hurt him.

After leaving the dressing room I was with my girlfriend of the time. She wasn't a WAG or anything; she had just flown out for the game that day. Obviously we're not together anymore, but she had to deal with quite a bit of scrutiny because of my penalty miss. I looked around and watched people wheeling their suitcases out, preparing to leave for the flight home and I was overwhelmed. I didn't want to affect anyone's plans, but I already had. Here we all were, leaving the tournament early and that was where I blamed myself. I felt like I had embarrassed my guests who came to watch me, when normally I didn't have many people come to my games. It was horrible. Danielle, Anthony and Nicki were all there for me. They were gutted, and I was devastated for them. I put them in an awful situation which is one of the reasons why I rarely had family and friends watch games. I was always the one with spare tickets for other players because I wasn't using mine. It was great they were there for me but I wished they could have had the opposite feeling to go along with the trip they planned. They must have been so scared for me taking that kick.

I don't think in that moment that I was handling things very well. We'd had such a great time in Portugal that I just didn't want to go home. I didn't stay long for dinner after the game as I just wanted to get back to my room, which I think was an understandable reaction. I was trying to work out what was happening next and I came to the decision, rightly or wrongly, that I didn't want to get on the plane. I just couldn't face it. There were so many sad faces around and I couldn't stand the responsibility. I had the discussion with my then girlfriend and I decided to inform the England staff via telephone conversation that I wouldn't be travelling home on the flight with the rest of the squad. Michael Owen had a property in Portugal and he was generous enough to offer me the use of it if I wanted to stay on and get my head down for a while, before returning to England for pre-season training. That offer was a big surprise for me, as Michael didn't speak that much. We all knew that he was such a quality player, but we hadn't started games together that often, so we didn't have that much of a partnership to be honest. I met Michael when I joined the senior squad, and even though we were the same age, he was always one step ahead of me within the England youth sides. He even broke in to Liverpool a couple of years before I did at Aston Villa. He wasn't my nemesis, but he was certainly a benchmark for me to match against. That offer from Michael showed what a special and close group we were. He was thinking of me straight away, and could probably see in my face that I felt sick.

Around five minutes later there was a knock at my hotel room door. My girlfriend answered as I was busy getting the suitcases packed and she was faced by David Beckham. I didn't believe her at first but she had asked him to wait and came back to the bathroom to finish getting herself ready and convince me it was him. I invited him straight in as I sensed something important was going to be said. He came through and sat on the end of my bed to chat with me. He explained to me his role within the team and the responsibility that we all shared to our colleagues and our country. He wasn't looking forward to travelling home, but he knew that we had to do it, and we had to do it together. I've never spoken about that moment, but his speech explained how much England meant to him and how it was the right thing to do. I knew instantly what I had to do; I had to go home with the team, there was no running away from it. David had experienced issues and difficulties in his career, so he understood exactly how I felt, and he knew exactly what to say. He didn't patronise me at all and he showed true leadership and character. He actually ended up taking more blame than anyone for his performances and for his penalty misses against France and Portugal. I felt that was hugely unfair. He's the captain and he's David Beckham, so I guess the focus was always going to be on him. I have nothing bad to say about him as a player or as a person. I believe that David Beckham is one the best captains this country has ever had, and I still have an admiration for him now. I have this feeling that he took the attention and blame away from me, almost to the point where people don't remember my miss. His post-match interviews were all about his own disappointment and the blame he placed on himself. That for me cemented the fact that he was and is a special person.

I look back now and wonder if I could have done anything different on that night in Lisbon. Apart from actually scoring my penalty, I wouldn't really change a thing. Ricardo, who I later played alongside for Leicester City, has since told me that he knew exactly where the England players were going to shoot, but that he had no clue with me as he'd never seen me take a penalty. He decided to take his gloves off, almost in an all or nothing gesture, as he didn't know what I was going to do. He guessed and he saved my penalty. Even if I'd have practiced day after day at the tournament, it may not have made any difference. Who knows? Missing out on going through to the finals will always be the big regret of my playing career though. Not even from the perspective of playing in the next round, just the feeling of wanting those guys to go on and win the tournament. I felt close to that group of lads, and even if I hadn't kicked a ball in the tournament and they'd have lifted the trophy, I would have felt like I'd won too. We were desperate to do it for each other, but it just wasn't meant to be.

When I say close, I mean in terms of an affinity to the group, but I wasn't a close friend of anyone when I joined the squad. I wasn't a loner, it was just that I hadn't played regularly in a team with any of them, I'd only played against them, and for England youth teams in the past. There was no one from Aston Villa in the squad, so I would bounce around speaking to anyone, rather than just being sat with the same group of people each day. Being away for that amount of time is not always a bed of roses either. Sometimes you are bored, but as a group we got on as well as you could. Those not in the starting line-up would train a bit extra and come back to the hotel later, so I was part of that, but I mixed with the regulars too. There was no hint of jealousy from those not playing; and I felt that too, especially given that Rooney and Owen were the starters, which I had no issue with at all. I knew I could help if I was needed and I had the habit of performing well for England which meant that Sven often wanted to start me, but he tried to do the right thing for the team and the right thing by everyone, which wasn't always easy.

Once it was time to go home and I'd come to my senses, I quickly composed myself and tried to move on. I didn't have the burning ambition to play for England that the likes of Beckham and Lampard had. That's not a criticism of me or of them, that's just the truth. Maybe I lacked a little something there, but it meant that I was able to return home and not be obsessed or consumed by the disappointment of the Portugal game. I think it may have been harder for them to deal with it. Maybe it was because I was a little more private as a person during my career? After scoring my first senior goals for Aston Villa in a UEFA Cup match against Strømgodset a reporter said to me, 'you don't really like doing interviews do you?' I replied, 'I just want to score my goals and then go home'. I don't know what he, or what anyone else made of my comment, but the truth was and still is, that I love football, but it was everything else associated that I couldn't stand. I knew I had to do certain things, but I fell in love with football through playing the game, not through the celebrity role that came with it.

Perhaps that helped me to process things after the Euros? I needed to get home and get on with my life. I just wanted to be away from it all, as I didn't want the reminder of our failure. I didn't envisage that the penalty would be my last kick in an England shirt, but I could cope with that, as I felt that I did a lot for England during that period. How could I be too sad? I went much further than I thought I would. I've been through something incredible, that people only dream of experiencing, and who knows, I may even be able to use my knowledge to help someone else in the future, which would be nice to do.

Until this day, the only person I have really spoken to about that fateful night in Lisbon in depth was my girlfriend at the time. As I've said, she was flown out for the game, which was a lot for her to go through at the time. She'd just come out to watch her boyfriend play a football match, and suddenly there was a level of scrutiny and exposure on her as well. Funnily enough, I remember waking up the morning after the game, beside her in bed, and I looked across at her. She was already awake, and the first words I said were, 'is it true?' We had to laugh really; perhaps that was a release of my emotions at the time. It all felt so surreal, like living out a dream that rapidly turned in to a nightmare. For that split second I really hoped that I'd dreamt it all and that the game was later that day.

When we returned home, my girlfriend had reporters calling up her work, my mom had journalists outside her house, even my old school friends were getting interviewed about me. I read stuff in the papers with people talking about me. I was asked to go on GMTV and I refused straight away. I have to say it was all very strange. I lived on my own at the time and I had a Lamborghini, a car which I rarely drove. I bought it as it was a beautiful car, but I'd just missed a penalty for England; I could hardly be cruising around Birmingham in it at the time. I kept it tucked away in the garage, and for two or three weeks I just saw the walls of my house and the local supermarket. I talk to myself quite often if there's no one around, or even talk to my grandma, just to find a reminder of worse situations going on in the world that make mine seem easy to deal with. That process helped me to adjust to being at home again, deal with failure and in establishing some form of normality. It was quiet again and I didn't have to see anyone or speak to anyone. I lived in a four-bedroom house, and remember playing Halo on the Xbox. My girlfriend could have told everyone that I was going crazy as staying in the house could be considered a sign to some people. My girlfriend would go to the shops and cook for me each night and she really looked after me, as I just wanted to rest and be at home. She never once spoke about the penalty, but somehow managed to make me feel so much more confident and better about it. I can remember her buying me some highlighter markers, she noticed that I was reading a lot and such a simple gift meant so much at the time. She showed that it was ok for me to just be me, even when I was printing out lyrics from my favourite artist just to understand the depth of what was being said. A task that would take hours as the music I listened to at the time was quite esoteric. It allowed me to relax and I was becoming a home person, and I wanted to relax before the new season started. I felt I really had something to prove.

My family just get on with things, and that was probably a good thing for me, rather than having people sulking around me feeling sorry for me. They were the best people for me to be around, for life to move on. Everyone came round for a dinner one evening and I remember my sister Vanessa took the p*ss a little, just joking around, and my dad was laughing. He asked me what it felt like for me to take the penalty, but I couldn't explain in any detail. He was wishing I hadn't taken one, as he was nervous for me. He didn't like the way he felt, so he imagined how I was feeling. Dad understood the game like me; sometimes goals just aren't going to come for you and sometimes the ball just isn't going to find me in the right location. Dad knows I'm only human.

I don't think it ever felt quite real what happened to me. I remember watching Gary Lineker in the 1990 World Cup in Italy, scoring two penalties against Cameroon in the quarter-finals. That was England for me, the likes of Gary Lineker; but I played 22 times for my country, scored six goals and played in two major tournaments. I was used for my ability and despite that night in Lisbon, no one could take England away from me. It may have flashed in front of me like a blur, but I was no one-cap wonder; I may have endured a penalty nightmare, but I lived the dream.

2

THE WONDER
YEARS

M ost of my early childhood memories involve my little sister, Vanessa. We were inseparable. I remember our first house, in the Castle Vale estate, a few miles from Birmingham city centre. It was a working-class upbringing, which I'll come to later. We had a back garden, but I was always behind the sofa playing 'cars', and the song that reminds me of those days is Culture Club's 'Karma Chameleon'. I couldn't get enough of Farley's Rusks either! I worked out where my mom, Jacqueline, kept them under the sink, and I would occasionally sneak in when no one was looking and get one.

This may seem like a big statement, but even at that age I can remember always striving to achieve a better situation for myself. Like the Farley's Rusks for example, I wanted more; I wanted better.

My little sister and I were like any siblings really. As the younger one, Vanessa seemed to get away with anything, and I was always the one who had to be told off and learn the lesson. I remember that it used to really bug me, but as an adult and a father myself, I can see why things were that way. Saying that, I think she got a lot of joy in winding me up. It might be funny now, but as a kid I felt more than a little sorry for myself. We were close, maybe because we were physically close to each other growing up in the same house, but I don't really remember my little sister being told off for winding me up; it seemed to only work one way.

Perhaps it was those early years that led to me becoming quite introverted as a child? It was easier for my mom to talk to me and tell me off, and to be honest my sister had this thing where if she decided she wasn't listening, then there was no getting through to her. I had to show responsibility in those early years as my mom and my dad, Courtney, or Vassell as he's known, split up around 1983, whilst we were still in the house in the Castle Vale estate. My mom took me and Vanessa to live in 462 Chester Road, with our grandad, and we stayed there until I went to school. It was a massive house, and seemed to go on and on forever. It was there that I realised I could do things, physical things. I used to climb over the stair rail and jump down. It was the highest I'd ever been as a kid, and I was proud of myself for not falling awkwardly. I started climbing on all of the furniture; the sofa, the cots and proving that I could do something, almost like a little challenge to myself. Vanessa would be following me around wherever I went, like little sisters do. We were looked after by an old friend of my grandad's called Joyce, who lived upstairs. She had sofas and a bed in the room and I was leaping between all three. Joyce said that I would be very fast when I grew up, but without saying anything I'd already discovered my speed, even though I didn't know what that would mean to me in later years.

At school, my speed began to have an effect at playtime. I soon realised that I was quicker than everyone else. I think that speed made it a lot easier for me to get in to football as well. I was certainly in my shell at this age; shy and introverted as I've said, but sport and particularly football, was the way that I started to belong. Teachers would be clapping and cheering me and I would feel really special in P.E., sports or playtime. I just didn't feel comfortable unless I was doing something sporty. It felt like I didn't quite fit in and that I wasn't saying the right things at the right time. I don't want this to sound like a sob story; it's the truth. My mom didn't have my dad around and she worked two jobs so rarely had a great deal of time with us. Mom was a social worker and now she works as part of a housing association. Back then, she used to take me and Vanessa as part of protest marches against the then Prime Minister, Margaret Thatcher. I think it was as a result of the Poll Tax being brought in and there was a real community spirit as we were meeting in people's attics ahead of the march. There's a photo of us somewhere holding up a banner and singing 'Maggie, Maggie, Maggie, Out, Out, Out!' Nowadays it would be seen as crazy. What parent would let their child be a part of that? But you have to understand that was my mom back then; she couldn't be like that now. It was a vibrant, different environment, where I was surrounded by lots of other kids I didn't know, and I tended to be one of the followers rather than a leader within those situations. Often, I would protect myself from being in a situation where all eyes were focused on me. Quite ironic when you think of the profession I'm known for.

Whilst living in my grandad's house, I would go to Chester Road Baptist Church, for boys' brigade every Friday night after school. I don't know why my mom sent me there, but we would play football and hockey in the gym, and all sorts of other games. My sister went to girls' brigade too. I grew up quite a lot there and discovered a certain level of independence; walking home in the dark on my own, crossing a main road and learning responsibility. The world is a different place now, but I felt like I had a lot on my shoulders then as my mom was so busy working and then looking after us, that I had to grow up quickly. Mom had a habit of taking me and Vanessa on expeditions when we were young. Be it marches and protests, as I've mentioned, or zoos or holidays; we even went strawberry picking on a number of occasions during the earlier years, which probably explains why they're one of my favourite fruits. I remember eating more than I'd put in the baskets.

After Chester Road, we moved to Emery Close in Erdington, when I was around seven or eight years old. I spent the majority of my childhood here, outdoors. Erdington is right next to Spaghetti Junction, and we were around ten minutes' walk from Villa Park. I suppose it was meant to be, somehow. Spaghetti Junction's subways and the canals underneath were my playground. I didn't just play football; it was hide and seek, we'd build dens, climb trees, play British Bulldogs, cricket, we'd even skim stones across the surface of the water, but mainly we rode our bikes through the network. That's why Spaghetti Junction is on this book's front cover; it's home and it means a lot to me. I would say that I learned a lot of my football skills around here without actually kicking a ball.

I haven't spoken too much about my dad yet. I have a great relationship with him. How do I say this though? He's never really been like a typical dad. We are great mates; he's a best friend. When we were living in Emery Close he would come over and pick me up at weekends to get my hair cut, buy me some chips and chat about football. It was great. He wouldn't tell me that he was coming though so it was always a surprise. Emery Close was on a hill with the cul-de-sac ending at the top, where I lived; it was just like a stadium with the houses surrounding us. We would play football until all hours there and I would see his car come up the hill. We'd go off to Aston and Handsworth where he was from for an hour or two and I can remember looking forward to him arriving every time.

I used to kick balls against the wall in Emery Close in our back garden as part of my practice. I had the same thing years later in Minworth, Sutton Coldfield, with a smaller garden but a concrete wall. It was my best friend, as I constantly played against it with a control and pass set up, practising when I got home from youth team training. I couldn't beat the wall and it was always going to give me the ball back. I would be stood there, alone, in this small garden, surrounded by concrete and I couldn't have been happier.

My relationship with my mom is a lot better now than it was back then. When I left the house at the age of 18 to sign professional forms with Aston Villa Football Club, we got on very well and continue to do so. As I've said, I always had the nagging feeling that Vanessa was getting her own way and I didn't feel as if things were going my way at that age; I felt hard done by. I felt that my friends were in a better situation than me. Their dads would pick them up from school in a nice car, they'd wear decent shoes and have trousers that fit them properly. Watching this, and growing up the way I did, it made me want the best. There's definitely a relationship between this and the way I have lived my life.

My mom was always protecting me though. She didn't let me go to some of the Romulus Boys' summer camps and the Church boys' brigade's trips around the age of eight or nine. I was gutted, but it was a way to protect me from embarrassment, as I was still wetting the bed. That lesson was probably what sorted me out. I used to dream that I was going to the toilet so therefore I would. I now appreciate what she was doing for me, but at the time I was so frustrated and upset.

Despite protecting me, I can still recall my first memories of experiencing real pain. I was born with a hernia and had a bubble belly, with my belly button sticking out. My mom didn't want me to go to junior school with it, for fear that I would be picked on so she took me to see our family doctor, Dr. Kumble, and I had a successful operation at the age of around five or six.

That wasn't the last I saw of Dr. Kumble though. I was so active after the operation, I managed to tear the stitches, so I had to return to the doctors. I had two choices; either have everything redone through an operation, or to have repairs done there and then. My mom said, immediately, "Let's do it now," as she was so busy with me, Vanessa and two jobs. Dr. Kumble laid me down on the treatment table, strapped me down and then introduced scissors with a hook on the end, which honestly still gives me nightmares today. He hooked out the clot and it felt like it took an age. I absolutely screamed the place down and afterwards he called me a brave boy, which I think was my first experience of someone giving me bullsh*t. I'm sweating as I write this now, but my mom and I joke about it today.

A few years later, when I was around eight or nine, I was back to see my old friend Dr. Kumble again. It was Christmas Eve and my sister, Vanessa and I were hyper with excitement and anticipation. I was chasing our cat, Tibby, around the house and, not looking where I was running, I went full pace in to the lock of the open living room door, which was broken so it stuck out. I connected with my right eye socket and chipped the bone and was knocked out cold. My mom and sister were in the living room watching TV, while the cat got away and I was told the rest of the story by Vanessa. She heard a noise, came running through and saw me lying on the floor with blood around me, and then frantically called my mom to come through, knowing that this was serious. Mom rushed me to A&E, we waited and eventually the wound was stitched but there was a small chip on the eye socket and I was warned not to chase the cat again. My mom, bless her, had been working so hard and didn't exactly get the relaxing Christmas she deserved. Sorry mom.

It didn't end there with me causing my mom trouble; Vanessa had a Game Boy and would never let me play it. My birthday was coming up, and I wanted a Game Gear, which was better than a Game Boy I thought, as it was in colour, so then I could enact revenge and not let her play it. On the morning of my twelfth birthday I walked in to my mom's bedroom, a place I rarely went in to, to receive my present. She passed me a wrapped package, which was the same size as a Game Gear box, but as I held it I knew it was too light. I ripped open the paper and it was a soccer kit; a fake kit, I think it was England, and it didn't look good, with the badge low down on the shirt. I went back in and said "Is this it?" and she calmly replied, "Happy birthday, son!" I stormed off to my room, crying, like a proper little brat and no one answered me for the next two hours. I eventually peeled myself away from my bed and went downstairs to the kitchen for a drink, and in complete disbelief there was a brand new mountain bike leaning up against the table. I certainly wasn't crying anymore. It turned out that she had tricked me, and taught me a lesson and I'd got a much better present than I could ever have imagined. The lesson I learnt was to be grateful. I apologised to mom wholeheartedly and I rode that mountain bike every day and all around the subways of the spaghetti junction for the majority of my childhood. It wasn't my first bike; my dad had got me a BMX when I was four but the seat couldn't extend anymore and I'd outgrown it. Living on a hill we would make ramps and perform mid-air stunts while trying not to break our necks.

Another great memory from my childhood was of the Italia 1990 World Cup. My mom bought me the first binder of the official sticker album, which was amazing, but I don't think she realised that you needed to keep buying the stickers and the issues to complete the collection, so my grandma, who I always spent Sundays with, would ask me and Vanessa what we wanted; I would get stickers and the next issue, Vanessa would get sweets or a toy. I remember that sticker album so fondly, despite only being ten years old. Lothar Mattheus was the first sticker I got and I read through each page, fascinated to learn about the players and the countries they played for. I was truly hooked on football.

I don't really feel as if I have strong similarities to my parents in terms of my character. My mom says I'm just like my Dad. My dad, even now, is constantly reminding me to do my best, to be the best I can be. He perhaps would admit that he didn't achieve as much as he would have liked, so he urges me on to do better. Saying that, he has always urged me to be happy, so he was balanced in his guidance. Neither are easy to do and you can't always have both.

I mean, take this for example; when I was around six or seven years old and I loved football, he told me that he played for Manchester United – and I believed him. He was my hero, so why would he lie? He explained that he didn't make it because of an injury, otherwise he'd have been playing alongside Mark Hughes. I didn't know much about football at that age, apart from two things; I loved Aston Villa, and Tony Daley was the best player in the world. I loved the game that much that I was practising my skills and tricks in my sleep; dreaming of what I would do with the ball, so that when it came to a game or a kickaround with friends, I would perform a piece of skill that no one else had seen or could do. I visualised everything and I'm sure all professionals must have done the same.

When my dad told me he was at Manchester United, I said, 'why didn't you play for Villa?' I just loved them too much and Man United meant nothing to me at the time. I was almost a bit disappointed to be honest. I used to tell all my mates that he'd been at United, and I began to think that because he'd played football, I was going to play for Villa. Soon after, I realised that he made it up. It wasn't the lie that was a disappointment; it was that it wasn't true that left me sad. He was so believable. He was such a good player too. He lives and breathes football and watches all the live games now. Maybe he had an ulterior motive for doing it; to inspire me, I don't know. Years later, when Jay-Jay Okocha was at Bolton Wanderers, Dad would call me up about this particular trick that Okocha did with a step-over, rolling the ball under his foot, and would ask me, 'have you done the Okocha? Have you done the Okocha yet? Try and score after you've done it'. That was his way of encouraging me to try and play some stylish football and enjoy it more whilst getting the recognition.

I soon worked out what school meant to me, and that I had to go. Did I enjoy school? Yeah, because I'd worked out the lessons that I liked, and made a contribution in those, asking questions and learning. I've always enjoyed learning. I didn't enjoy the time you had to arrive at school and the rigmarole of getting home. We were picked up from school by Sylvia, a child-minder and taken with around eight other kids to her home, where we'd wait for my mom, and we were always last to be picked up as she was so busy at work. We were that tired that poor Vanessa was sleepwalking to the bus stop. There was never any organisation or timing for the next bus and we'd be back home around 7.30pm. I remember those winter nights getting home late.

I enjoyed most of my time at school though; particularly music and sport, which I still do today. I started at Yenton Primary School, followed by Maney Hill Middle School in Sutton Coldfield for a year and played for their football teams, before going to John Willmott School, also in Sutton. I tended to struggle a bit with maths more than any other subject, and I can remember why. I didn't like having to keep things in my memory bank, go off and do another calculation and then come back to my original workings. I didn't trust myself that I'd got it right, so I'd be using the calculator anyway. I couldn't work out why we needed maths as well, which I appreciate now, but at the time I just switched off and lost concentration. The moment it was turned in to a competition for times tables, I was at the top of the class. I guess my competitive edge was beginning to come through. I ended up with an A and a B in English language and literature, and I got C's in everything else, so I didn't do too badly at school. It's a miracle that I did that well, when I consider that on one occasion I wagged off school with my good friend Jake Beach, as I was trying to break my personal record for keepy-uppies and Jake was the official adjudicator with a stopwatch, as he counted me through my effort. I think I reached 1500 in around 15 minutes, which we couldn't believe, but I had to stop as my eyes were watering from looking down and focusing on the ball for so long. Plus there were cars coming in and out of the car park. Thanks for putting me before your education, Jake. I owe you at least a pint if we catch up.

I'll always remember Miss Passley our teacher for science, who was the only black teacher in school. There was a trio of us; me, and my friends Danielle and Christopher who were also black, mischievous and always talking. We met her for the first time and we had been laughing and joking outside of the classroom before we walked in. She immediately split us up with Chris moved to the front, Danielle in the middle and me at the back, before we even knew her name. It worked though, as we were then not messing around. Today, she could be accused of picking us out as black kids up to no good, even though she was black herself, but what she did worked. I remember working hard that day, and I found her lessons after that quite interesting. It reminded me of my mom, completely no nonsense, with a lesson at the end. Education is something to be grateful for especially when it is free.

I played every sport at school and loved all of it. I couldn't get enough; obviously football, rounders, tennis, athletics, I even got trophies for the high-jump. Sport almost became boring for me as I was winning everything, so I'd try something new and then come first in that. My mom, who had been a good sprinter herself, would be there watching me and Vanessa, who was really fast too. There was something in our family, maybe in our heritage as both sides were originally from Jamaica. We would always watch the athletics on telly as a family.

I learned a very valuable lesson through sport as a youngster, something which helped me to avoid unnecessary confrontation during my career in the game. It was playtime, my favourite time of the day at school and I was sprinting around; any game I could play, I'd be the first in. There was a new boy at school, Simon, playing tennis, with a racket and ball that he had brought in himself. No one ever had anything like that; we'd make a football using whatever was lying around, or play British bulldogs, or hopscotch. I was confident and I had my mate, Adam Colvin with me, who got me in to Aston Villa. He was the friend who would dare you to do things and laugh his head off. So I ran at the new kid, grabbed the tennis ball off him and threw it on to the school roof. I thought it was hilarious that he had two rackets and no ball. I know it sounds cruel, but I thought it was great at the time. Simon shouted at me, and I stood up to him. I thought I was the King of the playground, a right little brat. The next thing I knew, he'd beaten me up, something I can remember clearly to this day. My head was banging on the floor, and this girl I fancied from the year above, Tessa, was crying and pleading for Simon to leave me alone. I hadn't realised that he was in the year above too. He had me in a headlock and taught me a lesson. I cried for the rest of the day and my friend Darrol Bradford was shaking his head, laughing at me in class. There was me thinking I was as cool as you like, and suddenly I'd lost my status. He'd truly humbled me in front of everyone. From that day onwards, through to the present day, I aim to be respectful when I first meet people and I take time to work them out. It was a huge moment in my life, and I was only seven or eight years old. I don't think Simon ever got that tennis ball back off the roof either.

Incidents like that didn't exactly help me with the girls either. I didn't have a girlfriend at junior school as such, although I did go out with a girl whose last name was Linford, and the reason I liked her was because my hero was Linford Christie at the time. Crazy I know, but I was only a kid. We used to walk home together, but then she'd run off and hide. I don't know if her family approved of her having a boyfriend or not. It was only pretend anyway because we were only seven or eight at the time. My first kiss was in senior school at John Willmott. I can't stress enough how uncool I was. I was like a cool dweeb I guess. The dweebs didn't socialise and would bring in an instrument with them. I was saved from that status by being good at football, so I was left alone; not quite a geek. I wouldn't get picked on as my name would be read out in assembly for scoring a goal or winning a trophy or something. I can remember hearing the word 'frigid' for the first time around then. People without a girlfriend would get laughed at. Kelly was a girl who I liked but she wasn't interested in me and I was too shy to say anything to change that. Though one time there was a perfect moment in between lessons, I was walking towards her in the school corridor, dragging my right foot so it wouldn't come off the ground. I was trying to hide the fact that my sole had separated from my shoe from playing so much football. I had hoped to speak to her, but sadly didn't as I bottled it. That sort of thing happened frequently and reinforced my feeling of a lack of confidence and not really getting what I wanted. It pushed me further in to being introverted. Then there was a whisper from nowhere that Louise liked me. She was a lovely girl and was my first proper kiss. I was amazed that a girl even noticed me. We spent the last few years of school together and I can remember her having a nice family; and there was always loads of food in their fridge, so I loved going round there. Our first kiss was in her bedroom. I'd heard people talking about 'getting off with you' and I'd feared that during my year at Maney Hill, as I didn't know what it meant, but I'm happy my first kiss was with Louise.

Louise played netball for the senior school team and I'd go and watch her, and she would come and watch me play football. We didn't speak about matches or have shared interests as such, it just felt right to be there for each other. You couldn't say a bad word about Louise, and no one ever did. Kids can be so cruel at that time, but she made me feel so comfortable and was such a good person for me to meet at that time in my life. Louise was a little bit like me; going by unnoticed, not the coolest at school, and

I guess that helped us to end up together at the time.

Music was a real passion of mine at junior school. I loved MC Hammer. I would borrow my mom's tracksuit bottoms, pin them and then imitate his dance moves as the pants were so baggy. Perhaps those moves helped me in later life to have quick feet on the pitch? Michael Jackson was a hero, and continues to be for a lot of people. Music was my thing. Whilst I was living in Emery Close, there was a group of us who were really in to music. In fact, we actually made out that we were in a group called ECP, which stood for Emery Close Posse. My sister was in it, Damian, my next door neighbour from both sides were in it too. They are going to hate me for revealing this, but we used to have dances we rehearsed, and people would jump in with a rap act and we'd make up songs. It would take up most of the day. I'm certain that some of my movements as a young player on the field, when I almost felt as if I was on auto-pilot, were influenced by dance and music. I was the kind of kid who would get an idea then really want to see it happen, this was just another example.

As I've said, Aston Villa were my favourite team. I loved the club so much and I still do today. Blue was my favourite colour, and I thought that claret and blue together was so cool. Obviously they were my local side too. I didn't just rate Tony Daley, I loved his hairstyle, how fast he was; I loved the style he brought. He didn't score that many goals but he had something special. I wanted to be exciting as a player and be the reason why my team scored, and that was why I copied Tony as much as I could. My friend Adam Colvin, who was a proper Villa fan and is still a season-ticket holder now, put his arm around me and told me to come with him to a game. I think my first game was with him and his dad, and I had never seen anything like it. I couldn't believe that many people were crammed in to one place. It took my breath away. I was scared of the noise, and then Adam grabbed me when we scored and we jumped up and down. I did it, even though I didn't really get it, but soon after I understood what was happening and it was incredible. Adam's favourite players were Alan McInally, and then latterly David Platt. They were great players back in their day; true legends of Aston Villa. I was watching these players as a fan in awe of them and never even dared to dream that I'd make it one day. I can remember being as excited as I'd ever been when I sat down to watch Tony Daley's England debut on television. Former

Villa boss Graham Taylor had picked him, and even though he didn't come on until the 70th minute, he had one run that was the best thing I'd seen that week. He was there next to Gary Lineker celebrating the goal that saw England qualify for the 1992 European Championships. I rang my friend Damian who lived ten yards away across the road, and we both couldn't stop talking about Tony Daley. He was my hero as a youngster.

I remember that around that time Adam and I would memorise the number plates of the Villa players. The club were sponsored by Rover at the time and if we recognised some of the letters on the plate we would run after the car and be waving through the window at one of the players whilst they were sat at the traffic lights. That was our thing, showing what true fans we were. It's humbling to remember those days when I think about people waving at me, or asking for my photo or autograph, especially if I feel in a bad mood or I'm in a rush to get somewhere. I was that kid, so it's important and I can't remember being let down by those heroes. Maybe I could have done more over my career when I look back? I would often just choose to come home, rather than do extra things in my career such as the players who have set up foundations and gone out of their way to do charitable work. I hope to do more in the future to help give something back.

My grandmother passed away in Jamaica when I was thirteen and she was the religious one in our family. She gave me a copy of The Bible and told me to read it, which I'm yet to do but will do one day I'm sure. Occasionally we would go to church, but she would have religious material around the house. It was a spooky place, on Trinity Road, around three minutes away from Villa Park and there were pictures of Jesus Christ on the walls and on a board above the door read, 'Christ is the head of this house, the unseen guest at every meal, the silent listener to every conversation'. She was very religious and even though I didn't read The Bible, I did go to the section about Darius, the King of Persia. I'm not personally deeply religious, but because my grandmother was, I know that there is something for me to explore there soon in a spiritual sense.

I think that religion was attached to me in later years as a young footballer. I was travelling back from an England under-18 match when I was involved in a car accident and I remember giving an interview where I just said that I thanked God I was still alive, like anyone would in a spur of the moment comment. It was blown out of proportion that I was highly religious. I didn't want to deny religion as that wasn't right in my view; my grandmother would turn in her grave if I'd have done that. Her daughter, my auntie Sandra, would take me and Vanessa to church with her on a Sunday in Handsworth after my grandmother had passed away, and she would look after us. I have to be honest and say that I didn't really want to go to church, but once I was there I would listen and try to gain something from the experience. I was a typical kid who wanted to play. Religion is not absent from my life, but I wanted to clarify that it's not as important as sometimes stated in the media.

Back to football and those early days, learning to play but also focusing on simply enjoying it. I used to play in the Armada Pub car park, right next to Spaghetti Junction and not far from Villa Park. The Armada was known for its concrete arches, and we would use them as goals. That was always the problem for us; jumpers for goalposts was never enough. I wanted to see and hear the ball go in off the post. The surface at the pub was great as the car park was flat and there were lights on, so we could play until late and of course we had the goalposts. Emery Close was just over the road from the pub, and obviously we played in our street quite a bit too as I've said. We caused so much damage over the years to houses, with footballs flying through gardens and smashing windows and we even used driveways as goals, so if a car was parked there that just meant the ball came back quicker to us. The neighbours didn't see it that way. Our instinctive reaction was to just run in to our house, but the neighbours knew it was us as we were always outside with a ball and because of the cul-de-sac shape of the street, they were sat in their living rooms looking out at us. There was nowhere to hide.

My friend Damian and I still talk about those days now and I feel I should apologise to those people who lived in the street with us. We were both so good at football and so in to it, so much so that we would buy particular footballs for different situations. For example, if we didn't have much money, we'd scrape 99p together for a 'flyaway' ball and work out techniques such as toe-poking the ball to get power and avoid the wind taking the ball in a different direction. We bought 'casers' which would curl easier. We were in love with the game. I actually learned a lot from Damian as he was huge compared to me and was really strong. We'd play as a two and the challenge for me would be to get the ball off him. I soon developed and was able to get low and steal the ball from him. I never found being physically smaller than people as a problem. Eventually Damian would go home as he'd had enough of me. He was p*ssed off that he couldn't get the ball off me. I knew I was doing the right thing and that practice with Damian was a great help.

At school we would set up for a game, maybe five against five, and it was difficult because people wouldn't even try to take the ball off me at times. I had to learn to pass more to involve others so I would get more enjoyment from playing. I would make a real point of celebrating when others did well too and I learned team skills rather than just focusing on completing the next 'move' that I had imagined.

When I look back at my childhood and relate it to my career in football, I wonder whether I could have achieved or done more. I wouldn't say a bad word about my family, but I do think about whether things would have been different if my dad had been around at home a little more. I didn't have lifts to play football, or advice at home when I needed, or maybe a bit of protection when I was in tears; like when I was substituted for the first time and I thought it was because the coach felt I was crap. The more I cried, the more some people laughed at me. I didn't understand that it was to give someone else a go and to give me a rest. The coach put his arm around me to explain, but that made me feel more on show, more vulnerable and I wanted to be anywhere else but there. I didn't like being the centre of attention and this is another example of how that became part of my character in later years. I'm not blaming my dad at all; it was just circumstances that dictated this was going to be the way things were in my family. I know he wouldn't have allowed me to feel like that and I think he wished he could have been there for me. We love watching and talking about football now and we like the same players and teams and have a close bond, which means a lot to me.

I do have a standout memory of those years which relates to my dad though. I was picked to play for the school's second team at Yenton, aged eight, wearing the blue kit and I was so proud and excited. Mrs Viles was my teacher and she did P.E. and I enjoyed lessons with her. She noticed me and praised me, and I could relate to her. It was Mrs Viles who gave me a chance, playing on the left of midfield as that was the only position left. I can remember running over to her in a panic and asking what offside was. She just told me to stay in line with where the ball was and I wouldn't go far wrong. There was no way she had the time to explain the rule just before kick-off! I was able to not know the offside rule for many, many years, based on Mrs Viles quick bit of advice. So anyway, that match was my first goal in a game and the first time I'd ever headed the ball. Two separate incidents that I'll never forget. The opposition goalkeeper booted the ball high in the air and as I looked up I realised I was right underneath it. I knew I needed to head it and I can still feel the pain today. I headed the ball on the top of my skull and it felt as if my neck was crushed down in to my body. I felt like my neck would never come back up; the pain was incredible. I vowed I would never head the ball again after that. Thankfully, after that incident and from an attacking corner, I reacted to the ball bouncing down in the box from the keeper's fist. Right footed and through a crowd of defenders I managed to score and my dad was there to see everything, which meant a lot to me. I love that he had seen me. I knew that he wanted to be there for me growing up, but I realise now, he just couldn't.

Despite wanting to emulate Tony Daley in those early years I only really wanted to be him within my own environment. I would tell everyone who would listen that I was 'Daley'. I never imagined reaching that level. At school I was told by teachers to pursue athletics as I was so fast. I went to train in Sutton with my friend Damian, and I would be sprint training or doing the high-jump, with people urging me to take athletics as far as I could. Obviously football stopped this ever materialising. In terms of careers away from sport, I was really interested in becoming a policeman. I loved the television shows T.J. Hooker with William Shatner and Street Hawk, which if you don't remember it, was like Knight Rider but with a motorbike instead of the car, and I loved Knight Rider too. Anything like that I enjoyed and the characters were my heroes. At the age of five or six, my grandmother asked me what I wanted to be when I was older. I said a policeman, and she replied, "No way, you don't want to be one of them," and the fact that I trusted her so much meant I changed my mind straight away. I don't know why she said that, but my short-lived interest in fighting crime was over before it began.

3

BALL CONTROL

I've mentioned before about how important my pace was to me as a youngster. It was as if I worked out how to be a football player by being quicker than my opponents, and therefore I could beat them to the ball and perform skills faster than them.

As a kid, in the school playground, we would play marbles on the drains or 'marleys' as we called it. If you won a game then the reward was the other person's marble to add to your collection. This other lad, who was really good at the game, had an amazing marble, but I knew I was faster than him; so I grabbed his marble and ran away as fast as I could. However, just like when I was beaten up at school by Simon in later years, I learned a valuable lesson; the other lad just kept running and I was shattered. He eventually caught up with me, gave me a few scratches for my trouble and I ended up having to give his marble back. I had no stamina, so I learned that I had to improve if I was going to last on a football field. It was all well and good being fast, but you needed to be able to sustain the pace. Later that same day, we were kicking a can around the playground. We weren't allowed any balls at infant school, and suddenly everyone wanted to play with this can, rather than with their marbles. There were loads of us playing. I managed to keep possession of the can for the whole of playtime. No one could get the thing off me and I had learned how to pace myself and felt like I'd really affected things, like something had clicked that would help me on the pitch. Back in class, the rest of the kids were still talking about how good I was with the can. It sounds crazy now and probably wouldn't mean much to most people, but it was a real breakthrough moment for me. I knew I had talent.

My first pair of football boots were Gola, with white soles and to be honest, I looked like Aladdin as they curled up at the top. I think they were too big so I would grow in to them and my mom didn't have to buy another pair for a while. I started playing youth football for Romulus Boys Club at under-9 level, and apart from school football, they were the only team I played for, before signing schoolboy forms with Villa at the age of fourteen. Romulus was a brilliant time of my life and I loved playing for them. Bob Ball was the manager, his wife Carol would do the oranges at half-time and treated us like extended family and their son Carl was the captain. They had watched me playing at school and I'd impressed them enough to be invited to come along and play for the club.

Phil Steele, the father of Chris Steele who lived near to me in Emery Close would pick me up for Romulus matches and training with no bother. I'm very grateful for that today, but I was probably too entranced in football at the time to express my thanks enough. Chris, Damian and myself loved playing for Romulus; we would discuss the match before and after together in the car. Then there was Dominic Reece's dad, Mark, rest in peace, who was first to pick me up if I was ever stuck. Dominic and I went from Romulus to Villa together, so again I had a lift to training if ever I was struggling. Dominic was a great talent and was unlucky not to get a professional contract.

My auntie Marion and uncle Steven also deserve thanks for all those lifts to and from football training. They now live in Scotland and get to visit a few times a year for updates on life and conversation about our shared interest in motorcycles and wines, and of course Persia. I actually took it upon myself to ride my first motorcycle 600 miles to Scotland and back alone. During my stay in Scotland with my uncle and auntie we all managed to ride from East Fife to the west coast and back in one day. My auntie rode pillion with my uncle riding, and I wasn't too far behind on my Ducati monster. My auntie still teases me today about the pair of expensive trainers she bought for me in my school days and how my tantrum after she refused at first forced her to overspend on her budget.

I knew what I wanted and also knew my mom wasn't going to buy me expensive new trainers anytime soon, as I kept wrecking them playing football. I must have been around 10 or 11 years old and my auntie thought I'd got the better of her.

Anyway, back to Romulus, where there was a real family feel, as we needed each other but as much as I loved playing for the club, I had a few difficulties, such as not understanding being substituted as I've mentioned, and on some of the team trips we had I experienced challenges. We'd go to places like Pontins as a team reward for winning the league or cup. There'd be the confident lads at the back of the bus, telling jokes and singing songs, but I was never one of them. I was always just watching, just being a little withdrawn and uncomfortable. I couldn't explain it, but the only time I felt comfortable was when we were playing football; the rest of the time, if we were at a disco or something I just didn't want to be there. I couldn't face people looking at me and the more uncomfortable I was, the more likely I'd be pushed in to it. You could guarantee that if there was a dance competition, or something like that, I'd be the first one called up. I felt like there was an inevitability about it happening. I felt just like that when I missed the penalty for England against Portugal in Euro 2004. Again, I hate saying all of this, but I hope people can understand that it's not a sob story, and I don't want people to feel sorry for me, but it's the truth.

I remember us being told that we had an hour to ourselves at Pontins, to go and play in the arcades and I'd be trying to enjoy it and then a group of girls would come along, and I'd be the awkward one again. None of the girls would want to talk to me, or look at me. I'm not angry about it, in fact I can laugh about it now, but I can remember that uncomfortable feeling like it was yesterday. Yet the minute a ball was in front of me, all was ok in the world. Another example of my awkwardness was when the kits were handed out, and my initials DV were embroidered on my tracksuit top, so everyone referred to me as a 'Divvy' from then on. It was crap and I'd go home thinking, not for the first time, why me?

Things didn't really change much at Romulus during my five years there. The manager and captain were the same, and I learned about consistency and continuity. I felt like I was an important fixture in the team and I improved with each season. In one of the seasons I scored over 40 goals, so I knew I was doing something right. I didn't really know what Romulus stood for as a club, but I knew that I enjoyed playing for them. Our home pitch was just off Holly Lane, quite close to my school and not far from my house on Emery Close. I can remember it all as if it was yesterday; the five-a-sides where winning meant everything to us, the cold showers which we'd do anything to avoid, the poor facilities and the hot dogs and chips after games, which was a real treat that Bob would buy for us if we had done well. It must have been pretty expensive for him as we won more often than we lost. He also let me off paying my subs, which would vary from 50p to around £1.20 depending on whether it was training or a game. Not being able to pay was never embarrassing and I'd be at the back of the queue, and I just wanted to play, but they were so good to me all those years. I must owe so much in subs now! Outside of football, those experiences and memories of being looked after and treated well, were something really special for me and I'm sure for the other lads too.

I was selected to play for the district, which was nice recognition and was also another step up in standard, but the Birmingham Boys League was pretty good anyway. There were five or six teams in the league who were competitive and we were one of the best. We'd either win it, or come second or third. There was a huge emphasis on trying to win the league, and goals against our rivals meant more and were received differently too. I think my time at Romulus helped to influence me; I mean I was always going to play football for my school, all you had to do was volunteer, but this was different, somebody wanted me to play and I learned a lot about the game in those five years.

I'm so proud of those days when I look back. Until I came to put this book together, I'd forgotten that I'd scored six in one game for example. At the time, you just want to play football and you don't think about the future. Now I realise how those days shaped the footballer and the person that I became. I remember Romulus desperately trying to keep me, almost to the extent of stopping me playing for Villa, which to be honest was never going to prevent me. There was a big emphasis, even back then, on not playing too much youth football. I remember asking Bob if he could take me to a Villa trial, and he couldn't. He did a lot for me, so I couldn't exactly moan about this. I knew that they wanted me to play for Birmingham City instead, as he'd taken me there at under-9s level, but once Villa came in at under-10s there was no stopping me. Just to wear the claret and blue kit meant everything to me. The guy who stopped me training with Birmingham City, Stan James, had scouted me. I was playing for a district side at Bodymoor Heath, Villa's training ground, and we won the game 3-1 and I scored two goals. Bob had taken me to the match, and Stan took me in to the Villa facility after the game, sat me down and he didn't exactly need to persuade me. I was ten years old, no parents with me, and the club I loved was telling me they wanted to sign me. I hadn't signed for Birmingham City, I was just training with them. My answer was always going to be yes, Stan didn't exactly have to twist my arm. I was being told by people that if I went to the Aston Villa School of Excellence I wouldn't make it as a footballer and that I would have more chance with Birmingham, but I was too young to worry about making it, I just wanted to play for the team that I loved. I might even get some kit or something.

I was given a black tracksuit, with the School of Excellence written on it, alongside the then circular Villa badge. I didn't feel like a professional, but I felt like I belonged there. I went back to school to talk to my mates about it, and I wasn't showing off, but I was so proud. Lads like Adam Colvin, who was a good footballer himself, were so pleased for me. Now I had the free tickets to take him and his dad, to repay them for the times they had kindly taken me to Villa Park. The perks were incredible; Stan James provided me with kit, boots, anything I wanted. They made it clear that they wanted me at Villa and I felt like I was in a dream. They really pulled out all the stops to make me happy. Stan got me my first Villa shirt, with Müller, the yoghurt company on the front, Vassell on the back and number 10, after Dwight Yorke. I treasured that shirt.

The first coach I remember at Villa was a guy called Warwick, and then I worked with Steve Burns. I remember him teaching me how to play as a striker with another striker alongside me; how to make runs, how to switch and match with another striker in a 4-4-2 system, which made me view the game differently. He helped to mature my game and improve my understanding of being a forward.

Bob Hazell, a former player himself, and one of my youth coaches, gave me advice that in a scenario where you are in a foot race with a defender,

I would need to get myself in front of and across him, as I was quick enough to do it. He was helping me to make it as difficult as possible for a defender to stop me. He also singled me out in training to advise me not to argue for the sake of arguing, as my teammate Steven had made around three comments to me in a row about what to do, and after the third comment I said 'I can't be fu**ing everywhere!' I was probably around 12 years old. Bob spoke loudly and I never did it again. The finger was pointing at me and it felt horrible. I knew the advice from Bob was right though.

Football was always enjoyable to me, but as I progressed and got older, suddenly there was more pressure and more structure to the games. No longer was it just a playground kickaround, or an easy win for Romulus; if I gave the ball away I was left in no doubt as to the severity of my error. I was bollocked and given how sensitive I was, I became scared of having the ball at first. I got over that, but it was a real change of pace for me to get used to. It wasn't the nicest way to learn, and now kids are not bollocked and we are a lot more inclusive and friendly, but I have to say that the fear really worked for me; suddenly, I valued possession of the ball and worked to ensure I didn't give it away as often as I had at Romulus.

I just wanted to play football matches. Training could be a bit of a pain at times, but at Villa I began to see how it could help to affect my performance in a competitive game. I would listen to the coaches, but all I wanted to do was play. I was counting down the time until the small-sided game at the end of training. We would train once a week, but then at the age of fourteen, when I signed two-year schoolboy terms, I wasn't allowed to play for Romulus anymore. Just a year before that I experienced a real setback, which I felt could have ended everything for my hopes of making it.

I was so proud to be playing for Villa and everyone around me was too. I was selected to play in a tournament in Sunderland, against Manchester United and I made an error, they scored and I immediately burst in to tears. I was the one in the team with all the negative attention on me. I didn't want to cry but I just couldn't help it, and everyone was shouting at me; it was traumatic. We kicked-off and the ball came to me and I just started running with it, skipping past players and getting closer to the United goal. I didn't know what I was doing, I was on auto-pilot, but no one could get the ball off me. I took a shot with my left foot from outside the box and it flew in to the top corner. We were level at 1-1 and I had made up for my mistake. I was crying throughout the run and then cried because of the emotion of the goal. I was a wreck. Not long after, I received the ball in a defensive position and I turned quickly and used my pace to create a counterattack. I then felt excruciating pain; a challenge from behind which caused me to fall and immediately grip my hands around my leg. I was soon taken off the pitch and I was on my way to hospital with the game unfinished. I didn't know what was happening and it was a real emotional rollercoaster. I can remember being given oxygen to ease the pain and I felt drowsy soon after. Bob Hazell, whom I looked up to, was there with a doctor and I saw the x-rays which didn't look good. I'd broken my leg and they explained the nature of the fracture. I was given a moment to come to terms with it, but I took the news to mean that I wouldn't play again. My teammates Aaron Hazell and Michael Blackwood came over to the hospital to see if I was ok, and told me that we'd beaten Manchester United 5-2, which was a nice touch. I was so happy to see them, it made me feel important.

I went home and was told that I wouldn't play for six months, but Villa looked after me really well. Des Cahill, the caretaker would pick me up in a minibus every day to take me to training, even though I couldn't take part. I was lucky as I was able to watch the first-team train whenever we weren't training. Ron Atkinson, who was the manager at the time, arranged for all of the senior players to sign my cast, which was amazing. Dalian Atkinson, who sadly passed away in 2016, was one of my favourite players, and I can remember him and Dean Saunders' signatures on the cast. The club even sent flowers to my mom, it was incredible. Before these fantastic gestures though, I was more worried about telling my mom what had happened. As I've said, I didn't have a great relationship with my mom at this stage. I was a bit of a handful at times with so much energy and attitude and she didn't have time for it. Football to mom was just something that occupied me, that I enjoyed and was safe, and also meant that I wasn't under her feet getting on her nerves by causing havoc. It tired me out and was a great way to learn a lot of team skills without realising. Having been away in Sunderland for a week, it must have been nice and quiet for my mom and Vanessa, and my little brother Jamie who had just come along, and then suddenly I'm back. Mom looked after me and her attitude changed towards me. I realised that my injury hurt her; her baby had broken his leg. I can remember for weeks afterwards, whilst I lay upstairs in bed, the egg and bacon sandwiches she made; I can still taste them now. She was up and down those stairs making sure that I was ok and I felt like the most important person in the house.

Things changed for me after the injury with Villa. Suddenly, when I came back, I was slow and I was the one that everyone was looking at. Not only was everyone stronger than me now, they'd all become men and had gone through puberty. There was hair everywhere in the showers, the talk was different, and yet I still felt like a kid. Even away from the club, my mate Damian could now beat me in a race under the Spaghetti Junction subways and that was a big blow for me, as I always used to beat him. I had a lot to do to get back to where I was.

I was worried that I was going to be released. Dave Richardson, the Head of Youth Development at Villa at the time, who now works with the League Managers' Association, and Steve Burns, who is now Head of Coach Development at Wolverhampton Wanderers, put together a list of players who they wanted to retain and sign schoolboy forms with the club. Dave then left the club and I was included on the list but from what I was told the new Head of Youth, Peter Withe, wasn't convinced and was looking to sign a lad called Nathan Lamey instead. It was crunch time, but I didn't realise it until I'd been asked to come in for a week's training and looked around and realised that the other lads, my teammates, had all been signed. None of the lads around me had any Villa kit; they were trialists, and effectively, so was I. There was a big question mark over me. The feeling was that I had gone in to my shell after the injury, and they were right. I don't think I've ever trained better than that week, throughout my whole career as a footballer. I worked so hard and everything just clicked again. Maybe the pressure of knowing that it could all be over worked in my favour, and suddenly Peter Withe was the new Stan James; my biggest fan. That week I was banging the goals in left, right and centre, and certain players were getting twisted up each time I got the ball. I could feel Peter Withe getting more and more enthused.

My mom had got me in to a Sutton school, and the lads I'd trained with, who had been signed with me must have thought I was posh. Some were talking in code, speaking in back-slang about how crap I'd become since my injury. They thought I didn't know what they were saying, but they didn't realise the background I had. There wasn't a back-slang term that I didn't know. They could call me 'itshay' as many different ways as they wanted, but I proved them wrong with my performances on the pitch. They had already been retained and in the space of a week, things were turned on their head for me as well. I'd gone from being moments away from being released, to being signed and being one of the favourites of the new boss. I was training with the youth team soon after. Years later, I was the only one who made it from my schoolboy year group to be signed professionally. All those talented young lads were let go or chose to play elsewhere.

I wasn't always destined to be a striker or a forward. My admiration for Tony Daley meant that I wanted to be a winger. People would tell me that I was skilful and I knew I had pace, so I focused on attributes such as beating the man and crossing in to the box. It was only once I had joined the Aston Villa youth team that I was morphed in to an all out striker. Maybe in those early days I would watch wingers on the television, and we were just encouraged to cross with height at pace. Now, as the game has evolved, it's clear that you don't always need or want height on a cross, and a ball fired in low can be just as effective. Back in those early days, I would even look up, just like the professionals did, before I crossed the ball in to the area. In fact, because of my pace allowing me to get past defenders, the only challenge was to lift the ball in to the air for a striker to attack. It was a skill that I became pretty good at, and it helped me in later years as a professional whenever I was asked to play out wide.

I remember my mom being with me when I signed YTS forms with Peter Withe. I don't really know what my family felt at this time. They didn't really put any extra pressure on me, I just got on with what I was doing and I would let them know how things were going. I guess they knew it was getting serious, but they never showed it. I had plaits in my hair around this time and I was very scared of the youth coaches Tony McAndrew and Kevin MacDonald. I wasn't used to their methods, and there was a lot of shouting and swearing, and they seemed very angry about things not being right. I thought to myself, 'I'm not up for this,' and on the day I went to sign my forms, I was photographed with Peter Withe and my mom, and my little brother, Jamie, who used to come and watch me play too. A few years earlier, I had been at my friend Matthew Aston's house when I found out that my mom was in labour with Jamie. My mom and Jamie's dad had split up before he was born. I was young and I didn't really know how to react. Matthew's mom asked if I wanted a lift to the hospital. I was so happy, and the three of us went there and we were the first to meet little Jamie, which was a really nice moment, something I will always remember. It was an example of my mom and I becoming closer – just like when I broke my leg. I was really grateful to the Aston family for everything they did for me that day.

After signing for Villa, we went off for the summer, before returning for pre-season training. At home, on the eve of my first training session at that level, I took the decision to shave my hair off. I was so scared that they would judge me for the haircut I'd had for the last three or four years. That was the moment when I knew football had become serious; it was now my job. My hair was my thing too. I looked like the guys on television in music videos, like KG Goldsmith from the group MN8 who were popular at the time, and I thought I was cool, but I didn't want to give anyone at Villa a reason to single me out, or to think that I wasn't taking things seriously. I was looking ahead at what I felt they wanted, and I'd hoped that the coaches noticed that I was dedicated and that I wanted this to work. I ended up being called 'Yeboah' after the explosive striker Tony, as I'd not shaved my hair properly and ended up with a dodgy hairline at the front of my head like he had.

Kevin MacDonald really gave me belief and confidence in my ability; he always said just go and score, which sounds simple, but it showed to me that he believed I could do that. I tried to do just that later in my career, against Coventry City at Villa Park in May 2001; straight from kick-off I ran with the ball and the defender Paul Williams gave me the worst tackle I've ever had, as I somersaulted in the air. He just about assassinated me! Needless to say, I didn't try that again. I can also remember being taken in to an office by Tony McAndrew who reminded me of what Dwight Yorke was achieving at the club, and he said I could have all of that and more. Dwight had become a hero of mine, so Tony's words meant a lot to me. I started believing in myself from there. Tony could be loud, shouty and would swear. He would often say to us, "You better perform or you'll be standing next to me." Michael Blackwood and I were both subbed after around 15 minutes of one YTS game for not applying what we were being taught and playing below the standard the club had set, and when we were stood next to him on the sidelines we realised it wasn't an idle threat.

One of the things that shocked me most was the amount of time we spent at football, without actually playing football. Michael and I would be in the gym any moment we could, kicking the ball around, playing head tennis. As soon as we heard the noise of someone coming in, we'd be back on our jobs, cleaning boots, sweeping the dressing rooms and making sure that kit was packed away neatly. We had to look after the first team, clean the dressing room, or even wash the manager, Brian Little's car, although on one occasion we managed to mess that up by stripping the paintwork off his car as we used the wrong cleaner on it. There were some moments of boredom, not much, but I guess that we were taught good lessons which helped to ensure that we were disciplined. I was given the task of cleaning Fernando Nelson's boots; a Portuguese full-back who was very religious and he was coming to terms with the English culture. He gave me a few tips, a bit of money for my work, I was so grateful and those days were amazing. We were always being told that our YTS days would be the best of our lives and they were really something. So many laughs and in-jokes, that only those twenty or so lads would remember and understand. They were great days. Not many of the lads made it professionally; Martin Ridley, who I am still friends with has done well for himself and was a professional golfer having caddied on the women's tour. He is now studying for his Masters. There's no great story of lads I am still in contact with, but for those couple of years we really did create some memories.

Gareth Barry, who was in the year below me in age, was given his professional contract a year before me, so he could have avoided doing the chores, but being the good guy he is, he helped us with our jobs. Gareth's age group were a lot more focused than ours, we were a group containing some contrasting characters and were difficult to handle. Only me, Martin Ridley and Michael Blackwood were retained from my group, and only I played for and made it at Villa. It was heart-breaking to see each of the lads go in to the office, one-by-one, only to be told that they were being released. I was gutted for my friend Dominic Reece, who was someone I felt should have made it. We'd grown up together and he was the one that everyone felt would go on to be a professional, so I was hoping he would make it through with me, but he didn't. His dad often picked me up when we were younger, as they lived in Aston, and would take me to games and training. I've kept in touch with Dominic a little, and he's in to motorbikes, which is a real passion of mine, and I'm pleased that he's done well for himself and has a family now. I can also remember Darren Middleton, who was in the year above me at Villa and how upset he was when he'd been released. He was such a good player but unfortunately he didn't make it. Fast forward to today and he's set up an academy for players who have been released, at Lichfield City. He's been through that experience, so he's able to give something back to help others and I'm pleased to be going along to hand out some awards soon and offer my support to him.

Tony McAndrew had spoken to me before my meeting which would determine whether I was being retained, and he made sure that I wasn't nervous, which I thanked him for. I respect him, not just because he signed me, but because he understood me and I think he knew that I had it in me to get worked up about the meeting and be uncomfortable. I was given the whisper that I would be retained, and I've never told anyone that until now. I think that people felt I would be signed, as I had scored goals and played well, but you can probably imagine that in my mind, until I actually signed I felt that something would go wrong. I can remember thinking to myself, 'you watch now, something will happen and they won't sign me, that will be just typical,' but thankfully that moment didn't come. Even today my wife calls me a pessimist, but I think I've always just been realistic. You can't always get what you want, and I had experienced disappointment and moments of real worry, so I was always cautious if something positive was about to happen. I didn't like having to face failure, so I was always guarded against it.

I have so much fondness for those days. One day it was a nightmare for you, with all the jokes on you and the next you were laughing until you had tears running down your cheek. We were like a band of brothers, creating real empathy and there was always something happening, most of it unprintable. It was a different time back then, and I understand that football has changed and that players have to be protected now. I got such a good grounding at YTS level; anything that was missing from my home life was made up for at YTS. Maybe kids today are missing something as academies are so structured, but that's not for me to say really. Even back then we had basic education, so the lads who had five GCSEs went to the clever college, which included me, and those who didn't went to the thick college as we called it. On one occasion the other lads had got in to so much trouble; our coach called us in to the gym at Villa and the Henley College lads, including me, were told to stand on one side and the other lads over the other side. They had caused so much mischief at college and the coach read them the riot act. They had to do extra jobs and chores, there was all kinds of language coming out and I can remember being so pleased that I wasn't in their shoes. We laughed about it afterwards though and there'd soon be another story or another prank going on.

On one occasion, we had to run around the boundary of Bodymoor Heath, in the snow, as punishment for bad behaviour. I knew I'd be at the back as always. We were punished as a team, but it was nothing to do with me, so I was even more distraught as this was as tough a punishment for me. Jim Walker, our physio, had to come out and run with me as I was crying. I was so tired, with snot dripping down my nose, which was frozen on to my face. Jim made sure I was alright. These things don't happen now, but they built up my hatred for long distance running. If there were no balls around at pre-season for example, you knew we were in trouble. Often we would train for pre-season at Kingsbury Waterpark or we would run along the canals. We'd be told on that morning we'd be doing it. I'd turn up, excited to play football and then be told we would just be running. I used to dread doing it – I knew I would be at the back, my heart would skip and my stomach would do somersaults as I hated being shouted at or singled out. I also hated that feeling when your back's about to cave in and you're still on the first lap.

Towards the end of my time in Villa's youth set-up two South Africans, Bernhard Coutinho and Bradley Blackburn were brought in. I immediately made good friends with them as they were living at the training complex and I was more than happy to stay late at the club I loved, while everyone had gone home. There were great facilities at Bodymoor Heath at the time and having the place at our entire disposal brought a lot of fun that only the three of us were aware of until now. We would drive the club minibus around the empty complex and help ourselves to Lucozade and cereal bars in-between bouts of head tennis in the gym, where the winner stayed on. When training started the next morning, no one, except Bernie and Brad, were aware that I'd been there all night, which was probably the reason why it took me a while to get my tempo right in training sessions as I was knackered from the night before. Those were the days.

I remember Paul Merson coming in to speak to the youth players about his problems with drugs and alcohol. It was really helpful and good of him to do, but my strongest memory of the chat was when he was asked how many England caps he got, and he said, "I should have got 50-odd caps, but I got 21 instead as Carlton Palmer had the rest of my caps from Graham Taylor."

At youth team level, managers and coaches' boots would be slung in to the dressing room if we were too loud at the training ground. As a youth team, it would remind us that we had to get our jobs sorted out. The training ground was always spotless, and we kept it that way. We learned real life skills there.

My job on away team duty was the medical skip, so I had a close relationship with Jim Walker and then later the first team physio, Alan Smith. Michael Blackwood had the worst job of all. He was on first-team footballs duty and he had to pump them up to the correct pressure. It was the hardest thing to get right and the moment a player made a mistake they would blame the balls. I was organised with my job; I had a checklist to make sure that everything was in the skip and got a pen, paper and ruler from Jim to do it and I checked everything in and out. My main concern was whether the Vaseline was missing or there being no tie-ups, and I was scared that the finger of fate would be pointing at me if I'd forgotten anything. Darren Middleton guided me through this as he'd done exactly the same job a year before and was now my mentor for the role.

There's a lot more structure now. I started doing my coaching badges back when I was in the youth team, for example, but as soon as I joined the first-team I was taken off of them, and I only returned to doing my badges once I'd finished playing. Now players are encouraged to do them whilst they play. It's not seen as a distraction; it's part of your footballing education and allows you to see the game from another perspective. I can remember promising Tony that I wouldn't go and spend my first wage packet on a brand new sports car. Instead, I got a nice Peugeot 306 to match my team mate, Michael Blackwood. It was all about music with us as we would fit the cars with sound systems, driving home from training was a concert on wheels.

Another funny story from those days happened when I was around 16 years old, when I met a girl named Stacey Bournes, who worked in the hospitality department of the club. I was there with my dad, watching a game, as I think I was injured. My dad started chatting Stacey up on my behalf, and asked her straight away, "My son wants your number," as I was painfully shy. She had a boyfriend at the time but gave me her number anyway, to be polite. The boyfriend got wind of this, got hold of my number and messaged me that he would blow my kneecaps off if I went near Stacey. I'd only just started using a mobile phone and trust me, I was scared. Despite this, I kept my kneecaps intact, and me and Stacey ended up best of friends, still in touch today, not living far from each other and sharing an interest in music. She spends most of her time travelling now but utilising modern technology I was given the opportunity to play guitar on one of her tracks not too long ago, I appreciate this a whole lot.

When I look back on those days, I don't really have any words of advice to give to my younger self; I just wish someone like me now would have been around then and watching over me. I needed someone if I was going to be a world class player, a little guidance and security. I didn't need someone to tell me I was good, but just someone to advise and encourage me off the field. He or she could reinforce what the coaches were saying and add more to it. Someone who knew the ins and outs of the game or had some experience. I took a lot on my own shoulders and had to rely on others around me so much, for which I'm grateful. I would use my imagination as much as possible. I loved my family and still love them now for everything they have done for me, but I could have done with someone from outside of the club and my family to help me adjust to my new environment. Little did I know just how different my life was about to become...

4

INITIATION

My two years as a YTS were incredible. We were thrown together as a group of young lads, and we became friends; we became a family. As I've said, only three of us made it through to receive a professional contract. I was given a three-year contract at the age of 18. Now it was real. I was a professional footballer for Aston Villa, the team of my dreams.

I felt like it was a just reward for my hard work. I'd come from the bottom of the group; both in terms of when I started, and then when I had to start again after the broken leg. Hard work and dedication and a little bit of luck was the only way I was going to make it. It was certification for everything I'd done. I kept saying the word professional in my head. It was something I'd heard throughout my amateur years, and now I'd realised my ambitions. For me, as a boy, to be able to say to people that I was being paid to play football, that it was a job but was still something I loved, really meant the world.

I knew before I signed that it was serious business now though. The first-team manager at the time was John Gregory, who had taken over following Brian Little's departure. I was so scared of John at first. It was pure fear, as I didn't want to let him down before I'd even had the chance to show him what I could do. He would have known a little about me from my time in the youth team, and I had trained with the first-team on a couple of occasions, but now he would be watching me up close and personal and I knew I had to impress right away.

I wanted to impress with how I looked too, so when I received my first call-up, me, Jlloyd Samuel and Gavin Melaugh went to buy my suit, which was a big experience for me. This was my first-team suit, and I was asking all of them for advice on what to try on and which one to buy. It was Dion Dublin who taught me to tie my tie properly, in a Windsor knot, a couple of months later when he joined from Coventry City.

By this stage in my career, I'd been given a few nicknames, which were all quite embarrassing; Droopy D for always looking sad, Diesel D because I was late for training yet lived the closest to the training ground and on one occasion I ran out of diesel in my car, so I had to park reluctantly just inside the front gate, in an odd position which everyone could see whilst we trained. I was even known as 'Uggers' for a while in the youth team as a nickname that was said to try and affect me by the older guys, and it certainly had me questioning whether I was ugly or not. A lot of people got this name at some stage. We were adolescent and there was this massive boil on my nose and I was so embarrassed. When a player took the p*ss it was strange because that's when it started to go down and then the p*ss taking player got it, right on their nose, and it was like we were being taught a lesson by this boil. I think five different players got it consecutively but only if they had took the p*ss. I was also known as 'Spiderman' for a while, as I tried to control a cross-field pass on one of my first training sessions with the first-team. As I stretched to control it, I kept the ball in play, but I was still falling backwards and landed on to the back of a 5-a-side goal net at the side of the pitch, getting tangled like a spider in a web in the process. Either Ian Taylor or Mark Draper shouted, 'there's Spiderman!' and it stuck for a while.

Jlloyd Samuel was known as J Love for a while, and I was called Woss, like we were in a band or a dance act. It all started when we were on a youth team trip to Germany, and when we took part in a penalty shootout the tannoy guy read our names out before we took each penalty. Mine was read out as Dar-ee-us Woss-all and Jlloyd was J Love Samuel, so it stuck from there. The youth team were all giggling at us, but we still had to take our penalties, which I missed by the way, as I hit it over the bar by trying to whack it.

INITIATION

Jlloyd and I would room together at away games in the first-team squad under John Gregory. The first time we were together we looked at the mini-bar and thought it was all free so we took everything home with us. The next week, Gregory called us in to his office to say they'd had a call from the hotel explaining that there was a charge for everything we'd used. He thought we'd got p*ssed before the game, so we had to explain that we hadn't and we'd just taken it home. I suppose it showed how young and naïve we were. When Jlloyd and I hit the town in those early days, he would say that he was a builder and that I was an architect. No one really knew who we were, but if we'd have said we were footballers then people would have been around us and we wouldn't have been able to dance. If you know any builders or architects then I doubt they will dance like we did.

I had noticed how good Gareth Barry was with both feet when he joined the club. Jlloyd was both footed, as a defender, which seemed weird to me at the time. I was similar and we appreciated that skill with each other and we would even label names of our shots. He was a hard-tackler, and we called those tackles a 'breaker', not to break legs, but just to be a perfect tackle that made that sound where you know the defender took everything including the ball. He would let the striker believe that he could beat him and then sense when the player was about to move, and that's the moment he would hit with the breaker. I would do the opposite with a defender, luring them in to tackle me and then I would accelerate past them. My shot was nicknamed a 'Schlazer'; I would strike across and through the ball with my left foot, and the ball would deviate in the air but stay on a general line. I did it for the England under 21s against Holland and scored with it. I believe it's important, especially nowadays, that you can be proficient with your weaker foot as well as your stronger one. Defenders should believe you will use it when necessary. It's a great foil if they don't know what foot you prefer to use.

I was named on the substitutes' bench for the first game of the 1998/99 Premier League season, for a 0-0 away draw against Everton. I was so grateful for the experience of being involved, without having to actually play. I know it sounds childish, but at the time I was simply scared. I was looking around at senior players like Gareth Southgate, Ian Taylor and Dwight Yorke, and I felt a little out of my depth. To be able to sit on the bench and soak up the atmosphere was so helpful in making sure I was prepared when I was called upon. The noise was incredible. I'd been used to playing in front of a few people, and now it was sell-out crowds of up to 40,000 and over. Gregory didn't call on me for the Everton game, as it was poised at 0-0, but in the next game, a 3-1 home win over Middlesbrough, I made my debut coming off the bench with nine minutes remaining and the two goal cushion already established. It was perfect. I was able to get a run out, breathe in the air and be a part of the team in front of the Villa Park fans. I can vividly remember walking off at the final whistle and taking it all in. They say you never forget your debut, and I can picture it all as if it was yesterday.

Having made my debut, I felt so grateful to Tony McAndrew and Kevin MacDonald and I didn't want to let either of them down. I would prefer them to be proud of course. They'd set such a high standard in coaching terms, that the longer I stayed in contention to make it as a professional, the more painful failure would have been for me. That's why my fear had grown. I would link this feeling to when I shaved my hair off so that I wouldn't draw attention to myself, and to avoid Tony and Kevin thinking that I was a trouble maker. I would worry about everything; I had to make sure that football would be the only concern. It took ages to get the hair done too and that time was no longer going to be available. They taught us well, and explained about responsibility and doing things right, but often I would struggle to just about get in for training on time. Now that I was with the first-team, there would be no room for error. I knew I'd had support from Tony, but I'm not sure if he even knew how much he'd supported me, as he was always so stressed from dealing with our group as there were some lively characters in there as I've explained.

After the victory over Middlesbrough, we won the next three matches against Sheffield Wednesday, Newcastle United and Wimbledon, without conceding a goal in the process. I had a four minute run-out against Newcastle, and all seemed to be going well at the club. John Gregory had taken over in the previous season after Brian Little resigned. He had been managing Wycombe Wanderers but he was well-known at the club having coached under Little previously. The club was in 15th place when Little left and Gregory got us up to 7th, which meant we had qualified for the UEFA Cup. Following the great start to the season, we prepared for the first round against little-known Norwegian side Strømsgodset. I was named on the bench, and we found ourselves 2-0 down. I can remember dreading the situation; we were in a mess and I looked around at the fans, who, had I not made it as a player, I would have been standing alongside, and I could feel the frustration and the anxiety. I was asked to warm up a few times, and then with ten minutes to go I was called over, and I replaced a good mate of mine Darren Byfield, who had played really well and was very unlucky not to score that night. Gregory got a hold of me and said something along the lines of, 'get in the mixer and get me two goals, son.' We were in a desperate situation and we needed a miracle to get out of it. I just nodded my head nervously, with my Villa shirt two sizes too big, and I ran on to the pitch full of energy. I had the words 'get in the mixer' running through my head, and I tried to stay in the box, without being offside. Again, I didn't want to let anyone down. Gary Charles grabbed a goal back for us as we lay siege to them, and then with moments left and the ball bouncing around their box, Lee Hendrie guided it towards me, I stuck a foot out and the ball was in the roof of the net. We were level at 2-2; I'd scored my first goal for Villa, at the Holte End. All I heard was noise, and I started running with my arm in the air. 'Where do I go now?' I thought. I was that shocked that I didn't really know how to celebrate! No sooner had we restarted, and Ian Taylor slipped the ball to Alan Thompson, who jinked his way through the defence, shot at goal, the keeper parried, and I raced on to it to stab it home. I knew as soon as he pulled his foot back that he was shooting so I was on my way to get the bits and pieces. A couple of us could have scored, but I was already in the middle of my stride and that goal was going to be mine. The Holte End erupted and I went wheeling off to celebrate. It was such an explosion of joy and relief. We'd won 3-2, and I'd scored two goals in the space of a minute. The final whistle blew and my second goal turned out to be the last kick of the game. Throughout the whole ten minutes, I was just acting on auto-pilot. None of this was in my plan for the night, I just expected to be sat on the bench and then I'd go home to have some late tea with my mom. Instead, I was leaving the pitch to congratulations from all of the senior players, the staff and the supporters.

After the game, I was surrounded by cameras and reporters, wanting to talk to the 18-year-old local lad who'd won a UEFA Cup tie. It was absolutely bonkers. I remember having a large zit on my head and I really didn't want to be in front of the cameras with that showing! The players who normally dealt with the media were walking past me and I was half expecting someone to tell me that they should be the ones speaking, not me. I said a few words and headed home. I walked in through the front door, and my mom was lying on the sofa, as she'd been watching her soaps after a hard day at work. There was a sports round-up at the end of the late news; she was watching and was about to fall asleep when all of a sudden my mug pops up on the TV! She rubbed her eyes and screamed at me, "Why didn't you tell me?" We sat up and watched the highlights on the midweek Match of the Day, which was hosted by Gary Lineker and Trevor Brooking, so it must have been surreal for her, as it was unbelievable for me.

Even though my life changed when I signed professional terms, it truly changed that night against Strømsgodset. I'd seen my name in the matchday programme, scoring goals for the youth team, but I'd never experienced that kind of adulation and media exposure. Grabbing those two late goals was enough to justify my involvement at first-team level; I'd taken my chance, but for me it wasn't anywhere near enough. I'd had a taste of the action and I wanted more. I looked back at the goals on the highlights and I felt like they were instinctive goals, but nothing more. I knew I could do better.

I was an unused sub in the next two league games; a draw at Leeds United and a home win over Derby County. The team was flying, and I managed to gain some further experience away to Strømsgodset in the return leg, coming on for Julian Joachim after 67 minutes, with us already 3-0 up thanks to a hat-trick from Stan Collymore. It was a weird experience for me, flying out to Norway with the first-team. There was a lot of focus on what to eat, staying hydrated and being comfortable on the flight, all of which seemed very professional to me. The game was a completely different atmosphere to the first leg, and I was just glad that I'd played my part in getting us through and avoiding any embarrassment. The joy of my achievement in the home game was over so quickly, and everything moved on. That was something I had to adjust to, as in the youth team we'd be talking about a successful game for months afterwards, but at first-team level you just had to move on to the next game and be professional.

I was an unused sub in the second round first leg against Celta Vigo, which we won 1-0, but then we were knocked out 3-2 on aggregate, and despite me coming on with just over 20 minutes to go I wasn't able to repeat the story from the first round. Celta Vigo then went on to knock Liverpool out, so they were a good side. I didn't appear again until the 23rd January 1999, as a second-half sub in a 2-0 home defeat to Fulham and again the week after in a 2-1 away defeat to Newcastle. I was then introduced as a substitute in the final three league games of the season against Manchester United at Old Trafford, at home to Charlton Athletic and away to Arsenal, all of which ended in defeats, but I felt like gradually I was gaining experience. We finished sixth that season and just missed out on qualification for the UEFA Cup. It was quite a year of change though; having sold Dwight Yorke at the start of the season to Manchester United, we had brought in Dion Dublin, Paul Merson, Steve Stone, Alan Thompson and Steve Watson to strengthen the squad. They were all household names and I was training with them every day.

I had been a real fan of Dwight's whilst playing in the Villa youth team. The ultimate accolade for a young player at that time of their career is to play well on the weekend for the youth team and then be invited to train with the first-team on a Monday morning. When it happened to me, I really began to realise what a superb player Dwight was. There wasn't a player in the team who could deal with how strong he was. He always seemed to be enjoying himself on the pitch; he was relaxed, playing with a smile and scoring goals. I didn't get that. I felt like for most of my career I had to be serious on the pitch, I had to concentrate and it was my job. The pressure of my role didn't allow me to relax and enjoy it, especially in those early days. He was untouchable in training and then when I watched him again from the stands, it all made sense to me. In fact, if I watched him in a game, as soon as I knew he was about to receive the ball, I'd take my eyes off him, as I knew he would control it and I'd be looking ahead of him, knowing that he'd play a great through-ball or start a one-two. There was always anticipation when he had the ball and that was really inspiring to me. He was also a very reliable player, and worked hard, so I knew I had to learn these skills and add them to my game if I wanted to compete at the highest level. I was gutted that Dwight had left the club, as a player but also as a fan, but those new signings, like Dion Dublin and Paul Merson, really reignited my love of the club and inspired me, especially as it was around the time I was breaking in to the team.

During the summer I went on holiday to Ayia Napa, aged 19 years old, for my first and only real lads' holiday. I loved the garage music, but I hadn't realised until then that I preferred going out with girls, rather than trying to find them on a night out. There was an almighty competition going on throughout the whole island for who could get the most girls. I was bumping into lads I knew through football and it felt surreal and uncomfortable at the time. I remember getting a call from a contact at Villa saying that Julian Joachim was possibly leaving and I used that as my cue to come home a week early, leaving five friends out there, so I could prepare for what I hated most; pre-season training. I was only a teenager at the time but football saved me from that awkward feeling I had on that holiday. It was the perfect excuse to come home, as I was too shy for all the shenanigans I was witnessing, whilst working out who I was.

In the 1999-2000 season we finished sixth again for the second season running. We finished as runners-up in the FA Cup to Chelsea, in the last cup final to be held at the old Wembley Stadium, and missed out on another cup final, losing to Leicester City over two legs in the League Cup semi-finals. We qualified for the Intertoto Cup, but I didn't manage to score that season. I was involved sporadically from the bench and made my first start for Villa against Chester in the League Cup second round second leg, in a 5-0 win, playing the full game with Dion Dublin alongside me. My first league start came a few weeks later, away to Sunderland in a 2-1 defeat, and I was gradually becoming comfortable at that level, despite only being 19-years-old. I was a player who could change the game, provide assists and spark life into matches. My team mates would encourage me to keep this going.

Dion sustained a serious neck injury in December in a 2-1 home win over Sheffield Wednesday after connecting with Gerald Sibon. I knew it was a bad injury for him and as soon as it became clear just how serious it was, we started to wonder whether he was in real trouble, not just with his career but with his life. It changed the pecking order at the club, as he would be out for a few months and had to have a titanium plate put in his neck, but all I could do was worry about him. I was worried that he was going to be paralysed and it was strange to see him so helpless, but full credit to him and his strong character that he made a full recovery and continued to have a great career on the field, and a successful one off it today.

I wasn't knocking at the manager's door at this stage in my career. I felt like I was ready to play, but that wasn't my style and I was still learning my trade. It appeared to me that Gregory knew that I was a good player, but we didn't have a relationship at this stage as such. He'd added his own players and to get his attention was going to be quite a challenge. He was very sure of himself and comfortable in the role as Villa boss. The dressing room and characters within there were strong, but he was always able to handle things; after all, he'd brought some very good players in.

Gregory was almost too cool for school and he always looked the part. I don't want to upset him when I say this, but his hair was never ever out of place. One story of our relationship is one that could so easily have ended things for me, before they'd even started. We'd find out we were in the squad, and normally if we didn't make the first-team then we'd help out with jobs around the place. We'd have the kit on and feel part of the first team and I absolutely loved it. I was on the bench for a first-team away game, my other youth teammates were sorting out drinks for the players and it was really busy, a hive of activity with massages, tape being put on socks and lots of shouting and motivating. Gregory was sat in the corner in his Italian suit, writing down instructions and set pieces. Me, Jlloyd and Gareth Barry were playing keepy-uppies. I got in to the game, lost control of the ball as I was in the zone and I stretched to save the ball from hitting the floor, and it was just too far away from me. The ball came off the end of my toe and as I was stretching I kicked it harder and the ball fizzed past Gregory and missed his face by a millimetre hitting the wall behind him instead. I was convinced that if it had hit him that would have been the end of my career. His head probably would have hit the wall behind him and I'd be in all sorts of trouble. It seemed to take an age to reach him, by which time Jlloyd and Gareth had moved away and looked as if they weren't even playing with me. I would have been in the sh*t if the ball had struck the boss and sent all his team sheets in the air, I just knew it. It was a real thank you grandma moment, something I would always say if I had any fortune in life. It's the image I tried to recreate on the book front cover, 'thank you, Grandma.' It wasn't a one-off though, as on another occasion at the end of training, Gareth pinged an 80-yard ball across the pitch and it hit Gregory flush in the face. I looked straight towards Gareth, but he was looking in the opposite direction to the incident, far in to the distance, as if he was pulling a 'Blue Steel' pose from the film Zoolander. It was one of those moments, like when you were in a classroom and something funny happened, where I had to do everything possible to stop myself from laughing. 'That's out of order, it's not funny,' I tried to tell myself. As it was from so far away, Gregory had no clue as to who did it and he just went red-faced, muttered something and walked in to the training ground complex. We had got away with it. Sorry gaffer.

Gregory was a good player and he would join in in training, and he'd be in the passing drill line as part of a pre-match warm-up. The point being that you could never hide. He'd shout, 'How's your touch?' just as you were about to receive the ball. You couldn't even lean on walls as a youth player. He always had us on our toes and that was good. He wasn't past it, he could do what the other players could do with the ball and I made sure my touch was spot on whenever he passed it to me.

I was contributing assists, or playing solid cameo roles at the end of the game and I felt like Gregory could rely on me. I didn't allow myself to go crazy about not scoring in the first half of that season as I was still young and there was less pressure on me to get the goals. I was coming off the pitch with the team talking about how I'd caused havoc, or provided a good cross for the goal. It felt like I was able to make a difference. I guess when I look back, this was a time that I was perceived as a substitute, with multimillion pound players ahead of me, and it was up to me to prove that I deserved a place in the starting line-up.

Unfortunately, the chance to further prove myself was taken away. I'd already limped out of the action with a hamstring injury at Sunderland in a 2-1 defeat, which was the second time I'd suffered that injury, worked hard to get fit again and was back on the pitch just over a month later, before my bad luck with injuries struck again just over a month after Dion's injury. I was stretchered off on Saturday 22nd January 2000, after coming on as a half-time substitute for Julian Joachim in a 0-0 home draw with Chelsea. It was a strange injury really, as I slipped in the corner of the pitch, in front of the Holte End. Our physio, Jim Walker, had initially thought that my ankle was badly twisted, but just a week later the scans showed that my ankle was fractured. This was the second time I'd suffered a major injury, after breaking my leg as a youngster, before I became a professional.

The injury meant that I didn't play again that season. I can remember the amount of extra training that was needed and watching the team go out to train each day while I was on the exercise bikes in the gym. I also missed the chance of playing in the League Cup semi-finals against Leicester City, which were just after my injury and the FA Cup final that season, which was against Chelsea. I went along to watch as a fan and support the team, but I was gutted to miss out. Gregory joked that I was made of glass, but I was desperate to prove to him that I could remain fit and injury-free for a whole season and show the team that I was reliable. In the 2000-01 season I began to play more of a part in the first-team. We finished eighth that year, were knocked out of the domestic cups quite early, but reached the semi-finals of the Intertoto Cup before losing to our European foes Celta Vigo again, this time 3-1 on aggregate. It felt like a long time and in fact it had been two years and four months since my first goals in a Villa shirt, but I was finally on mark, helping us to beat Newcastle 1-0 at home in the FA Cup third round replay, my first FA Cup goal in the process, even though it did come off my thigh. They all count, anyway. It was kind of a lucky goal, but Paul Merson swerved the ball in, which he always had a way of doing, and Dion attacked the near post. I sprinted my guts out to get to the back post, again out of fear for not doing my job and getting a bollocking from Gregory, but I arrived too soon, so had to adjust and guide it in with my thigh. Gregory wasn't someone who would destroy you, but there was a lot of talk of the term 'Billy big-time' around then, and I was desperate not to be seen as that. I then grabbed four league goals towards the end of the season; two away at Bradford City in a 3-0 win in February, one in a 3-3 draw at Charlton Athletic in April and then finally one in a 3-2 win over Coventry City in the final home game of the season. Things were starting to look up for me. These goals were also the start of an unbroken run in my career. I scored in 46 Premier League matches and didn't lose any of those games. When I announced my retirement as a player in January 2016, I was told that this was a record. I suppose a defender could have a similar statistic, but only with less goals scored, but it's a nice stat either way.

At this stage, we had attacking players such as Dion Dublin, Paul Merson, Juan Pablo Angel and David Ginola. I was surrounded by talent and experience, so some of it was sure to rub off on me. There was great competition for places, which really helped to raise the bar. I was integrated in to the squad, and I was bubbling under the surface, getting closer to becoming a regular fixture. I spent a lot of time on the bench, and some players wouldn't have settled for that, but for me that represented an opportunity to influence the game with fresh legs. I began to get that 'super-sub' tag around this time, and it probably started with the Strømsgodset goals and I guess I never really shook it off, right through to my England days under Sven, but it didn't faze me, I was just pleased to play my role. I think I often gave managers a headache at just the wrong time. A manager would bring a player in for a lot of money, and then I'd grab a goal or have a great game just after the new guy had arrived. It was the same with England; Wayne Rooney and Michael Owen were the obvious pairing, but I'd score an important goal, or link up well with Wayne, and it would cause Sven to think about including me from the start. I didn't do it on purpose, but maybe sub-consciously, when I knew there was extra competition for places, I would step it up another level somehow.

We started the 2001-02 season in the Intertoto Cup again. I have to be honest and say that the competition never really registered with me in the way that a league game, the FA Cup, or playing in Europe for real did. Having said that, we won it that season, and I think it helped to be the catalyst to a year that really saw me become an established Villa player in the Premier League, and helped me to claim a place in the England side. I scored 14 goals in 33 starts, with 12 of those goals coming in the league. My goals against Rennes and Basel helped us to lift the trophy and qualify for the UEFA Cup. It was incredible just how many European games we seemed to play in every season. Maybe the Intertoto Cup affected our league form in some way, but all I could think of at that time was playing, scoring, and helping us to win.

I won't list my goals from that season as it's there for people to see online, but I was proud of scoring against Manchester United at the start

Jackie and Courtney, Mom and Dad

Grandad's back yard, with my little sister Vanessa.

Modelling Mom's idea of a 'Villa kit', with Vanessa laughing at my expense.

One of Mom's great expeditions, Bronx Zoo in the school holidays. Well done Mom!

Picture Day at Yenton Junior School.

Grandma Vassell (RIP),
and Grandad Vassell.
Parents to Romy, Eric,
Courtney and Sandra.

Yenton Football Team with classmate, Adam Colvin, far left on the back row.

Still working on my footballer pose a year on. Classmate Darrol Bradford (back row, middle) nailed his! Tony Capaldi (Cardiff, Wales) front row, right. We went to the same after school child-minder and both ended up playing professionally.

Mrs Viles far left, taught me the offside rule and head teacher Mr Spall (far right).
We had a pretty good team if I remember and it also looks like we won something.

Yenton Athletics/Sports Team. I competed in high jump and
sprint events. Back then I loved to participate in sport.

My class at Yenton Junior School over two years. Mr Fowkes (below, far right) had his work cut out that year I seem to remember.

I thought the braids were cool, ok?
John Willmott School 1992-1996

Mom on her school photo, studied at
Riland Bedford now Plantsbrook School,
Sutton Coldfield.

Receiving a trophy at a Romulus Boys awards ceremony. Very proud days.

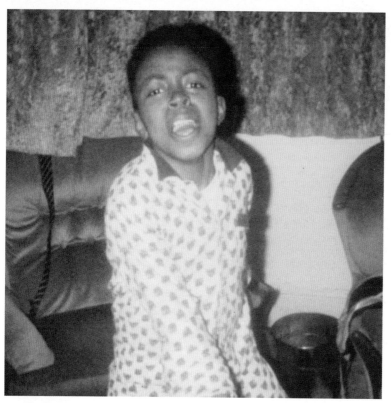

I think I'm trying to sing in this one. Emery Close, Birmingham and I think it's past my bedtime.

'Mom tell her to stop wrinkling my Villa training gear! Doesn't she realise I'm in the 'School of Excellence!'

Dad showing me how it's done. At Mom's house in Minworth, Sutton Coldfield. I used to pound the football against that wall all day, I remember.

Mother and son on another expedition. I can only assume Vanessa is taking the picture. She was usually never too far away.

Little brother, Jamie, at a few weeks old on the doorstep at our Emery Close home. I doubt he remembers Vanessa and I taking, in turns, to change his nappy.

The Girls and Boys brigade annual photo, guess who forgot their uniform? (Front row).
See it's not always me! I can remember getting to play indoor hockey, football and many other
sports during the weekly meetings at Chester Road Baptist Church.

Nursery days at Tyburn Road Daycare
Nursery, not too far from Villa Park.
1982/83 Villa were European Cup holders

Brothers in Portugal; didn't realise I'd be coming back to take an important spot kick years later.

My sister and brother out on a family occasion at a restaurant in Birmingham.

More awards at Romulus Boys club with Bob Ball in the background. Bob gave me a great opportunity to play Sunday League football, where I learned so much from him and the team.

Major cup winners with Romulus. I was tiny back then, as you can tell by the size of my shirt.

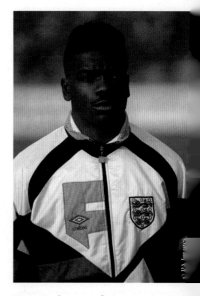

Tony Daley; my favourite Aston Villa player. I loved his pace, his skill and his haircut, and as a youngster I copied his every move, hoping to one day emulate him for Villa.

My Villa Youth team mates; we had a great squad back then and so many memorable times.

Abroad with the team. Michael Blackwood, Gareth Barry, Michael Standing and Jlloyd Samuel. Congratulations to Gareth on becoming the third player to make over 600 Premier League appearances, alongside Ryan Giggs and Frank Lampard.

gain, great times. I'm in there somewhere.

I should be booked for this dive! A break with the family abroad during pre-season.

Kev, Malcolm and Tony. My Villa coaches enjoying the festival on the last day of our team trip to Germany.

Mom taking brother Jamie on another one of her expeditions.

Aston Villa really looked after me when I broke my leg at 13. They picked me up every day and sat me in the company of Ron Atkinson and the Villa first team as they prepared for training during the week.

A big day for me, signing Aston Villa YTS contract forms with Peter Withe and my family at Villa Park.

of the season and then in the next game, a 3-1 win at Anfield. I finished as the joint-top scorer with Juan Pablo Angel, but in late January, John Gregory was sacked. Despite a decent start to the season, we recorded only one win in eleven matches from November 2001 to January 2002, and we were dropping like a stone. We halted the slide with consecutive 2-1 wins over Derby and Charlton, with Juan Pablo and I getting a goal in each, but it was too little too late to save Gregory who was replaced by John Deehan and Stuart Gray on a temporary basis, before Villa legend, Graham Taylor was appointed in early February. We finished in eighth place again that season, for the second year running, but ultimately I think it was deemed as a disappointment for most people, almost like we had underachieved.

I felt that John Gregory had got the recipe right for me as a player. He signed Juan Pablo Angel and we developed a great understanding and a successful strike partnership. For some reason, we just clicked. He was deceptively effective in the air and had exceptional timing. I think that helped him to beat defenders who simply weren't expecting him to be that strong, and that good. We always had a feeling that he would score if we could get a cross over to him. I became quite cute as a player at this time, using Juan Pablo's presence to help create space, so he was a great foil for me. He was always looking for me when he had the ball, and that connection meant so much. I mean, he was a world-class footballer, who Villa had splashed millions on, and I was getting his respect and attention as an equal. It's a truly great feeling.

That made me feel like I belonged, and for the first time in my short Villa career at this stage, I managed to become a first choice on merit. Any time he had the ball, he would flick it around the corner and in to space for me to run on to. We were a proper partnership and it showed on the field. Juan Pablo was a really good person and we got on well off the pitch too. He was a family man, with a quiet wife and a little baby, and he was trying to learn English and adapt to the culture of our country and the style of play. The fans really took to him too, and I think that they sensed something special with the two of us playing together at times.

I think that there was a real growth in my development as a player and as a person at this time as well. I'd been used to playing alongside Dion, who had been like a big brother and is that kind of character to anyone he plays with, exactly the kind of guy you want alongside you. Dion allowed me to relax; nothing could happen to me with Dion alongside me. He won everything in the air and made life easy for me, always encouraged me and I could always hear the guidance. Defenders such as Sol Campbell, Matt Elliott, David Unsworth and midfielder Thomas Gravesen who were all huge, were now not a concern for me and I owe that to Dion. Watching someone as big as Dion apply so much technique to his game was inspirational and I realised that my small size could still protect the ball and knock defenders over. Dion would always make a big deal when I shrugged off a defender, and this was while we were playing. Now, with Juan Pablo, I had to take a bit more of a lead and come out of my shell a little more. I had to find my voice. Dion was a real mentor, and it was time for me to stand on my own two feet and show people what I could do. I even took a couple of penalties that season, and knowing how uncomfortable that made me, it shows that I was in a good place.

I'd worked with John Gregory for around three-and-a-half seasons and I'm not sure we ever got past me being fearful of making mistakes, but as I've said he certainly knew how to get more from me. One example of this was in my early days in the Villa side, when he lambasted me at half-time in a game for giving the ball away and not being available to pass to. We were all sat in the dressing room and he looked at me and his opening line was, 'for fu**s sake DD,' which was one of my many nicknames. Ian Taylor stepped in and said, 'You can't blame him all of the time, it's not his fault, he's only 18.' Nothing was said after that and I knew at that point that the lads had my back. Reflecting on this today, I believe that Gregory was just trying to motivate me in a different way, trying to get a reaction from me and everyone else. Under Gregory I had so many good games where I was assisting without scoring and it's a shame they will be forgotten forever. As a striker, people only seem to remember the goals.

Graham Taylor came in and we only managed to win three out of fourteen matches, and two of those wins were in the last two games of the season. I managed to grab three goals in those last two games, both goals in a 2-1 home win over Southampton and one in a 3-1 win at Chelsea. I know it meant a lot to the supporters and the timing was perfect as Sven was always watching via himself or his good friend, Tord Grip.

In hindsight, I feel that maybe Graham Taylor shouldn't have come back to Villa Park. He was an absolute hero for the job he had done in the late 1980s. I loved him as a kid when I was a fan on the terraces, so I was obviously excited at his return with me now a player. As I've said before, there's this thing with me and heroes, and I don't always think it's a good thing to meet them. They are just human like the rest of us, have good days and bad days, and meeting them removes the mystery. I felt that Taylor had inherited a very good squad and a strong team, full of powerful characters. He seemed to want more out of me and often seemed to be frustrated with me. Admittedly, there had been question marks over me during my time at Villa, and people wanted me to realise my potential. I just wanted to enjoy my football and was beginning to do that in terms of the partnership with Juan Pablo, but Taylor was still trying to get more out of me. I could see it when he looked at me. I remember being questioned whether things were ok, and he had a sports psychologist spend time with me too. Gregory had left me alone in that sense. I remember John asking to speak to me in his office, when I went in, there was just a guy sitting there and it wasn't John Gregory. I realised it wasn't a psychologist either when he asked if I was signed with an agent. It makes me laugh to think back. Gregory would have a word with me if I gave the ball away, or if I wasn't running at defenders otherwise I was left to get on with it. I understood Graham's approach, as he felt he should be the one to unlock me. He was the manager of my favourite player of all time, Tony Daley and he also selected him for England.

Graham was protective and didn't want people to rave about me too much; it was like he was trying to keep me level-headed. He spoke about how I needed to be an outlet for the side, to run the channels, buy us time, get on the end of flick on headers and initiate each attack with a forward run. I feel like it may have worked against us at times, and it led to people knocking it long for me, out of fear of giving the ball away with a bad pass if I came short. Then it was labelled as a long ball 'style of play' creating negativity amongst us. Dropping deep and trusting that I would spot something running forward with the ball, is part of my game and I needed to be doing this more. The combination of both is what fools defenders. Whereas me losing the ball whilst trying, was not a risk Graham was going to take when there was so much on the line. He did not like to lose football matches, that's for sure. If you hadn't given your all for Graham Taylor then you wouldn't figure in his thoughts. He made this clear quite often in meetings.

It wasn't only Graham who was frustrated with me, Andy Gray, the Villa legend made his feelings clear. I was sat next to him at an awards dinner and I went along with Nicki Clarkson who was PA to my agent Neil Fewings at the time. Andy was chomping my ear off with frustration that I didn't score enough goals. It was one of the first times I'd met someone who could easily relate to what I was going through, and I could sense his frustration as he knew there was something more to come from me. It's not the feeling I wanted people to have when they watched me play, it made me frustrated. I knew that I needed to listen though, I needed to take in and filter as much advice as possible especially when it was coming from those with more experience than myself.

One of my overriding memories of Taylor and his time in charge was of his attitude towards the media. We would often be told not to speak to them, or be given instructions of what to say and what not to say, whereas it was a lot more relaxed under Gregory. I was younger with less expectation. I'm certain that this was a hangover from Taylor's period in charge of England, where he was treated poorly and with a total lack of respect at times. All the offensive 'Turnip Taylor' headlines were unnecessary and maybe he was never the same again with them? I couldn't be, that's for sure. Some trust was perhaps lost. Taylor was still a big character in my eyes, but I witnessed the effect that England exit had on him. He knew he was in the moment and it was a big chance for the whole country. I watched that documentary of him with the England team and I love how football was back then, there is something about that era. "Do I not like that?" All of those experiences are bound to have caused him some strain. That's why he knew so many different psychologists I guess? Either way, he had seen it and come through it all with some valuable nuggets of information that I needed to apply to my game.

The job at Villa was huge and it was a difficult time for him to come in, halfway through the season, and inherit Gregory's players. There was an impression at the time from within the dressing room that we would be going 'old-school' in our style of play, and I don't think that the team were particularly excited about playing this way. It didn't matter what league Villa were in, I wanted to play, but it felt like I was being told how to play and that my time was running out. Honestly, I've never completely known how I've done the things I've done on a pitch, I would just do them in the moment.

The next season, Taylor's first full season in charge during his second spell at the club was a disaster, as we plummeted down the league and finished 16th, just two places above relegation. We started off in the Intertoto Cup, as became pretty standard for my years at Villa, and we beat F.C. Zurich, before being knocked out by Lille. In the League Cup, we reached the quarter-finals losing 4-3 to Liverpool, in a game where I scored a penalty, and we were embarrassed 4-1 at home to Blackburn Rovers in the FA Cup third round. Taylor changed the squad dramatically with eight players signed and ten sold, including big names such as Merson, Taylor, Stone, George Boateng and Peter Schmeichel leaving. We only survived relegation on the penultimate game of the season, beating an already relegated Sunderland. I managed eleven goals in the 2002-03 season, with eight coming in the league, but there wasn't much reason for us to celebrate.

My partnership with Juan Pablo had been effectively ended; we would still play together, but not on a regular basis, as Taylor had brought in Peter Crouch and Marcus Allback, and we already had Bosko Balaban by then. We lost at home and away to our city rivals Birmingham, who had returned to the top flight, and that was hard for me as a Villa fan to take, and wasn't much fun for those living and working in the city either. People automatically assume that I hated Birmingham City but that wasn't the case; I just hated losing to them because I could never live it down. Birmingham is my home and believe it or not, I am proud we have two teams and a rivalry to go with it. It's something I'm always asked about.

We lost 3-0 at St. Andrew's on 16th September 2002, in the first ever Birmingham derby in the Premier League era. I came on as a sub at half time with Dion, to replace Angel and Allback and we were 1-0 down at that stage after a Clinton Morrison strike. I quickly got in to the action, and had a goal disallowed on 57 minutes for offside, and then soon after had a header which went narrowly wide after a looping cross where Dion was being a beast in the air as usual. We were looking like getting back in to the game and then out of nowhere Olof Mellberg took a routine throw-in back to our keeper Peter Enckelman, who made an error of judgement and allowed the ball to roll under his boot and in to our net. Immediately the home crowd celebrated and Blues fans streamed on to the pitch and sadly confronted Peter. It took a while for everything to sink in, and the ref David Elleray went over to his linesman to consult on whether or not Peter had actually touched the ball. They decided he had and in the most embarrassing of ways for Peter, we were 2-0 down. Steve Staunton was booked in protest at the decision. Peter was a good guy and a talented goalkeeper who had made many good saves for us; he didn't deserve this, but we all have moments in our career that we remember for the right and sadly wrong reasons, and this, just like my penalty miss against Portugal, will be associated with him, especially given the importance of the game.

The return fixture in March 2003 was another firecracker with Dion Dublin's infamous head-butting of pantomime villain, Robbie Savage. Only Dion knows what he was doing at the time. I think that Robbie overreacted to a late tackle from Dion, and then it looked as if he said something to him, which resulted in Dion, shall we say, leaning in on him. I think he would have got a yellow for the tackle, but the ref, Mark Halsey was left with no choice but to give him a straight red card. It affected me as I was up front on my own for the next 40 minutes, having to chase long balls, win the header and then chase my own knock down. I think Dion would have known he had let us down, and he apologised to me personally for the position he'd left me in, as that's the kind of character he is. He contributed so many more positives than negatives in his career, 200+ goals but we lost the game 2-0 and Blues had completed the double over us in their first season back in the top flight. Taylor did make sure we weren't relegated and he will never receive credit for that which is a shame. As players we knew deep down that we came close. Thank you, Graham, and everyone associated with the club at the time for sticking together and avoiding it. For example, Taylor would stop training for long periods and talk to us, leaving nothing to chance. He would tell me to make certain runs and get me to do them there on the spot as a demonstration but the restart didn't feel natural. I would always do as he said, as I respected him and I wanted training to resume quicker, but I knew in my heart that the set-up wasn't right and that some sessions seemed unrealistic in training. The defenders were standing there listening to what I was being asked so they were ready for it when the coach restarted the sessions. Then it looked like I wasn't applying myself or I had lost a yard or two. Perhaps if I had been a bigger character, I would have stepped up and told the coaches I felt something was wrong, but that didn't come naturally to me and I sidestepped any form of conflict with staff. It's not a good method of getting yourself selected.

It was truly a season to forget for me, although one story stands out from that year, all for the wrong reasons. I can remember heading in to training with a sore toe one day, and I went to see the physio, Alan Smith. The top corner of my toe nail was sore to touch, and once Alan pressed on it there was a lot of pain. He took a haemodril nail trephine out of its case, which is used to drill a hole in your nail if you have a blood blister. He began to drill down on to the toe nail, in order to release the blood and ease the pressure and the pain that it was causing. It was excruciating though, and I yanked my foot away from him a few times and explained that I'd have to do it myself. I had done it many times and I thought I could control the level of pressure I was gradually exerting, without being in agony. We agreed that I would take the haemodril home with me, which is just a small battery powered drill, like a wall nail or screw, and come in early the next day. It was still throbbing the few hours between training and getting home and when I tried to do it once again there was still too much pain in that area to even contemplate applying pressure. I rested up and went back in extra early to training the next day to get the physio to take a look at it, by which time he could confirm that it had been infected all along. That was why I wasn't able to stand the pain of the drill, so I was given a toe injection by the physio, who also removed the infected nail and all of the puss which was underneath it, which obviously meant I was going to be out of action. I am thankful to Alan because I haven't had a problem with that toe since and I wasn't an easy patient to deal with; he needed a very steady hand that morning. Taking the nail off the day before would have still meant that I would have missed the game.

Meanwhile, Graham Taylor was asked in the media as to why I wasn't available to play, and between him and the physio, all he'd heard was that I'd taken a drill to my toe at home. I can imagine his face as he was listening to the physio report, knowing he had to explain it all five minutes later in an interview. It came out as if I'd grabbed a Black and Decker out of the garage and hacked away at my toe, with blood flying everywhere! I've been asked so many times about this story, and the whispers around it have turned it in to something hilarious. There's even an animated video on YouTube about it, and it's always listed as one of the strangest injuries in football history, alongside the ones where players get injured getting out of bed in the morning, or something like that.

There was interest in the story that was reported, put it that way. The best thing I can say is that Graham asked me to come in to his office afterwards, and apologised about the way it came out in the press. I just wanted to move on with things, get back to fitness and play. I don't know if he'd spoken about the drill and my toe to distract from on-field problems, or maybe to try and lighten the mood a little, but the fact that he apologised shows that he knew the real story and was indeed a true gentleman. The truth of the matter is, that it's a story that has stayed with me throughout my career, and this is the first time I've been able to put things straight. As it was such a funny story, I did try and laugh about it, but I knew that the people involved knew the truth. I guess the football world needs these kind of stories, otherwise the character is lost from the game and it just becomes like any other business.

The incident also uncovered another issue; the size of my feet. The physio discovered that I had a slightly larger left foot, creating extra pressure on that area. It was a chronic problem that I'd been self-managing for years, an ingrowing nail that had aggravated the whole big toe. Obviously, I'd been buying football boots in equal sizes throughout my career, so it's something I struggled with until I found a size ten boot that was loose enough on the left foot, but tight enough on my smaller right foot.

The toe nail issue, and a few other things, had left my dad concerned about me and my relationship with the club and manager. At the end of a game around that time, Taylor was asked a question about me during this season and said that I wasn't the finished article or something to that effect. I don't remember anyone saying that I was and I knew that I wasn't also. I was fine with what he'd said, just didn't feel that it needed to be said that's all. As long as he was trying to help make me the finished article it didn't matter too much to me, but my dad felt that something like that should have been kept in-house. Dad knew I wasn't very confident and he was looking out for his boy as best as he could I guess. He cited Arsene Wenger, who would be publicly supportive of his younger players and encourage their development when talking to the press. My dad really didn't take to Graham's approach on that occasion. Whilst I had communication with him, I never felt like I could speak up to him as such. I'm not sure whether it was because he was 'Graham Taylor', the ex-manager of my favourite player for both Villa and England, or whether I wasn't sure enough about myself and knowledge in the game. A combination of both I guess and like I said before, I didn't really know how to describe what I was trying to do on the pitch. Graham took it upon himself to help me figure it out. He definitely had good intentions; bringing in Peter Crouch, for example, where he could develop us as a big man and little man combination, which made sense on paper. I enjoyed playing with Peter, we had good moments but just not enough. Something wasn't right at Villa in general and the team could all feel it. We were probably getting weaker as others were becoming stronger. There just wasn't enough left in the dressing room to quickly turn around the slump we were in and that included me. We were not getting much luck in matches either. It hurts me to say that, as I'm a Villa boy deep down and I'm partly to blame.

We were in a difficult period, with many changes and it was probably one of the worst times I experienced at the club, as relegation felt like it could become a reality. That was unthinkable, unacceptable, but recent events show that a club of Villa's size is not above losing their Premier League status.

Thankfully, we survived and I thought my goals may have helped to save him but Graham Taylor was replaced by David O'Leary in the summer of 2003, but we did little to change our fortunes at first, as we were rooted in the relegation zone around Christmas time after a poor first-half of the season. My own form, in terms of goal scoring at least, mirrored the club as well, as I only scored one goal before Christmas, which came against Wycombe Wanderers in a 5-0 League Cup win. I remember my contract was running out and I had to start adjusting to the feeling of uncertainty leading up to January. I certainly didn't want to go anywhere. I needed to do something. It seemed that as I came good, so too did the team. I grabbed eight league goals after Christmas, kick-started by a double against Fulham in a 3-0 home win and including a goal in a 2-2 draw at home in the Birmingham derby. Those goals helped us to finish a remarkable sixth, just missing out on a place in Europe, whilst we reached the League Cup semi-finals, losing agonisingly 5-4 to Bolton Wanderers on aggregate.

Despite the previous season's failings, I didn't necessarily expect a change as Graham Taylor was a Villa legend and both he and I seemed to be 'working on something'. We were starting to trust each other and hopefully he would eventually get the very best out of me. Therefore, when O'Leary joined it was a bit of a surprise, but we all knew his reputation as a great player and a talented manager. He'd done very well at Leeds United so whilst there was some uncertainty around the players and the staff, there was optimism too. He brought a sports scientist in called Steve McGregor, who went on to work with the golfer Rory McIlroy, and there was a very new and professional, modern approach adopted off-field. I also noticed that O'Leary tried to be closer to, and on more familiar speaking terms with the players than I had seen previously. My good friend, Jlloyd Samuel and he were thick as thieves together, and were coming out with slang terms, fist pumps and I'm sure they were sharing tracklists on their iPods. O'Leary settled in quickly; there was a lot of work to do and he had a team including Roy Aitken that were up for the task.

I think that because David O'Leary had played to such a high standard, and worked with quality strikers such as Ian Wright and Robbie Keane, he knew that I should contribute a lot more goals. He told me this and would have video footage of me to help me visualise the good things more, while eradicating the bad. Like Graham Taylor, he identified my importance pretty quickly, but I just don't feel he had the patience to get the best out of me. He knew I'd been at Villa for a while and I think he probably saw that he'd got a bit of money to spend, like new managers do, and perhaps felt the urge to change things and bring his own men in. I never once felt that he was going to base his side around me. I felt like I had to reinvent myself again, as I'd done previously, as I didn't want to leave Villa. I would have ended my career at Villa if my contract wasn't almost out.

There were a few fixtures during my time playing under O'Leary where I was completely left out of the squad, and there wasn't a clear reason. It happens to players now and again and it's a horrible feeling that I just wasn't used to at Villa. I didn't expect to play every game, but I should have made the squad. For me, I was playing at the same club, with a similar bunch of players, and yet I was being left out of the team. It almost felt like I was being blamed for our poor form at times. I'll never understand why the partnership I'd had with Juan Pablo Angel was allowed to break up instead of it being reinforced. We'd had that great season in 2001/02 under John Gregory and then under Graham Taylor after Gregory was dismissed, where we scored thirty goals between us, and then quite predictably, as during the rest of my career other strikers were signed and we didn't get that run in the team together. Juan Pablo was left out under O'Leary and it was a transitional period for certain players, and perhaps he didn't cope as well with it. I know Juan would have had his own issues too after adapting to a new manager whilst still trying to settle down in a new country and the uncertainty that brings.

The change towards a more scientific approach, whilst I understand the reasons, also seemed to take some of the enjoyment and the smiles out of the training ground environment at first. Suddenly, it was more about numbers, such as your heart-rate, rather than how you were playing and how everyone was interacting with each other. The second-half of the season saw us improve beyond recognition, but I honestly never really felt comfortable playing under David O'Leary. Even if I got a well done from him, it felt that long-term it wouldn't really matter. It's difficult to describe but I could tell that he wanted more quality and was looking forward to bolstering the squad. It should have worked with Graham Taylor, with him being a Villa legend and having that relationship with the club and the fans, but with O'Leary he had stepped in to the role, would make his changes and move on soon after.

Things got progressively worse in the 2004/05 season, which was a largely forgettable campaign for me and for the club. I broke my ankle on the 23rd October 2004 in a home game against Fulham. At the start of the game I was worked up and anxious; I was fired up to prove a point to David O'Leary, to show the Villa fans that I could still do it for them and I was playing against a former colleague from my youth days at Romulus, Zat Knight, who was normally a substitute when we were younger, which he'll admit himself, so I wanted to be on form on that day, knowing that he would be coming for me. He had done really well for himself and I wanted him to think I'd done the same. On my mind at the time was the disappointment of my penalty miss for England against Portugal at Euro 2004, so I was carrying around with me the need to prove people wrong and show that the miss hadn't affected me. The ball broke towards me, and this is one occasion where my pace was a problem for me as I was too quick and got to the ball first ahead of a slide tackle from Papa Bouba Diop, nicknamed 'The Wardrobe' due to his size. All of his weight went through my standing leg and that was it, I was out of the game. I was taken off after 62 minutes and replaced by Carlton Cole. I didn't play again for another four months. The pain wasn't as intense as previous injuries I'd had; my ankle went stiff immediately and I felt the sensation of pins and needles. I couldn't move and I knew I wouldn't be playing again for a while, but found out later that my ankle was broken. My next game was at the end of February 2005 against Everton, and it felt like an age. The problem was time; I didn't have long to show O'Leary and Villa reasons why they should extend my contract, but already by then, it had begun to feel like my last season at the club, which was the last thing I wanted. O'Leary hadn't been happy with my goals return, and in fairness I only scored three goals in my final season, so he had a point, but the injury had ripped my season in to shreds. I'm not blaming anything, but I feel like that year I was just trying too hard; whether it be to score, to win the ball back and to defend for the team, and maybe I should have been a little more selfish, but that's easy to say in hindsight. After the Everton game, I played during the rest of the season and got myself fit and made myself available to compete up until the end. We finished tenth in the Premier League and were knocked out of the FA Cup and League Cup in the third rounds. It was a disappointment after finishing sixth a year before, especially as we'd ended that season strongly and had momentum coming in to 2004/05.

I'd suffered a broken leg and two broken ankles in my career, so when the Liverpool striker Djibril Cissé broke his tibia and fibula I decided to write to him. I was learning French from Lorna McClelland at Villa who was the player liaison officer, another close friend of the family who came to our wedding. I wrote Djibril a letter as I'd been through it all and also we both had pace and were strikers, and I wanted to practice my French. Lorna checked it over and we sent it to Liverpool as fan mail. I didn't get a reply, which was understandable because I'm not the greatest at that either. I didn't mind that I didn't get a reply, but I just wanted to know whether he'd received it or not, whether it made any sense and to show him the support of a fellow footballer.

INITIATION

After coming back from injury, I was filmed while driving my Lamborghini through Birmingham and the footage ended up as part of a DVD that was said to glorify gang culture. My image had been used without my permission or knowledge and it put me in the difficult position of having to defend myself when confronted about the news reports surrounding this 'DVD'. Come to think of it, I was listening to one of my favourites of the time, Tupac Shakur, on the stereo during that recording. It was all such a bad look for me. David O'Leary spoke to me briefly about it and the matter was closed as soon as I had explained the unfortunate misunderstanding. He knew that It wasn't a story with any worth, I could tell by his face. It was still something that he would rather not have to deal with though. I sold the Lamborghini after this, which was a beautiful midnight blue. It was never the same and I felt like a right clown driving it after those reports. In fact, I can't believe I bought that car but It was just too irresistible at the time. A year later I posed for a group photo with my best friend Nathan at Miss Moneypenny's nightclub and then all of a sudden that photo is printed in the local papers, with reports of other people in the image and at the event allegedly being linked to gang culture in Birmingham. I knew the guys in the photo, in fact I knew Nathan very well, but didn't have any real knowledge of what gangs anyone chose to represent. I was out to have a good time, not to investigate in to everyone's character and background. The papers made it sound terrible to me, as if I was a criminal involved in gun crime, which couldn't have been further from the truth. My friends and family were extremely worried about me but the more local people I spoke to, in and around Birmingham, the more the tension eased. I carried on going to my local barber shop and I had youngsters asking me whether I was part of a gang. I can understand how and why they drew the comparisons after those original reports, but it did upset me as that wasn't the kind of image I wanted to portray, especially with it being false. Birmingham is my home, but these incidents and the attention I received changed the way I saw my city and I had to think twice about going out at night. There was no way I was going to start refusing photos if people asked. I had a fairly decent reputation before this as a good footballer and now I was being asked if I was in a gang. I didn't have time for that. It was starting to get ridiculous and to control it I chose to stay at home more and more.

I wasn't fully aware of the gang culture in Birmingham, but this had opened my eyes more. It wasn't a good time for me and my city but I'm glad the rumours all fizzled out as there was no real gain from those stories, only confusion. Nathan was a good friend, his mom would cook me dinner after a youth team match and we were great mates at Villa. His Dad would always help me out if I needed anything and we were quite close when I lived in Birmingham. He and I certainly had no dealings in gangs; neither would we have what it takes to do so. We're not in as much contact these days unfortunately but that's life and down to this footballing journey I guess. This whole episode had led to some pretty horrific chants aimed at me when Villa played Birmingham City at St. Andrews. I was called a murderer, a gang member and was sworn at with every word imaginable as I warmed up running up and down the touchline. This was one match I wished I was starting in. It was beyond anything I'd been called before; it was horrible and really affected me on the day. I've never really mentioned the affect it had until now. I was thinking that I was named sub just so I could go through that, I wanted to do a 'Cantona' so badly but it just wasn't and isn't in me. I had to accept it and concentrate on the game. The thought of how the world is changing and how quick a story can spread if it has the right ingredients is a scary thing for a footballer.

I went in to pre-season for 2005/06 full of optimism. Now I was fit again I was determined to enjoy a strong period of training and be as sharp as possible for the competitive stuff. Unfortunately, O'Leary had other ideas for me. It's really hard for me to speak about, or even to explain what O'Leary was like to be honest. I mean, I guess it is incidents like this that sum up the situation? He was a footballer himself and he knew what that was like, and knew full well that I had been at the club all of my life, and yet I didn't even hear it from him once that Villa were on the verge of selling me. My agent at the time, Neil Fewings, called me whilst I was in Sweden for the club's pre-season tour. That was the first I'd heard of it. I remember him saying, "Villa have agreed to sell you," and I felt that sinking feeling. I was so fit, running ahead of everyone else in the bleep test, despite the fact that I didn't like that kind of training, so it shows the mindset I was in at that time. I didn't want to hear from Neil as I didn't want to even contemplate leaving Villa. I couldn't even think about moving away. I eventually spoke to Neil and explained that I didn't want to leave. I had another year left on my contract and I was determined to stay, earn another contract and stay with the club

I loved. We'd always fought for a contract that we felt I deserved. Neil was able to benchmark against other players, and we felt that I deserved more security, at least equal to those around me. We never made a wage demand, we wanted to see what the club valued me at. An offer didn't come and I'm not complaining; I was paid well by the club and loved playing for them, but at this stage it seemed clear to me that I was being forced out, and that other players were considered more suitable. David O'Leary came over after one of our training sessions, and draped his arm around me and intimated that I was talking to my agent about leaving the club, acting as if he knew nothing about it and that I was instigating it. I was so uncomfortable with the thought that he knew more. I was certain that he knew all about it and that he wanted me to leave so he could bring someone else in. He had to know surely. I could feel it and I felt it when he arrived up until this point. I want to call this a betrayal, but I don't regard David O'Leary as an Aston Villa legend, and I assume he feels the same about me, so I can't really call it that. He owed me nothing and maybe in his heart he just couldn't handle me expressing my complete disappointment to him.

It was time for me to move on and get my head around it all. Once I knew that O'Leary wanted me out, and that no one was going to stop this happening, I had to come to terms with it, rather than feeling sorry for myself. My agent called me and said that there was interest from Stuart Pearce at Manchester City. This whole scenario convinced me that it was right to go. I allowed myself to dream that someone at Villa would come out and publicly state that I wasn't going to be sold; that they would keep me until my final days as a player, but I needed to be realistic with myself. Villa had changed and it was time for me to change too. I can admit now that I would have loved to have signed an extension with Villa, as I was desperate to stay at the club. I hadn't thought about going anywhere; it was my life and Aston Villa Football Club was my extended family.

Once I'd been sold to Manchester City for £2million, Kevin Phillips and Milan Baroš were immediately brought in at Villa, so it was clear that my departure hadn't appeared from nowhere; it was planned. I don't think that anything I did at that time could have made a difference.

I think that given some hindsight and perspective here, I should, however, offer the other side. O'Leary was entitled to do what he wanted, and I hadn't scored many goals the previous season, and had suffered a serious ankle injury, which I had recovered from, but he chose to let me leave. Looking at the statistics, he can say that I wasn't producing the goals, but I knew that I was still able to do a job for Villa. I suppose, in the long run, it makes no difference how you leave a club; but I just felt like I loved the club more than the people who were selling me.

I left pre-season in Sweden early, to fly back to the UK and then head to Manchester to meet with City's manager, Stuart Pearce and representatives of the club. The situation I faced there couldn't have been any more different; they were the opposite of Villa, making it clear that they wanted me, offering me a good deal, whilst talking about what a key role I would be playing in the side. For all my sadness at leaving Villa, I felt wanted again. Pearce's face as I walked through the door was a picture. His smile was from ear to ear. It was exactly what I needed. On my first day of training I was late, totally my fault, but they didn't mind and made a joke of it. I saw Trevor Sinclair, Danny Mills and Robbie Fowler, who I'd played with for England and I felt at home. I was asked by the press when I left Villa how I felt about joining City, and I said I was pleased to be joining a big club. I'd spoken with my agent about it beforehand and what I meant to say was 'another big club', but it didn't come out right. It was printed as if I was bitter towards Villa, and I wasn't at all. I just wanted to score a few goals past O'Leary for the troubles, that's all. I don't feel I need to apologise, but I wanted people to know the truth. I'm not a media person; I don't call up journalists and ask for a retraction, I just answer people when they ask me a question in the street around Birmingham and that's me.

Just a week after I was signed, Andrew Cole (Coley) was brought in on a free transfer from Fulham. If I was happy already then this really was the icing on the cake. I think that at this stage, the move was exactly what I needed. I wasn't going stale at Villa, although people may have felt that, but I just felt that City made me more complete as a player and as a person. In fact, it felt like I was suddenly being treated as a big player, on a full length contract, playing alongside one of my childhood heroes, Andrew Cole, not just coming off the bench to play at the end with him. He was also one of my favourite players of all time. Those Newcastle days remind me of when I was at school, our kit was very similar and he just couldn't stop scoring. It was just incredible. I'd played my whole career, to that stage, as a graduate of Villa's youth set-up, so this was my first experience of being bought by a club. I can honestly say I was delighted to have that feeling; to be wanted again.

Villa had been such a huge part of my life though. It was like a relationship breaking up. I look back so fondly on my time at the club, and I still love Villa just as much today as I did when I was a boy stood on the Holte End. I'm still in touch with Dion Dublin and Jlloyd Samuel, and I'm hoping to be playing golf soon with Gareth Barry, who I was good friends with when we were younger. Lee Hendrie's a good guy too and I stay in touch with him. Dion and I have this cultural thing, I guess; we laugh at the same jokes and he understands me. He's a genuinely good guy and someone I would go to if I needed guidance. He's an important figure in my life. My Dad said he's got style and presence, and deserves a lot of credit for his work off the field and on TV. I would have to agree, plus he's scored over 200 goals in his career.

I would make quick judgements about players in my early days, and I think a lot of footballers would admit they did this too. I'd look at players and work out whether they were any good from how they stood, appeared or sometimes what boots they had. I'd give them a nervous up and down with the eyes to work out the competition. For example, Peter Crouch, when I first met him at England youth level, didn't look like a typical footballer to me, but when I saw him play he showed that things aren't always as they seem in football. He could manoeuvre the ball cleverly and was always a good finisher. As a young kid, I would hear the name Matthew Le Tissier read out frequently on BBC1's Grandstand show; he sounded so exotic, like an expensive foreigner. I couldn't wait to see what he looked like because he was scoring week in week out and it was getting ridiculous, then when I saw him he was nothing like how I expected. He was so much taller, what a player he was though. I wish I could have scored those types of goals week in week out, the combined freedom and bravery to try such things. I understand that prejudices do exist in the game but in many different forms, not all of them are harmful. The game can bring everyone together a lot more efficiently than it can divide us.

On the field at Villa Park, I've already spoken of the understanding I had with Juan Pablo Angel, which was as good as I'd had with any player I played with. Paul Merson was a special guy to play with too. It didn't matter where you were on the pitch, he could find you with a pass. The only problem would be the amount of spin on the ball. You had to be on your game if you were playing with Paul Merson, as he was different class; another football legend. I'm pleased for him that he's working as a pundit and I think people like him as he's naturally a funny guy and he's easily relatable, especially with his comical pronunciations! As a 17-year-old at Villa, the first-team bus was an awesome place to be. I can remember those big players at the back of the team bus with their card schools, a huge stack of cash on the table and a load of laughter. It was strange to witness and quite daunting at first. I couldn't tell if they were really that angry when they lost or really that happy when they won, there was just so much noise and banter. That environment certainly helped me to grow-up faster, though I never ever caught on to the idea of gambling. There were so many talents I played with, such as Stan Collymore, Nobby Solano with his trumpet, who would be jamming with Dion, what a character Nobby was to be around. I remember him organising a BBQ at his home for the whole team and it was just us all there munching and chatting away. Olof Mellberg was a great person to talk to whilst learning from and Lee Hendrie was often involved in my goals and often knew exactly how to find me. I owe a lot of goals to Lee and his creativity. It would be hard to pick out the best player I played with at Villa, but those I've mentioned, along with defenders like Gareth Southgate and Ugo Ehiogu, and George Boateng and Ian Taylor in midfield were all exceptional. On a team trip to New York, George and I decided to go on a helicopter ride across the city during our free time. It was then that it dawned on us that we were both scared of heights! George remains a good friend and he attended my wedding. He's a really good guy with a passion to help others improve.

As a youth team player, I got the opportunity to train with the first team, and people were questioning whether I could get past the likes of Paul McGrath and Ugo Ehiogu. Ugo was in the gym and shouted me over and said: "I'll give you 50 quid if you can get past me!" My heart was beating fast, and I looked at the size of the gym, looked at the size of Ugo and worked out that I could control his pass heavily so it would ricochet past him, I'd then sprint by him picking up the ball and collect my winnings. He passed me the ball and my plan worked a treat, but I wasn't allowed to do it that way and he made me do it again properly, with the ball under my control. By this time, the whole of the youth team and some other players and coaches came in and were watching, so I was really feeling the pressure.

I don't know what I did, but my footwork and turn got me past him and the place was in uproar. Alan Wright was there laughing at Ugo, who saw the funny side of it and paid me the £50 too. I had a fresh £50; to the rest of the youth team and for the rest of that day, I was a legend. I'll always remember that day and I was in Trinidad with Ugo recently just playing golf, talking about his coaching career, and you just stop and think, where did all the time go? David James was quite a character too, and I remember it being publicised about his addiction to playing computer games, late in to the night before a game, which drew a lot of attention. You would have thought he would have been good given all the time he spent on them, but he wasn't very good at all. Lee Hendrie was the star of the consoles. It was either Fifa or Pro Evo, but honestly Jamo wasn't the best. I can't forget to mention David Ginola as well. What a nice character he was to be around. Every time he walked in to the dressing room, there would be something different; like he'd have groomed his eyebrows, or had a new hairstyle. He treated me so well, and I really looked up to him. He was such a name, he had a real aura around him, but he was still such a good guy. David would receive a lot of stick from the rest of the squad for the attention he got from females, but it was all in jest. Talking of that, Ian Taylor was definitely the joker of the group, and then Alpay was a really lively one. He was hot headed and in training he would shout, moan and kick you, but he really took to me. He always made time for people and he never wanted to injure players, but he was just so strong and competitive. He had altercations all the time, but what a cracking player. Thomas Hitzlsperger was a lot quieter and I roomed with him from time-to-time. Obviously, he's come out about his sexuality, which received a great deal of coverage. I'm not going to lie, I was shocked but I hope he's happy now and has come to terms with everything in his life. I remember the 'Hammer' of a shot that he would practice in the gym. Him at one end and me at the other; the whole wall was the goal and we would blast the ball across the gym at each other. He had that cheeky grin as if to say 'Stop! Hammer time' every time he scored. Another foreign player who joined us, but sadly didn't have a happy spell was the Belgian striker Luc Nilis, who suffered a double leg break against Ipswich Town in September 2000. I actually replaced him as a substitute so didn't see what had happened, but I really felt for him. We also had two Moroccans, Mustapha Hadji and Hassan Kachloul, who were good guys and they helped me with my French. They both spoke highly of Dion Dublin and Hadji was an ex-teammate of Dion at Coventry City, prior to joining Villa. There were a lot of players at the club connected in similar ways, so the banter got very loud at times.

I guess I'd pick Juan Pablo out as the best player if I had to, for our work together, and that special season where we scored goals and enjoyed fantastic away wins and great bus journeys home, but there were simply too many good players for me to name just one. I don't think I knew how to keep that partnership with Juan Pablo going. There was a lot of freedom to the partnership and we really did click. What I never considered was his own personal situation, away from his home in Colombia and him being worried about his family and integrating them all into an English way of life. I knew we were good together in the 2001/02 season, but I don't think you stop and consider it all at the time, as there's always another game to come.

As for the fans, I met so many different sections of them. There would be the players' families, close to the dugout and you got to know them and see them at home games, who my dad would sit amongst and listen to what they would say. Sometimes he'd hear praise for me, and sometimes criticism, but he'd always sit there quietly and listen to it all. Then at the other end of the scale were the fans in the Holte End. If they had a problem with you, you would know about it, but you always wanted to score in front of them. If I could have that feeling all over again I would. Then there were the really extreme end, the Villa Hardcore, or Villa Youth as they were also known. I met some proper Villa supporters on a night out in Birmingham, after I'd left the club, and once I spoke to them they saw me in a different light. They were not happy with me at first. It's hard to explain, but I found joy from the fact that they turned from maybe questioning me, to just talking about my time at the club and us respecting each other over a drink. I guess they knew that I was a Villa boy at heart, doing what many of them dreamed of doing and pulling on the claret and blue shirt. Their perspective changed completely when they realised that I didn't want to leave the club, and to add to it O'Leary didn't last long in the job after I left. That was no consolation for me though.

5

DREAM WITHIN
A DREAM

I was fortunate enough to represent England at under-18 and under-21 level and I enjoyed every moment of that period of my career. I played five times for the under-18s under Howard Wilkinson, scoring five goals, with two in Dublin against the Republic of Ireland, one in Rome against Italy and a goal against Andorra and Israel.

Howard was a very thorough coach, who believed strongly in preparation with lots of meetings and his tactics were always precise. I began to understand how important everything was with England under him. He was actually quite innovative and at training once he used a headset which was linked up to speakers around the pitch and he would communicate to us, changing the system and monitoring how we reacted. He was always looking to get the best out of training and meetings; anything off the pitch and he would ensure it was the best it could be for us as players on the pitch. Howard felt that we had a great squad and that we should have done better and could have won something, but it's all over in the blink of an eye and players disperse back to their clubs and some move up to the under-21s. I, like Steven Gerrard and Joe Cole, was lucky enough to do that.

I made my England under-21 debut in Budapest on 27th April 1999, in a 2-2 draw with Hungary, ironically as a substitute for my Villa teammate and England roommate, Gareth Barry. The team on my debut was Richard Wright, John Curtis, Andy Griffin (Wayne Bridge), Luke Young, Danny Mills, Gareth Barry (Darius Vassell), Jonathan Greening, Hayden Mullins, James Beattie (Carl Cort), Jason Euell (Richard Cresswell), Curtis Woodhouse and our manager was Peter Taylor. Everyone got on well with Peter, and Gareth Barry already had experience of working with him and spoke highly of his coaching skills. He was hands on with the players, always praising and wanting input and feedback, so we were always valued. He was down-to-earth, and was different to managers I'd worked with.

When Peter left, Howard Wilkinson stepped in for a while, before David Platt took over as under-21s boss. I knew I was doing ok in the under-21s. On one occasion, Howard shouted during training to everyone, "Pass the ball to Darius, he's a magician," and when he said that I looked at other people's reactions and Frank Lampard, who didn't know me that well at the time, had a look of disbelief on his face, along with a few others. I found it funny too. Gareth Barry was winding me up in the hotel room, calling me 'magician' all the time. We were told to read out a poem one day as we were late, and Frank refused to do it. I was helped to find one by one of the coaches and I read it out in the team meeting room, in front of all of the staff and players. It was almost like a walk of shame to be honest. I wished I'd stayed strong like Frank as it was embarrassing, but I did feel better once I got back to my seat and I vowed I would try harder not to be late again.

Platt was a legend; remember, he was my school mate Adam Colvin's favourite player and we'd watched him play at Villa Park and really admired him. I scored in a 4-0 win over Holland at Reading, with a great goal, a 'Schlazer' as me and Jlloyd Samuel would call it, and that game was the making of Platt in his role. He was modern and understood the game and what players were trying to do, almost things you can't teach, and he would encourage us to try things and continue to try things even if we'd made an error. He was always one step ahead and had put together a strong squad which was always going to benefit the senior side.

Platt had worked under some quality managers and he took all of that knowledge and experience and developed a great relationship with his players and his own staff. He was an iconic player and a real standout figure in football. I can remember being in training listening to him speak and all I could think of was that amazing volley he scored for England against

Belgium in the last 16 of the Italia '90 World Cup, and it took me straight back to my sticker album.

I played eleven times in total for the under-21s and scored one goal, and my final game was a 2-1 win over Greece on 5th October 2001, with Wayne Bridge also playing in that game with me. Players like Ashley Cole, Frank Lampard and John Terry came through that set-up and went on to play for England for many years, so I was in very good company.

There had been word for a while that I was going to be called up to the England squad and Platt had said to me, on a couple of occasions, that if I kept playing the way I was I'd get my chance for the national side. I tried not to dwell on this too much. Being the way I am, I convinced myself that it wouldn't happen for me and just focused on doing my best for Aston Villa.

When the announcement was made and I was named as part of the squad for an away friendly against the Netherlands in February 2002, I was honestly shocked, but so happy. I was immediately unsure of what I needed to do. Did I need a suit? Thinking back, I can't even remember if I had one at the time! I have always been terrible with names too, and I didn't know where anything was, so it wasn't the easiest of starts; almost like a first day at school revisited. As soon as I was called by the England staff though, everything was taken care of and organised and I need not have worried. I was so thankful for the staff behind the scenes for England. I got the feeling that they knew I was nervous and their organisation and efficiency allowed me to just focus on training and playing. There were many people there who I'd like to thank, but I can particularly remember Michelle Farrar and Ann King née Romilly, who were both fantastic.

I was out on the training pitch for the first time, with household names all around me and I didn't know what to call people. I shouted out "Beckham, pass it here." Everyone stopped what they were doing and burst out laughing at me. David called me over, and said, "Just call me Becks, Darius." I didn't feel so bad then, but I hadn't wanted to just call them all by their nicknames, like I was trying too hard to be their mate.

Joining up for training left me with the feeling I had all those years back with Romulus Boys. I was out of my depth, surrounded by the biggest players in English football, some of whom were the biggest names in world football. What helped me was that there were a couple of others in the same situation as me, but there was a real shock factor when I turned up that first time, even though I'd played against them at Premier League level. I guess my feelings reflected those of other people at the time, and there was a lot of scrutiny on the decision to call me in to the squad. A footballer I admired greatly, Jimmy-Floyd Hasselbaink, was talking on television ahead of the game and commented that he was surprised I had been called-up and felt it might have been a little too soon for me. I knew that from that moment on, England wasn't going to be fun; it was going to be about answering people and proving that I belonged at that level.

I was so thankful to Sven for giving me my chance with England, as there was such competition for places with England around this time, with many quality players in each position, battling it out to be picked. Sven was always pictured attending Premier League games and I can remember him coming to Villa Park to watch us play. We were often on Sky against the other big clubs, and I would tend to play well on those days for some reason, it may have been a coincidence, I just don't know? We were made aware by our club manager if Sven was attending and there was a lot of focus on him by the media at the time. I wasn't used to having people come and watch me play throughout my life, so it was nice that Sven was there, even though I knew he wasn't there just to watch me. If I made a mistake I would always want to put it right to show him what I could do and that I was a good team player as well.

I was desperate to prove myself at England level, to everyone, my friends and family and particularly to the other England players in the squad. I didn't want to contemplate people thinking I'd failed, and then the sympathy that would come with being a one-cap wonder. The squad at the time all played for the likes of Manchester United, Arsenal, Liverpool and Chelsea, and I was at Aston Villa so I wasn't sure what they knew of me. Once we were in training together, seeing that they accepted me and that they felt that I could offer something was perhaps the biggest satisfaction I gained from my time with England. It wasn't intimidating to be around David Beckham or Steven Gerrard, but when they were pinging 80-yard passes towards you, and everyone is watching to see whether you can get the ball under control, you know that the stakes have just got a lot higher. Just knowing that they trusted me to cope with the pass was enough for me to believe that I belonged amongst them, as they never stopped pinging those passes in my direction.

DREAM WITHIN A DREAM

It was strange around Aston Villa after the announcement, getting a load more 'well done's' and lots of taps on the back, which was something I had to get used to. My close friends from my youth days would be asking me if I was alright and how I felt about it. I could sense that some of these guys, who I'd played football with at YTS level, were feeling my news as if it was them, which meant a great deal to me. I think that I played it down a lot at the time, but just to play once for England would have been pretty amazing in itself.

I can remember looking at the squad as it was listed on Sky Sports and then later, seeing the team named and I think there was a real question mark over it. We were a few months away from the 2002 World Cup, being held in Japan and South Korea, and our manager, Sven-Göran Eriksson, named an experimental squad. It was a friendly, so it was normal for him to give people an opportunity to claim their place in the squad, and there were the usual big names in there too, but Sven was very good at judging people on what they had done and their recent form, rather than just picking people on reputations. I felt like I would be given the chance to play my usual 'super-sub' role, especially as I was yet to make my England debut, so I felt quite comfortable about the prospective of that. Then, all of sudden, I was told I would be starting in a front three alongside Emile Heskey and Michael Ricketts, who was also making his England debut after a run of goals for Bolton Wanderers had seen him called-up by Sven. He was on fire, and we'd grown up not too far from each other; Michael playing for Walsall while I was at Villa and there was a battle for who could score the most goals in the West Midlands in those early days. Wayne Bridge also gained his first full England cap in Amsterdam. The team that night was Nigel Martyn in goal, a back four of Gary Neville, Rio Ferdinand, Sol Campbell and Wayne Bridge, a midfield three of David Beckham, Paul Scholes and Steven Gerrard and then the front three of Heskey, Ricketts and me. It was a strong team, with an experimental strikeforce, so we knew that all eyes would be on how we performed, more so than the regulars. Even though it was a friendly, there was no element of taking it easy.

I knew I was a good player and that I could perform at this level; but I always had at the back of my mind this thing about making a mistake and ensuring I put it right, so I think that helped me to cope with making my debut for England. Then that's all forgotten as you look across and

Edgar Davids is stood there, getting ready to compete against you. It was a humbling experience to see world stars on the same pitch as you. Having said that, I won a one-on-one battle against Davids and came out with the ball, which helped me to stop running around the Amsterdam Arena like a headless chicken. I began to react properly and felt in a good frame of mind.

My debut will always be remembered for my goal. I guess that if I hadn't have scored, no one would have talked about me. I felt I played well and contributed to the team, playing on the left and on the right, rather than as an out-and-out striker, but we fell behind to a first-half Patrick Kluivert strike. I didn't want to let people down, and I tried a trick after receiving the ball from Scholes and I gave the ball away. I can remember turning to see Steven Gerrard shouting and screaming at me. If I didn't realise the standards expected and the level of responsibility on me, then I did now. I knew Steven from playing for England youth teams, but seeing his face like thunder really opened my eyes. In terms of my goal, it was just so natural, like a lot of my goals I didn't really know what was happening and just reacted, almost in autopilot. In the second half we had numerous chances; I hit one of my 'Schlazers' from outside the box which Edwin Van Der Sar saved, and then a Beckham free-kick was saved before Chris Powell, who had come on at half-time, volleyed over. I was linking up well with Heskey and also Kevin Phillips who had joined the action with Powell at the break, but it was Beckham who was involved in everything. On 61 minutes, he got the ball out of his feet, wide on the right and whipped one of his trademark crosses in to the box. I'd seen him do it thousands of times. As the ball curled I had to adjust myself, as perhaps with my eagerness to get on the end of it, I was ahead of the ball. I held my step and must have been in a good place, playing what I would call happy football, to even try what I did and I connected perfectly with my right foot and acrobatically volleyed the ball home. I'd scored for England. The dream of so many young boys and here I was living every minute of it. I ran away to celebrate with the fans and then remembered we were playing away and our fans were at the other end of the ground, so I just looked for my teammates. I remember Paul Scholes and David Beckham celebrating with me and whispering something to me, and it dawned on me that I'd made an impact in my first game. That could have been my only chance and I'd taken it.

I can honestly say that goal changed my life. Just in the way my first goals for Villa had done a few years earlier, this took things to another level. It's one of the main wishes of any young boy who plays football. That goal gave me an immediate connection to every football fan. Did it matter whether I played well on the night? Yes, of course, I was a professional, but people simply don't remember that; they remember my goal. My debut goal for England and people still ask me about it today. Even though it may sound a little unprofessional, I honestly don't know what to say to people about it; it just happened and before I knew what I'd done, I was wheeling away celebrating. Obviously I meant it, but it was an instinctive reaction.

At the end of the game I can remember going over to my Villa teammate, George Boateng, who had made his debut for Holland in 2001 and had come on at half-time in this game, and he was so pleased for me. He treated me as if I was equal to everyone, as if I belonged there. I think it helped that he was there, a familiar face, as everyone else was swapping shirts and speaking to Dutch players they knew, and I didn't want to be the only one at the end looking like I was out of place. I felt just like a trialist that day, doing everything I could to impress people. On the bus as we left the stadium, people were singing my name and Gary Neville came over and congratulated me. I was handed a debut present later, with framed photos and signatures. It was like I had truly arrived and everyone had accepted me. Any training session or game from that day on, I felt like the rest of the squad realised what I could do to help the team and they would look for me on the field and use me as an attacking threat. Before then, I was just someone on the periphery. It's not their fault that I felt that way; these guys were used to debutants coming in to the squad and not being seen again. They were the core players and now I was being welcomed as one of them. That bond doesn't really get spoken of very often, it just happens.

After all the media hype for a day or two, I returned to playing for Villa, so there wasn't really time to let it all sink in. All I took from the experience was that the goal and my performance had given me a very good chance of being named in the next England squad, and that was quite a calming feeling. It meant that I didn't need to worry so much, I could go off and play for Villa and let England worry about itself. No one could claim it was a bad decision to pick me now, or that I didn't belong at that level. That night gave me such belief and it was a real career highlight for me. I think that the real shock was that so many people had seen the goal. I guess that naively, I hadn't accounted for the reach of an England game and the impact that it would have. The game was followed with a trip to Old Trafford and a 1-0 defeat for Villa, before I scored for in our next home game, which was a 2-1 win over West Ham, and the focus remained on me. This was the season where I grabbed 14 goals for Villa, and my partnership with Juan Pablo Angel was flourishing.

Timing is everything in football, and my timing in 2002 was pretty good. Those Villa goals and the strike in Amsterdam meant that I had a chance of going to the 2002 World Cup. I didn't think of it that way though. I didn't allow myself to look that far ahead. There were two friendlies before the squad was named, the first of which came just over a month after my debut. It was at Elland Road and I came on as a substitute in the 51st minute, replacing Emile Heskey in a 2-1 friendly defeat to Italy. Robbie Fowler had given us the lead soon after I came on, but a Vincenzo Montella double, including one in the last minute meant we were beaten.

My final chance to impress ahead of the squad being named came on Wednesday 17 April, against Paraguay at Anfield. We won 4-0; I started the match and scored after 55 minutes, with a deflected shot to make it 3-0. On the evening, Ray Wilkins who was co-commentating for Sky Sports highlighted how hard I had worked and that I deserved the bit of luck for my goal. It seemed like people were happy for me to be involved and after my goal the whole team came over to celebrate with me. Pundits began to name their predicted squads for the tournament and I was being listed in many of them and people were taking notice. I felt like it was certification of my ability, and having been doubted, people began to say that they would prefer to have me there. It was a real turnaround for me.

On Thursday 9 May, I was named as part of the 23-man squad to travel to the Far East for the World Cup. I had played just 190 minutes of football for England, aged 21, and I was there, heading to a World Cup. Sven saw what he needed in training though, I'm sure. Whilst people may say two goals in three games did it, I'm certain that my work in training with England convinced him of what I could do and he knew what he would get from me. I could be relied upon and I communicated with him, so I could do the job he needed me to. His style of management allowed a player to play their natural game. I was playing with better players than I'd ever played with, and yet it was all kept so simple. That's no disrespect to the players I had played with at club level at all. I don't know how Sven did it, but he created a great recipe with England.

I think that people often have a perception of Sven being on the phone in an office, away from the training ground, but whenever I worked with him, he was as actively involved as possible. He always had his boots and tracksuit on and he was out on the pitch working directly with his players. He was and still is, from what people tell me, a guy who loves football and loves coaching. With England, there was such a standard on the field that he must have loved every minute of working with those players. I think any manager would have given anything to work with that squad and that level of talent.

I understood my role under Sven completely, it was just that at our team meetings, I was trying to understand other people's roles as well. Sven had a habit of experimenting with me out wide, in midfield, but it was always obvious what I had to do under him. In the meetings though, I used to come so close to falling asleep, I was concentrating that hard. I counteracted it by sitting at the front, right in front of Sven, knowing that I wouldn't get away with dozing off. He wasn't the only one talking, and it wasn't his fault at all though. Everything I tried to do to stop me falling asleep seemed to put me in to even more risk of getting in trouble. No stone was ever left unturned at those meetings, it was very thorough, with Gary Neville, David Beckham and Rio Ferdinand often speaking.

Sven took five strikers to the tournament, meaning I was joined in the squad by Michael Owen, Emile Heskey, Robbie Fowler and Teddy Sheringham. The players who just missed out on the squad were Ugo Ehiogu, Frank Lampard, Jamie Carragher, Darren Anderton and Andrew Cole, who then retired from international football. Matt Jansen came very close to making it, and Steve McManaman was linked with an inclusion too, with Danny Murphy named as a stand-by.

It was a youthful squad with the likes of Wayne Bridge, Joe Cole and Owen Hargreaves younger than me, but there was experience too and as I looked around at them all, I knew that without any doubt, this was the best group of players I had played football with. Names like David Seaman, Gareth Southgate and Teddy Sheringham, who had such experience and a wealth of caps to their name, were alongside me. It was incredible. There was a genuine belief in the squad that we could win the World Cup.

Once the squad was named, we had two warm-up games ahead of the competition itself. The first came against South Korea, a 1-1 draw, just ten days after my season had finished for Villa with a 3-1 win at Chelsea. Just Heskey, Hargreaves and I played the full ninety minutes, with Michael Owen opening the scoring, before Park Ji-Sung equalised. We weren't at our best against South Korea who ran us very close at the end, but Sven used the game as an opportunity to make eight substitutions and give as many players as possible a chance to be involved. Our final friendly was against Cameroon, five days later. Samuel Eto'o put them ahead, before I grabbed my third goal in five appearances on 12 minutes. Geremi put them ahead in the second-half and I was taken off after 77 minutes for Robbie Fowler, who scored in the last minute to save our blushes. History has shown that both South Korea and Cameroon were better sides than perhaps people first thought, but we were not at our best, which must have been a frustration for Sven and his staff. We were just itching to play competitively at this stage but there was a real weight of expectation on us too.

We only had to wait a week, as anticipation built, and our opening game was against Sweden in Saitama, Japan. I felt like I had a reasonable chance of being named in the starting line-up and it was confirmed as Sven asked me to play up front with Owen as Heskey filled the wide-left role. I didn't mind where I played; I just wanted to be a part of the side and was happy to do whatever job was required of me. I was used to being the super-sub throughout my career, but this was the World Cup and I wanted to be involved as much as possible. Again, we weren't at our best and after Sol Campbell put us ahead, Sweden equalised in the second half through Niclas Alexandersson, after Danny Mills gave the ball away. I can remember feeling really sorry for Danny who got a lot of stick in the press for that moment, but he had worked very hard to be a part of the side, replacing the injured Gary Neville and deserved his place. The reaction to that game was very strong back home, but I can remember saying to my colleagues that we hadn't lost, and I felt like people were treating the result as a defeat. I was replaced by Joe Cole with 16 minutes to go. Michael Owen seemed very disappointed in himself after the game, and he hardly spoke to me on the day. I didn't see that as a negative as such, I think he was just so focused on his own game. We never really had the break-the-ice conversation though, not until much later in my time with England, and we were considered as very similar players I guess.

Being in Japan was quite an experience for me, especially at that time in my life. It was nothing compared to what it was like for one member of our team though. It was complete Beckham-mania whilst we were out there. This is not the only reason I admire him, but he took all of the attention away from us and handled it all so professionally. He was always first off the coach, speaking to the press, signing autographs for supporters and posing for photographs, with a smile on his face at all times. It was like a Konica advert from years ago, with thousands of people in a small place and lots of vibrant colours, like a carnival, with David Beckham at the centre of it all. I'd never seen so many non-English people holding England flags in one place. It was surreal. The rest of us were just laughing, but also imagining what it would have been like to have to cope with all of that. The chants of 'Beckham, Beckham, Beckham' were almost tribal. He was always humble and always gave them what they wanted. The rest of us would leave the coach and have an almost free walk in to a building because of him. It made the whole experience a lot easier for us, especially the other big names in the squad. Our hotel was cordoned off for our use only, and we had posters on the wall of us and a games room to use, and Sven would organise dinners for us. We didn't want for anything, but we had free time to go out and shop and do some sightseeing. In fact, I now have a Japanese-themed room at home, which is made up of purchases from my time out there. I didn't mind being in the hotel though, as there was always plenty to do. I was never bored out there. I was writing and I remember reading a psychology book whilst I was in my hotel room, which Joe Cole, who I knew well from our England youth days, took a look at too. I think the only feeling I had was missing home a little, which I don't think should be made a big deal out of. It is part of what makes you the person you are and shows that you have a comfortable and happy home life, and I think it's important to have that in your heart. At the time, I had my dog Germaine, my two cats Xena and Chanelle, and my then girlfriend waiting at home for me, so when I had spare time, I'd be thinking of them.

I knew a few of the guys, like Gareth Southgate for example, who had moved on to Middlesbrough and he was always very supportive, but I felt comfortable with England, so he knew that he didn't need to look out for me as such. I got on well with Joe Cole and Owen Hargreaves, but the squad got on well as a unit. There were groups who played together, so they would hang out with each other, but nothing unusual. I didn't really forge new or strong friendships but I liked everyone in the group. The mood lifted to another level though as we faced Argentina in our second and ultimately defining group game. I was left out of the side, and that day belonged to our captain, David Beckham. His penalty, just on half-time, gave us a 1-0 victory and lay to rest his demons from the 1998 World Cup and his sending-off against the same side. You only have to look at the emotion in his face after his goal, to see exactly what it meant to him. It was total vindication of him as a player, as a character and as our leader, and was probably one of the most remarkable turnarounds for an individual sportsperson on the world stage. It was such an intense atmosphere on the day, and there was a real edge to the game and around the stadium. Most players would have been gutted to be left out, but I didn't feel like that. I was so happy to be part of the squad and I understood my role. What bothered me, more than anything, was if people had any form of sympathy for me. I hated that feeling. What a result that was for us though and it certainly helped to add to Beckham-mania too. People were everywhere, desperate to grab a glimpse of David, or to get close enough to touch him or speak to him. That left us on four points with a final game against Nigeria to play, with Sweden also on four points, Argentina on three and Nigeria yet to get off the mark. We were held to a tense 0-0 draw, and I was introduced for Michael Owen with 13 minutes remaining. The draw saw us through with five points, and Sweden and Argentina's draw meant that Sweden went through as group winners due to scoring more goals than us, whilst Argentina were knocked out. It was very nervy, and a goal or two here and there could have changed things, but we were just glad to get through to the knockout stages. The game was largely forgettable as Nigeria had nothing but pride to play for, and we were expected to make it through following the win over Argentina. I can barely remember a thing from the match though. The next day was my 22nd birthday and I can recall being presented with a cake, with the squad singing happy birthday to me, which was nice, if a little embarrassing in front of everyone. If we'd have been knocked out that wouldn't have been much of a birthday as we would have been flying home, but instead we were preparing for the last 16.

My first goals for Villa against Strømsgodset in 1998. There's no feeling like it!

Spot a young Daniel Sturridge in the bottom row in front of me. A great day at Villa Park where we got to play 5-a-side against some of the local talent.

Those were the days; the arrival of my big bro, Dion Dublin who was a great signing for the club and for me personally.

Dion in action for England; a true leader.

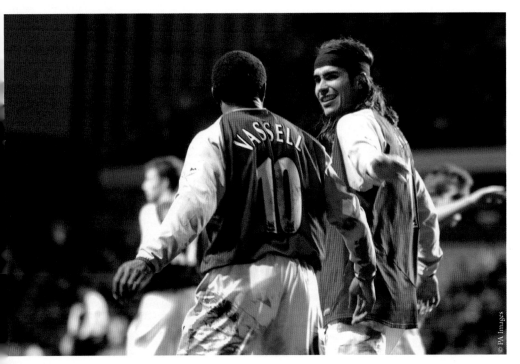

uan Pablo and I at it again for Villa. The number 10 shirt at Villa was worn by many legends including Dwight Yorke. It was an honour to get the opportunity.

owzers! An infamous moment in football history. Big characters in big matches are always bound clash. Dion Dublin and Robbie Savage demonstrating the tension between two rival clubs.

© PA Images

The return of Graham Taylor (RIP). Despite the disappointment of us underachieving as a club, I'm proud to have worked with Graham during his return.

When incidents like the Peter Enckelman 'throw in' goal go against you (below), there is little anyone can do to reverse that momentum.

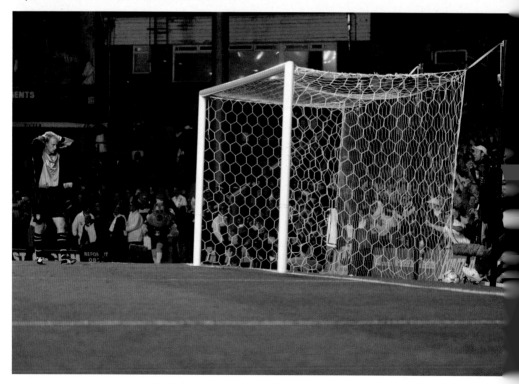

Papa Bouba Diop managing to break my ankle in this challenge. The feeling of being injured and no use to anyone is the most sickening feeling to a footballer, especially when you want to prove a point to a new manager.

David O'Leary having played against and worked with the legends of the game and of my position, wanted more of a return from me.

No matter how down I got at Villa, England were calling and from my first training session there, it became refreshing to meet the England team and forget about Villa for a while.

Debut Day I will never forget.

I must have felt comfortable and relaxed to have tried this on my first game. Credit to Sven and the staff, as well as the players, for creating an environment in which I got to show what I can do with no fear.

Congratulations from Sven, and me starting to contemplate what I've done and the potential headaches caused regarding future team selections.

Gary Neville and Robbie Fowler; two legends who were quick to congratulate me on another England goal, this time against Paraguay at Anfield.

Emile Heskey recognising my finish against Cameroon ahead of the 2002 World Cup, after a great through ball from Paul Scholes. We were sweating buckets in the afternoon heat. That goal meant we got to rest for a few minutes while Cameroon setup again.

Beckham-mania in full effect; it was like this most places we went while in Japan and South Korea.

The chants sounded like Beckha, Beckha, Beckha! They woke me up as I slept with my headphones on the coach, these chants meant that we had arrived at our destination and it was time to get cleared up and be ready to depart the bus. Very useful.

Spot the ball! Looks like I flicked it over the head with the back of my left heel, then volleyed it into the top corner. Yeah, that's what happened.

The perfect birthday gift from the players and staff at the FA; June 13th was always great to celebrate with the England team and it made me feel very special, and was greatly appreciated.

Owen Hargreaves and myself with a game of two-touch in a pre-match warm up. A great teammate and player for England. I'm sure our paths will cross again soon.

The 'Schlazer' in full effect. A favourite shot of mine but this time performed on the volley. I like to imagine it going in off the post with a bit of right to left swazz.

Not quite Passenger 57. The travelling does take it out of you. Zzzzzz.

Visualisation. Each player mentally going through the strategies and techniques that will be required to perform the next day.

A little more Beckham-mania. Our skipper will be kicking himself that he didn't get to lift a major trophy during this generation.

Danny Murphy and Jermaine Jenas in footballing discussion as we get ready before kick-off.

Dejected; a cruel way to leave the tournament. A missed opportunity for us all.

Three days after the Nigeria draw, we faced Denmark, with the winner to play Brazil or Belgium who played two days later than us. I was an unused substitute in Niigata, and we comfortably disposed of the Danes 3-0, with goals from Rio Ferdinand, Owen and Heskey all in the first half. Whilst I wanted to play, I was so happy that we had made it to the quarter-finals, and I was really pleased for Emile, who'd had quite a bit of stick for his time with England, so I was delighted that he was able to shut people up and show them what he could do. I learned to deal with being left out, as I didn't want to be a bad influence. I knew that if Sven needed me he would call on me from the bench. Brazil beat Belgium 2-0, so we knew that on the 21st June we would be facing them. If we had won our group then we wouldn't have had to face Brazil until the semi-final stage at the earliest, but there was no point thinking like that. I can remember walking back to the team bus on the evening before the match against Brazil. We were both using the stadium to train and they were scheduled after us. On the way back to the coach I was alone and I noticed three figures walking towards the pitch we had just finished training on. It was only Ronaldo, Rivaldo and Ronaldinho walking together, about to get ready for their session. As they passed me, all three gave me the nod of respect and a smile. I immediately nodded back and it further dawned on me that this was real and no sticker album whatsoever. It was so nice to have that exchange with them, even though it was brief but back to the football. I was on the bench again, and Michael Owen put us ahead after 23 minutes with a calm finish under pressure. It felt like we were getting stronger as the tournament progressed. In first-half injury time, Ronaldinho created the space with a couple of amazing dummies, which had those of us on the bench wondering where the ball was going to end up, allowing Rivaldo to equalise, which was a hammer blow for us and meant we went in level at half-time. On the bench I was so excited at what I was seeing and what may be possible in the next 45 minutes; surely I was going to score and completely shake the whole tournament up. Going in square at half time became crucial to the game. Five minutes in to the second-half and with a free-kick out wide towards the right touchline, Ronaldinho put Brazil ahead with the most unusual goal I've probably ever seen. His looping cross went over David Seaman's head and in to our net. I don't think people could quite believe their eyes. We were absolutely shell-shocked. I didn't think the ball had gone in at first.

I was sure it had hit the top of the net and rolled down the back. It just didn't make sense and there was a real silence on the bench. Ronaldinho was sent off seven minutes later, which meant we had over 30 minutes with an extra man, giving us hope, but we never really did ourselves justice. I always felt that they could score throughout the game, as they had players who could do the impossible at any time. At 1-0, rather than feeling in charge, I felt like we were playing out time to hold on. I can't speak for the others, and for those on the field or for Sven, but that's how I felt. We needed to get in to the dressing room 1-0 ahead and in the space of just minutes we were 2-1 down.

There was a well-used quote from one of the lads, in reference to the half-time team-talk given by Sven in the Brazil quarter-final, as follows, "We were expecting Winston Churchill and instead got Iain Duncan Smith," who was the uninspiring former Conservative leader. I totally understood what was being said, but in fairness, if Sven had got up and starting shouting it wouldn't have been right. He never struck me as that kind of person and I think it would have been funny. I don't think I would have wanted him to do that. My view was that if we needed to be motivated and inspired by him at a World Cup quarter-final against Brazil, then perhaps we should have been asking ourselves questions?

In any case, Sven's actions in terms of his substitutions, suggested that he was doing everything he could to get an equaliser. He brought Kieron Dyer on for Trevor Sinclair, and then late on I was introduced for Michael Owen and finally Teddy Sheringham came on for Ashley Cole as we threw caution to the wind. It wasn't enough though and with ten men, Brazil were heading for a semi-final with Turkey, and we were heading home. It just wasn't meant to happen that day. I know that there was a deflated feeling and especially back in England, where people didn't feel we had attacked Brazil enough. I felt like the game passed me by at the end and that ultimately it just wasn't our day. They kept the ball well, and prevented us from gaining any momentum in the game, or from making our extra man count. In the dressing room afterwards, there was real sorrow from the more senior and older players, for whom perhaps it was their last chance of glory with England. I deliberately tried not to be disappointed, as I was at the World Cup, we'd just lost to Brazil, who I'd watched and admired since I was little, so what did I have to be disappointed about? I'd only just got in to the squad in February, and here I was in June in Japan, playing at a World Cup. I was gutted for the team and for the country, I want to make that clear, but it was incredible just to be part of an occasion like that. I hope it doesn't come across as being flippant, but I had to be realistic. My family and friends were shocked that I had been picked, so I was coming home having played for England at that level, and they couldn't wait to see me and hear all about my experiences. One of them would ask me about the football, and someone else would shout at them for talking about football. It really changed the way that people behaved around me, with those close to me just trying to show me their love and support, but naturally things were never going to be the same again.

I think that given hindsight now, we also need to put in to perspective that Brazil went on to win that tournament and they had the likes of Ronaldo, Rivaldo and Ronaldinho in their attack, who were almost unplayable on their day. It's also worth keeping in mind that Sven's record of reaching quarter-finals, doesn't quite look so bad these days, given recent tournament failures. Knockout football is brutal, which is why it's so exciting, and sometimes it just isn't meant to happen. I think we can all look back at that Ronaldinho goal and say it was a bit of a freak occurrence. What could David Seaman have done to prevent it? If he'd have remained stood on his line, it would have opened up the space for a Brazilian attacker to reach the cross. No one could have expected what Ronaldinho did. I really hope that David isn't losing any sleep over that incident. He had a fantastic career, and goes down as one of our country's greatest ever goalkeepers. It's just a shame that people remember that incident, as in my opinion, it really wasn't his fault.

The best way I can describe that whirlwind four months in my life, which changed things forever, is that I still feel like an England player today; like those days remain a part of me now and that I am defined by what happened whilst wearing the three lions on my chest. I'm recognised today, in the same way that I was recognised when I returned home from Japan. I'd never craved the fame, or the celebrity culture, but it's nice that people remember those days and the small part I played. I haven't played football in a few years now, but these days, these unbelievably special days, seem like they were just yesterday.

6

I'M SUPPOSED TO BE HERE

After the disappointment of our World Cup exit, I felt that with some of the senior players moving on and retiring, it was my time to step up and play a little more than a bit-part role for England. I had more to offer and felt there was more to come from me. I attended Wimbledon for the tennis, as a guest in the Royal Box, although my friend Nathan and I were late, so they held up play for us. My England teammate Martin Keown went along too, but it wasn't long before I was back to Villa and putting my heart in to performing with them, in the hope that I would continue to play for England. In honesty though, after I broke through at international level, Sven always seemed to judge me on my performances for my country, knowing that I could deliver what he needed from me. I had a responsibility to ensure that I was still playing well for Aston Villa, but I didn't feel as if my England place was under threat at this time. It may have been frustrating for some strikers, as after that whirlwind 2001/2002 season with Juan Pablo, where I was scoring left, right and centre, I never really hit the goal trail to that extent again, but Sven kept on picking me, right through to the Euros in 2004. I think that as I continued to play well for England, either by scoring, or making a contribution, I made it difficult for Sven to drop me. I had that super sub tag, being able to make an impact from the bench too, and I was versatile in the sense that I could play out wide or up front, so that must have helped. I never felt like I was an automatic pick though; I knew I had to work hard, do what Sven said and that helped to keep me grounded and maintain my standards.

People always say, or presume, that I must have had this great relationship with Sven. I mean, I did get on well with him, but never for one moment did it feel as if he would do me any favours. If I wasn't doing what he needed, he would have left me out at the drop of a hat. I gave him a headache by always performing for him, despite there sometimes being speculation that he would pick someone else instead of me.

I was an unused substitute for a 2-1 qualifying win over Slovakia, which got our Euro 2004 hopes off to a good start, but we were brought back down to earth quickly when Macedonia came to St. Mary's Stadium, Southampton and earned a 2-2 draw. I came on with around 30 minutes to go, and the result put huge pressure on us, given that we still had to play twice against Turkey, our main rivals for qualification. It was a remarkable period of time in history to play for England, given that Wembley Stadium was being redeveloped, so we toured the country playing at provincial stadiums, which was reintroduced ahead of Euro 2016, which I feel is a good move. It created a special bond between the players and the supporters in that era, which was obviously helped by the fact that we won more games than we lost. In fact, it's because of this that Sven never managed at Wembley, and I never actually played there, which is probably a surprise to people. I think that period allowed more people to get their opportunity to see England play, and I can remember seeing Villa fans in the crowd with their flags, there to support me and the team, which was a great feeling. It was peculiar, as I was used to going to these grounds and getting booed or jeered as a Villa player, and now I was seeing support. It showed to me that football shouldn't be taken that seriously, and that it's a game we all love, regardless of who we play for or support.

In November, the squad were fortunate to meet the Queen at Buckingham Palace, which was quite an experience for us all, before a three-day training camp at our base in Hertfordshire. After the Macedonia setback, we were hit with another blow. We faced Australia in a friendly at West Ham's former stadium, The Boleyn Ground, a game which has become infamous for a couple of reasons; the debut of a certain Wayne Rooney, and the day that Sven fielded two different teams in each half. We were beaten 3-1 and the press really went after Sven and the team. I came on at half-time, with us losing 2-0 with a more senior line-up, and we did slightly better in the second-half, but not enough to rescue the result. It was Jermaine Jenas' first game and another debutant, Francis Jeffers, who I'd played regularly with at under-18 level and had the nickname 'Fox in the Box' amongst his teammates, grabbed our only goal in his only appearance for the senior side. The half-time substitutions, with Sven making eleven changes to completely alter the side grabbed all of the headlines though. Premier League boss, Richard Scudamore was particularly critical of Sven, blaming the deals done by Sven with Premier League managers to only play players for a certain amount of time and urging him to be stronger with club bosses. You could make the argument the other way though; that many players may have been pulled out of squads for friendlies, so at least this way Sven ensured that he had a strong squad to select from and was able to give everyone some game time. I never had that problem, as I always went along when selected, unless injured, and Villa were always supportive of me playing for England, but for some players it was different I'm sure. It seemed that during Sven's time with England there was always something in the media. If we'd beaten Australia then there wouldn't have been an issue, so the result just magnified it. At least the likes of Rooney were able to play, probably earlier than they would have without those changes.

A month after the friendly defeat, I travelled but was an unused sub in a 2-0 qualifying win over Liechtenstein, which was followed a few days later on 2nd April 2003, by the crucial home game against Turkey at Sunderland's Stadium of Light. Just like my debut game against the Netherlands, this is another match I'm asked about by people to this day. The atmosphere was cauldron-like; the kind of thing you would expect from Turkey themselves, which we experienced six months later in the return fixture. You could sense that something was boiling on and off the field. It was a frantic game too, with chance after chance going begging. I was brought on after 58 minutes for Michael Owen who went off injured, and Sven had given Rooney his full debut, leaving Emile Heskey out.

Wayne was absolutely unplayable that night, and being alongside him in that mood was pretty special. Turkey were very dangerous and they had reached the semi-finals of the World Cup just months earlier, losing to our conquerors and eventual winners, Brazil, so we knew just how tough it would be, facing players like Tugay and Emre, especially given our dropped points against Macedonia. As much as the night is remembered fondly, it could have been very different if not for David James who had replaced David Seaman after his international retirement, and was really on form, especially right in the dying minutes with an amazing save from Nihat.

On 65 minutes and with the frenetic pace not letting up, I forced a save from their keeper, Rüştü Reçber, with an impulse shot, which earned us a corner and Beckham came close with a free-kick, but we just couldn't get through. Another ten minutes of pressure and after Rio Ferdinand's shot was saved, I was in just the right place at the right time, and I drilled the ball low and hard underneath Ruştu and in to the net to give us the lead. It was such an important goal, and before I had the chance to properly celebrate I had players and fans jumping all over me. It was crazy. Once again, I felt like it was one of those moments in my life where a finger was pointing down at me and I had to deliver. My frame of mind that night was to simply be direct and hit the target. I felt that Rio was going to score, so I was just following in and as it broke off Ruştu I just wanted to keep my shot down. I'd always believed that I was part of the England set-up for a reason, and that goal justified it.

England was so much more than just the game; it was meetings, it was media interest, it was the people shouting your name on the street. There was always a big build-up and the people behind the scenes work so hard, as true professionals do, and therefore you really feel the weight of expectation when you're on the pitch. That day against Turkey, I watched for 58 minutes from the bench and I knew that until we scored, there was always the risk of all of that expectation blowing up. We'd been accused in the build-up of not being a passionate enough side and of Sven being too laid-back and I think we answered those critics, quite emphatically, that night.

After David James' great save, Rooney left the pitch to a standing ovation and was replaced by Kieron Dyer, who won a last minute penalty, which

David Beckham blasted home to seal a 2-0 win and wild celebrations. At the end of the game, David allowed me to just head off the pitch and get on to the bus away from the limelight; he took the interviews and I was grateful to him as the exposure that night was extreme. It was like he knew. I had the feeling of really enjoying scoring the first goal, winning the game and celebrating with everyone, without having to deal with anything afterwards.

At the end of the 2002/03 season we had a couple of friendly matches with England, with the first a trip to South Africa. Playing for England was a real dream for me, but there were times when the off-field side of being with England was just as incredible, and this was one of them. Before our friendly in Durban, the squad went to meet Nelson Mandela. We were asked if we wanted to meet him, and we all travelled to the Nelson Mandela Foundation in Johannesburg. Not one person said no to that opportunity. As we walked in to the room to meet him, I saw his face and there was a moment of disbelief, where I had to actually convince myself that the man sat in front of me, looking back at me, was in fact Nelson Mandela. To see him was enough for me. We were all whispering to each other, when Beckham stepped forward as captain to speak to him, which broke the ice. We all then shook hands with him and posed for a photo together. I remember us being with him for a while and each player had the chance to speak. I was one of the last, probably a little shy, but he seemed content and happy to be there, and to be honest, I think he was just as happy to meet Beckham as we were to meet him! I don't think the occasion really hit home until I received the photos of the event and showed them to my friends and family back in the UK, who couldn't believe that I'd met him. I guess it just shows where football can take you. This little lad from the streets of Birmingham made it to South Africa and met Mandela. I still can't believe it today, really. Oh, and we beat South Africa 2-1 in Durban and I came on for the last 25 minutes. Our second friendly, a few days later, saw us take on Serbia & Montenegro in Leicester, with our second consecutive 2-1 win and I got another 30 minutes under my belt at the end of the game, in another match where Sven made use of the substitutes' bench. Those two friendlies were warm ups for yet another 2-1 win, this time over Slovakia in a qualifying match at Middlesbrough's Riverside Stadium. I came on, again as a substitute for the last 30 minutes, and at the end of a long season we'd got the win we needed ahead of the summer break.

I wasn't involved in the side for the next three matches; a 3-1 home friendly win over Croatia at Portman Road, Ipswich, in August, followed by back-to-back qualifying wins 2-1 in Macedonia, with Rooney's first goal for England, followed four days later on 10 September at Old Trafford by a 2-0 win over Liechtenstein, as I was recovering from an inguinal hernia operation. That final result meant that a month later, we needed a point in Turkey to qualify for the 2004 European Championships in Portugal, something that Turkey would be even more determined to stop us doing after the hostile atmosphere they experienced in Sunderland. If we thought that was hostile, it was nothing compared to the reception we were given in Istanbul; the noise was deafening and there were no England fans in the stadium, so it was as partisan as could be. We went there to play for the win and that was emphasised when Steven Gerrard won a first-half penalty after Tugay caught him, which Beckham stepped up to take and slipped as he struck the ball and blazed it over the bar. The reaction of the Turkey players, led by my Villa teammate Alpay, in ridiculing Beckham, resulted in a nasty ten minutes leading up to half time, which was then followed by altercations in the tunnel area after Alpay poked Beckham in his face as they left the field. It felt like the devil's own arena, it was absolute mayhem everywhere. As we sat in the dressing room, the noise from the stand above was like an eruption. The colours of Turkey, red, with the noise, would probably have been enough to intimidate a weaker squad of players, but we had experience and leaders in that dressing room, and everyone remained calm to get the job done in the second-half. I was brought on with 23 minutes to go to replace Heskey, and then four minutes later Dyer replaced Rooney, and we were told to run and occupy the Turkish defence. Both Kieron and I nearly grabbed a late goal each, and Kieron was offside as Beckham had a late goal disallowed. As the final whistle blew, we had done it. A 0-0 draw was enough to see us through, and the team converged in the centre of the pitch, and as one, in a huddle, we jumped up and down. The noise of the stadium boos were loud, but we drowned them out as we all screamed and celebrated. We'd gone unbeaten in the group, winning six and drawing two of our eight games, and had finished a point above

Turkey. We were going to Portugal.

I'll always remember that game, not just for the achievement of qualifying for a major tournament, but for Alpay Özalan. His actions that day led to his contract being terminated at Aston Villa, as an effigy of him was hung up in Birmingham city centre a day after the game, and life in England would have been difficult for him after that night. He was my friend at Villa; he didn't speak fluent English but I understood him and he was clearly improving, and he didn't always get on with everyone but he liked me and I classed him as a friend. There was always something annoying him and his fiery attitude on that day was typical Alpay. He marked me when I came on and he gave me a little tap before the game and wished me the best, but the moment the game started he was angry. I mean, he used to kick people at Villa in training, so this was just normal to me, but I can remember the England lads on the bus back to the hotel in Istanbul, asking me what was wrong with him. They couldn't believe it and thought he was crazy. He wasn't crazy just fiery, and he was alright when he was on your side. I had one chance to beat him, when I was running with momentum at him at the end of the game, and he guessed the right way as I was about to pass him with just the goalkeeper Ruştu to beat. I was gutted, as I knew I could beat him in training, but he just managed to stop me.

Alpay's disappointment didn't end with that result, or him leaving Villa, as Turkey were knocked out 3-2 in the qualifying play-offs by Latvia, who reached their first major tournament in the process. Alpay went on to play in South Korea, Japan and then Germany. It would be nice to see him again and I hope he's happy and enjoying life.

I missed out on playing in a 3-2 friendly defeat against Denmark at Old Trafford, in November 2003, through a knee injury I'd picked up in Dubai, against Al-Nasr, scoring four goals in the game, on a midseason break with Aston Villa. Then in December it was announced that Rio Ferdinand would be banned for eight months for missing a drugs test in September. I can remember Gary Neville asking the group what we wanted to do. Gary was known as being busy with the organisation side of things, but in an affectionate way as he got everything sorted. I like him, he's a good guy, and we needed him as a group. We were all prepared to go on strike in support of Rio, and we agreed we would do this as a team, and whilst it never got that far we still wanted to show our support to him. James Beattie spoke about the incident at the time, as part of a documentary called Three Lions, which probably wasn't wise as we were keeping our views in-house, but he wouldn't have wanted to cause any harm as I know his character, yet he never played for England again.

I missed a 1-1 draw against Portugal in the Algarve in February 2004 through illness, but I was back playing for England a month later in Gothenburg for a 1-1 draw against Sweden. I was taken off after just 12 minutes though, with an ankle knock, after my Villa teammate and exceptional club captain, Olof Mellberg challenged me. I tried to stay on and run it off, but it just wasn't happening for me. Jermain Defoe came on and did well up front with Rooney, and I was forced to watch from the sidelines, with my good friend Jlloyd Samuel, who was an unused substitute, which was his only involvement for the England national team. When I've spoken to him about it, he says that it wasn't enough and I guess to have the taste of working with the team, just that once, must have been very frustrating for him.

Jermain Defoe had always been pretty special in my eyes and he's proved it by staying at the top of the game late in to his career. Back when we played for England under-18s together, in a friendly at Lilleshall, I was named in the starting XI and then those trying to get in to the side were on the bench. It was 1-1 at half-time, and our team was completely changed, with Jermain being my direct replacement. We were waiting on the coach having had our showers, when someone came on to the bus and told us that Jermain had scored five goals in 45 minutes. I was quite happy with my own performance but that soon changed once I knew he'd scored five!

There was only a month and a few days between the knock I picked up in Sweden and the squad being named for the 2004 UEFA European Championships. There was some concern that I wouldn't be completely fit for the tournament, but I worked closely with the medical teams at Aston Villa and England and was declared as fine to play. I felt fine too. I had a great working relationship with Jim Walker and Alan Smith at Villa, and they were always supportive of me and my England prospects. There was some speculation that Defoe would be taken, and he was in good form and was pushing hard for a place in the squad, but Sven decided to go with those who had been involved over the past couple of years and Jermain unluckily missed out on Portugal. There were four strikers in the squad; Rooney, Owen, Heskey and myself. It was such a strong squad, full of real quality such as Gary Neville, Ashley Cole, John Terry, Sol Campbell, Frank Lampard, Steven Gerrard, David Beckham, Paul Scholes, Owen Hargreaves and the strikers I named earlier. We were certainly considered as one of the favourites to lift the trophy, but before the competitive action, we had two final warm-up friendlies, hosted at Manchester City's stadium as part of the three-team FA Summer Tournament, against Japan and Iceland. We were held 1-1 by Japan in a pretty uneventful game, where I came on for the last 13 minutes, before we hit the goal trail with a 6-1 win over Iceland. I came on at half-time and grabbed two goals and it was a nice send-off for us before the competitive stuff started. We collected a trophy and medals, which was a bit of a surprise to be honest as I was just focused on the football itself, rather than trying to win a trophy, but it was nice, and we all just hoped we could replicate it when it really mattered.

Going in to the opening group game against France, we were without Rio Ferdinand for the tournament, and with John Terry struggling with a hamstring injury, Ledley King started alongside Sol Campbell. Frank Lampard gave us the lead in the first-half with a header from a Beckham free-kick, and then just a couple of minutes after I came on for Michael Owen, a blistering run from Rooney in the second-half earned us a penalty, which Beckham saw saved by Fabien Barthez after 73 minutes. No one spoke about the fact that I was clear through on goal, just to Wayne's right and all he needed to do was lay the ball on to me and I would just have Barthez to beat and two-thirds of the goal free. I guess that Wayne was just completely focused on one thing – the goal – and he did earn us a penalty. We held on until the final moments, when a stunning free-kick from Zinedine Zidane levelled the score at 1-1 and in injury-time, a penalty from Zidane won the game for the French, after a Gerrard backpass fell short of David James and as he tried to reach the ball his momentum took him through Thierry Henry giving the referee no option. We were absolutely shell-shocked. Wayne had once again been unplayable that night, with no fear, he was on fire. That penalty miss would have killed them off, but David struck it almost too well, and it was a comfortable height for Barthez to save. I remember thinking how quickly everything had changed. We were professional footballers; the best group of players selected to play for England and yet we'd conceded two goals at the death. The guys who had started the match, the senior players, were gutted and almost inconsolable. I took the view that we still had two games to play and just needed to beat Switzerland and Croatia, which I felt we could do. Those guys had three points ripped out of their hands, whereas watching from the bench for the majority of the game left me with a different perspective. France were still a very good side with Zidane, Henry, Patrick Vieira and Claude Makelele and it showed how close we were to beating them. The next day, the mood was a lot lighter and Sven talked us through what we needed to do to put things right.

As a group, we all moved on and looked towards Switzerland, where we knew there was no room for error. I had 18 minutes of action, coming on for Michael Owen at the end of the game, which we won comfortably 3-0, thanks to two goals from Rooney, and a Gerrard strike late on. It was over 30 degrees that day, and I think the players were affected by the temperature, and that meant a lot of possession was given away. You could tell from these games, once again, that Sven was keen to use me as an impact player, and I was able to influence the Switzerland game even more so as there were some tired legs out there. I knew that Emile Heskey and I were options to replace Rooney and Owen if they needed resting or if they were injured. I agreed with that approach as those two were truly world-class strikers. I think it was always the plan that if I was to be brought on, it would be for Owen as I've previously mentioned we were quite similar.

Our final group game was against Croatia; an end-to-end game that we had fallen behind in, but eventually won 4-2, thanks to another two goals from Rooney and one each from Scholes and Lampard. I came on for Rooney this time, with the score at 3-1 and with 18 minutes remaining. Again, Wayne had been unplayable and Croatia just couldn't handle him. I'm sure that Sven took him off to protect him for the quarter-finals, and afterwards he was quoted as saying: "I don't remember anyone making such an impact on a tournament since Pele in the 1958 World Cup in Sweden." Strong words, but no one would have disagreed at the time. He was only 18-years-old, and yet played like a man at the peak of his career. With Wayne with us, we felt we could go all the way and I'm sure that we would have. He had become a world star in that tournament and really announced himself with goals, lung-bursting runs and all-round football ability; he was so much more than just a goalscorer. Croatia had pulled it back to 3-2, but then I was involved in our fourth which sealed the win. I was really pleased for Frank Lampard that he got the goal. He contributed so much to England over the years, but often the press or the public would sing the praises of Beckham, Scholes and Gerrard ahead of him. I would put him in that bracket with those players, as fantastic midfielders for England and for their clubs. For me, he was an equal of them.

Going in to the quarter-final, we were to face the hosts, Portugal. I didn't feel that we had anything to fear by playing them. Most of the lads were involved in the 1-1 friendly draw against them in February and they had lost their first game, against Greece in Group A, but still went on to win the group after knocking Spain out in the final round of games. Our game placed Sven against Luis Felipe Scolari again, who had knocked us out of the World Cup with Brazil just two years earlier. Michael Owen had put us ahead with a hooked finish past Ricardo, before Wayne Rooney went off injured with a broken metatarsal, and I replaced him. We were just seven minutes away from the semi-finals, when Hélder Postiga's header levelled things, but there was still time for Sol Campbell's header to be controversially disallowed, so we were left to face extra-time. A stunning Rui Costa goal looked to have put Portugal through, before with only five minutes remaining, Frank Lampard swivelled in the box and smashed home an equaliser and we were heading for penalties. In the shootout itself, Beckham slipped and missed, and then Owen, Lampard, Terry and Hargreaves all scored, before Ashley Cole scored the first of our sudden death penalties, and then I missed our seventh penalty of the shootout. Portugal were through and ironically they faced Greece in the final, just as they did in the opening game of the tournament, and incredibly Greece pulled off one of football's greatest shocks by winning Euro 2004.

Our fans were simply incredible during our time in Portugal. The sheer number of flags, from so many clubs across England, and the noise they created was really special. They followed us around and everywhere we went in Portugal there was a strong England presence. It was always like that, throughout my whole time with England. What effect does it have on us as players? I always felt like I just didn't want to disappoint them or let them down. None of the players did. We went out there to entertain, to win and to deliver for them, and I know the other players felt the same too. I didn't feel the weight of expectation with England in the way that the press categorise it, I just felt the frustration of us coming close, but not quite achieving the success we could have. I never believed that people felt we had a divine right to win anything, they just hoped we would. I know I'm biased and likely to say this, but that Euro 2004 England side is as good as you're going to get at international level. It had everything; a great captain who kept everything together and was well-supported by the other senior players, along with talented younger players coming through and an experienced coach, who had won so much in the game. You could see the disappointment on his face in the Portugal game, as he knew how close we had come, which was not an emotion we often saw from Sven. Football is a great game, but it also has the power to leave you distraught and it just wasn't meant to be for us on this occasion. Even without Rooney on the field, we showed real character to take them right to the wire. We all left everything on the pitch that night in Lisbon and I think you could see that by our reactions. That's where the frustration comes in, as we probably just needed that bit of luck to see us through.

After the tournament, I was involved in five further England squads, but never kicked a ball for my country again. I was an unused substitute in a 3-0 friendly win over Ukraine in August 2004 and watched on from the bench as we drew 2-2 in Austria in a World Cup qualifier and again for a 2-1 win in a qualifier in Poland. I was then a squad member for the 2-0 win over Wales at Old Trafford in October and the 1-0 win in Azerbaijan and that was my final involvement. Just 12 days after the Azerbaijan game, I broke my ankle playing for Villa against Fulham, which meant I was out of action at the exact time that Jermain Defoe was beginning to play for England and he was in very good form too. Sven called me around that time, which he didn't have to do, but that showed the kind of manager and person he was and I knew that my England chances were fizzling out. I didn't return to Villa action until late February 2005, and missed two England friendlies against Spain and the Netherlands, and I only scored one further goal that season for Villa so my form didn't give Sven a decision to make on whether to bring me back in to the fold. Things just weren't going that well for me at that time and Villa were struggling a little too. I couldn't really complain and I didn't, as I'd never imagined I would even play for England just once, so it was such an honour to do it 22 times. I know it could have been more, and given that I played for England when I was so young, perhaps I could have played again? I suppose if I'd have scored the penalty against Portugal and we'd gone through, then there would have been a chance of me starting the semi-final with Rooney out injured, and who knows what would have happened next? But it's not worth me considering any shoulda, woulda, coulda factors. In fairness, I played with Jermain Defoe at England under-21 level and throughout his career he has been a fantastic striker, so he deserved his time after Euro 2004 and Sven made the right decision to give him his chance. I couldn't begrudge anyone that opportunity.

I look back on my time with England with great fondness. The only small concern I have is when other people don't, in the sense of being sympathetic to me, and express that I was unlucky or perhaps could have done more. I understand why people say it, but I consider those days as an amazing experience, and a big part of what has made me the person I am today. I loved playing for England and I will always cherish those memories; that debut goal, the 2002 World Cup in Japan, meeting Nelson Mandela, my strike against Turkey, qualifying in Istanbul and Euro 2004. I couldn't have even dreamt of those days, and with hindsight, I'm so proud to have worn the shirt for my country.

SVEN-GÖRAN ERIKSSON

I gave Darius his debut for England in 2002 against the Netherlands in Amsterdam and he really took his chance. He scored a beautiful goal and made the perfect start. That game showed just what he was like; he did everything I asked of him and tried from start to finish.

Darius deserved his chance with England as he was a very good player, one of the best we had at the time. I picked him because technically he was very good, with real pace and huge strength. I think he was a lot stronger than people realised. Darius had a great understanding of the game, something you have to have if you want to play at the top level and for your country.

In our Euro 2004 quarter-final defeat, David Beckham and Darius missed their penalties and Rui Costa missed for Portugal. In a shootout it can happen to anyone; Messi, Gerrard, Lampard, it has to be someone and on that night it was Darius. Everyone was devastated as we felt we could win the competition and I felt personally sorry for Darius. He was extremely sad, and after the game he came to me and told me that he wanted to stay in Portugal. I asked him if he had a holiday booked and he said no, just that he didn't want to face the press. You could see how much the experience had hurt him. He asked for my permission and I said it was fine, it was his decision, but that we really should face the return to England together. I explained that it was better to get it over with now, rather than delay any longer. I'd never heard of a request like this, but I understood it completely. It showed just how much playing for England meant to him and how he didn't want to let anyone down.

Darius was never a problem on or off the field. He always did exactly what I wanted him to do as his manager. He gave me everything, with great professionalism. He had the biggest heart.

I managed him for England, Manchester City and Leicester City, so people will always associate us. We had a professional working relationship; we didn't go out for dinner together or anything like that. He was quite quiet and polite, but was always very nice to work with and well-liked by everyone. I would say that he was a good influence on younger players and he is someone I trusted and relied upon.

I have lots of memories of Darius, especially during our time with England; from his wonderful debut, to his important goal in Euro 2004 qualification against Turkey at the Stadium of Light, and his pace and skill beating players either through the middle or out wide. I hope that these memories stand out for Darius over his penalty miss, but an event like that will always stay with you, especially for someone as dedicated as him.

How many people play for their country? Just once maybe? Darius, you did it 22 times, scoring 6 goals and you didn't let anyone down. You should be very proud of what you achieved, just as I was proud to manage you.

Football is like a drug, and I really hope that you stay involved in the game Darius as before you know it, you will miss it. You are a role model, the perfect professional, and I hope you are able to pass on your knowledge and your experience to help the next generation of footballers.

Good luck for your future and take care Darius.

7

SKY BLUE
HORIZON

Given the last year I'd had at Aston Villa, I felt it was time to redeem myself. Villa had always been my safety net; even when I missed the penalty for England in Euro 2004, I always had Villa to go back to. It was my home. My sole aim had been to get that contract extension at Villa and see out my career there, so I'd built up a great deal of anxiety focusing on that at the time. I felt like I had a clean slate again, having recovered from injury and being as fit as I could have been. I was ready to show everyone what I could do in pre-season.

At the time, I was living in Shrubbery Close, Wylde Green, near to Sutton Coldfield. Whilst Villa was my home, that had become my sanctuary when things were not going as well as I'd have liked on the field. The house was nice, but I needed an incentive to make things work for me in Birmingham, so I bought my current house, in Knowle, in order to show how determined I was to stay at Villa and to live here on my own at the time. There was a lot of stress happening at that time for me, and I guess I feel like I'm betraying Manchester City by stating how much I wanted to stay, but at that time I didn't have an affinity to City; I just knew that they were about to sign me, whereas Villa had been there since day one. That call to tell me I would be staying never came, so I had the new house in Birmingham, but I was on my way to a new life in Manchester.

As I left Aston Villa, I felt the heavy weight of failure on my shoulders. It was my hometown club and I felt like it would be difficult to look at my family and friends; almost as if I was a reject of the club. Of course, that wasn't true, but that's how I felt at the time; a failure. There was the look of sympathy from everyone around me, and it really affected me. Around this time I also broke up from my relationship with my then girlfriend, and I didn't get to move in to my new house. The support system that I had been used to wasn't going to be there anymore, I was off to City and I was truly on my own. If it hadn't have been for the amazing welcome I received from City, my mood would have remained at a real low.

I took my place in the City dressing room, sat next to Trevor Sinclair, who everyone knows with his great big smile, and it was comforting to see some familiar faces from my England days. My first year at City was a real whirlwind and I look back on it as being pretty similar to my 2001/02 season with Villa and Juan Pablo Angel, as I was playing alongside one of my favourite players, Andrew Cole. It was just what I needed to make up for the disappointment of Villa and even though it may seem like a strange thing to say, Coley was on the pitch with the ball at his feet, and he was looking up to find me. It was incredible, having watched him play with Dwight Yorke at Manchester United, and yet here he was with me. I had great support from the manager, Stuart Pearce as well. Everyone knows about Stuart from his playing days, for all he did at club level and for England. His grit and determination really shone through. I think I probably missed that in my latter years at Villa, and he was a little more like John Gregory had been for me, where I had the same feeling of not wanting to let him down. Little, almost inconsequential moments, like a tackle or a header that I would win, I'd put down to Pearce and his way of working with you and motivating you on a one-to-one basis. Whereas Graham Taylor had said I wasn't the finished article and put in the extra hours to get my head prepared for a relegation fight, Pearce really encouraged me from the go and did everything he could to highlight any positives I had contributed to the team in matches, without ever claiming that I was the finished article. I was a product at City and a prospect at Villa; I loved being both.

I remember when I was first settling in, we went to watch the boxer Ricky Hatton fight, with his entourage. We were behind the scenes, and I was with

Trevor Sinclair and a few other players. It was that kind of club, with a real spirit and togetherness. We went out and ended up dancing in Sheffield afterwards and it was a great night and helped me to get to know everyone. Ricky was a real legend, and Trevor was great and really welcoming. The night nearly took a turn for the worse though, when a group of guys seemed to be deliberately pushing us off the dancefloor. Trevor, who is the nicest guy you can imagine, has another side to him as well and we had to leave early as he was ready to get physical. I tried to calm the situation, and we all agreed that it was time to leave, but if something had happened, Trevor was ready to take four of them on, on his own. I could sense that he was looking out for me as much as himself.

Being in Manchester was almost a case of me becoming a man and growing up. I wouldn't say I cut my ties with Birmingham, but I had to learn how to do things for myself a little more, in a new place. It naturally gave me some distance from home and probably gave me more independence than I'd had before. It felt different to wear a new shirt. Was this suddenly work? It had always been love with Villa, but I fell in love all over again with City, as I had all the ingredients there in front of me. We played some decent football during my time in Manchester, and I can always remember looking forward to playing at the City of Manchester Stadium. It was a really special time for me. Manchester City is a huge club and there was such an attraction about playing for them. Even the incentive of being told I'd play alongside Andrew Cole was enough to convince me.

I also used my time in Manchester as a chance to learn to play the guitar. I was so determined to settle and for everything to work, that I needed an off-field focus, so I learned with a brilliant tutor called Jason Brown. I would take that guitar everywhere with me and I really got in to playing.

I scored ten goals in my first season, making 41 starts, which disproved any injury or fitness question marks people may have had over me at the time. We were a real work-in-progress as a team though as we struggled and finished the campaign in 15th place. That was a disappointment when you consider that the team from that 2005/2006 season included the likes of David James, Danny Mills, Sylvain Distin, Trevor Sinclair, Joey Barton, Claudio Reyna and Andrew Cole and I up front. There was a turning point for me in that season though, as Andrew picked up an injury after Christmas and we lost nine of our last ten games, which saw us slide down the Premier League table. The dynamic of the team changed a little and that left me sometimes playing out wide. That's not to offer an excuse; it's just to say that I wished I'd had the chance to play alongside Coley for the whole season, as our partnership had looked so promising.

In the January transfer window of that first season, Stuart Pearce signed Georgios Samaras for £6million. I understood that competition was good for the team, but started to question whether that would leave me out of the side if everyone was fit. I was used to big name strikers coming in at Villa though, and it just ensured that I got my head down and worked as hard as I could for City.

My first goal for City had come in a 2-1 away win at Sunderland in August 2005. I deliberately toe-poked the ball in to the corner, a skill that I'd practiced before so I was delighted I managed to score with it. A month later I scored an extra-time penalty away at Doncaster Rovers in the League Cup, which we then lost on penalties, with me missing our first in the shootout. In October, I grabbed another in a 2-0 home win over Everton and at the end of the month I really made my mark at the club, live on Sky Sports, in a 3-1 home win over my former club, Aston Villa. I really wasn't looking forward to the game, and that was not just for the fear of being booed by the Villa fans, it was because I was playing against my former teammates, the club I supported, but mainly because I was just plain angry. You can see in the video footage from that night, just how determined I was to prove a point. No one was going to stop me. I scored just four minutes in to the game, after a defensive mix-up between my good friend Jlloyd Samuel and the Villa keeper Stuart Taylor, leaving me with an open goal to slide the ball in to, but prior to that I'd beaten Liam Ridgewell in the air and had chased the ball down. I think I was almost too angry that night, and needed the goal to settle myself. People often say you shouldn't celebrate against your old club, but I did, as it was just what I needed. Twenty minutes later, and I can't really put in to words the second goal; it was like the perfect training ground move, as I linked up with Coley who lofted the ball over to me, and I struck it first-time on the volley, across the keeper from an angle inside the area and in to the far corner. I couldn't believe it. I'd only left Villa a few months earlier, and I'd scored two goals against them inside 26 minutes. Ridgewell grabbed one back for Villa before I turned provider with a header back to Coley, who finished things off securing the three points for us.

That night against Villa was a great example of how good the partnership with Coley could be. I look back now at photos of us playing together and honestly wonder how I'm stood next to him. We didn't have a relationship off the field, so to speak though. We were always polite and there was a really strong football understanding, but he was one of my heroes and I didn't really want to get too close to him. He was incredible on the training pitch as well, and I wanted to show him that I was willing to do the hard work, as he was getting on a bit at that stage, which I'm sure he won't mind me saying. I was desperate to win his approval and I remember him absolutely hammering me in a game against Birmingham City that season. I was booed by their fans, even though I'd left Villa, they were still at me. Coley had put me in on goal and I opted to shoot when off-balance and it was a poor effort. He shouted words to the effect of 'if you're going to shoot like that, don't bother, just give me the ball back and I'll score,' which you can say if you're as good as Andrew Cole. It felt like my dad had scalded me. Coley went out of his way afterwards to allay my fears in the changing room and told me not to worry about him shouting at me, and it was just what he did to ensure we won. I took it on board and everyone was happy, but I think he'd realised that he'd got to me. He's still one of my heroes today, but we weren't best mates at the time or anything like that. I absolutely loved playing with him, but he was quite a quiet guy, perhaps a little like myself I guess.

After being sold by Villa, I was determined to not allow that feeling of failure to creep back in again. In a moment, by myself, I came up with what was almost a personal motto, S.K.A.T. F.C. where every letter had a sentence coming off it and stood for the following:

Shoot on every occasion
Keep moving to keep up motivation
Always look around to know the situation
Toe-poking is effective but not part of education
Follow-up shots so goal chances are never wasted
Close down defenders but red cards need evasion

I used to say this to myself just before every game after joining City. I must have made it up during preseason in Sweden with Villa. I think it stemmed from people questioning the number of goals I scored, and I felt that if I did everything on that list, I'd be noticed and people would realise that there was more to my game than just goals. I wanted to show that I'd made a worthy contribution, even if we'd lost a game I had to give myself the best chance of coming off the pitch having felt I'd done something if not score. The feeling of making a contribution as a team player is invaluable. This process focused my mind, calmed me down and was a form of self-management and it was a way to ensure that I was a valuable part of the team. No matter what I'd done in the past, people would always judge me by how many goals I'd scored, or the lack of me being a 20-25 goal a season man.

I scored my fifth City goal in a 5-2 away win at Charlton Athletic in early December and then on 14th January 2006 we welcomed Manchester United to the City of Manchester Stadium. I'd experienced my first Manchester derby at the start of the season, a pretty non-eventful 1-1 draw, with Joey Barton rescuing the point for us after Ruud Van Nistelrooy's opener. The return fixture had so much more to it. We came out on top with a 3-1 win. I'd been used to volatile derby atmospheres in the Villa vs. Birmingham games, but this was just as charged. Within the city centre itself, it was all that people talked about in the build-up and after the game. Walking out on the pitch to that sea of sky blue was incredible and I felt like I had to perform that day for those fans. That United side was pretty special and included the likes of Gary Neville, Rio Ferdinand, Cristiano Ronaldo, who was sent off after 66 minutes, Wayne Rooney, Ruud Van Nistelrooy and Ryan Giggs amongst others, but through goals from Trevor Sinclair, myself and Robbie Fowler we sent one half of the city home happy. Scoring in this fixture was a special moment. We all combined as a team that day and in each goal. I can remember the joy in both mine and Trevor's faces as we celebrated with supporters.

Sadly, our season never really kicked on from there as it should have. I scored a couple of weeks after the United win, in a 3-0 home win over Newcastle United, but I saved my last two goals of the season for one club; Aston Villa. We drew 1-1 against them in the FA Cup with a last-gasp headed goal from a young Micah Richards, who then infamously swore on the BBC in the post-match interview. Micah was so bubbly and that goal meant a lot to him as he has family from Birmingham, and the lads had quite a good laugh about that afterwards. It's funny how he went full circle and ended up at Villa himself. In the replay at home, I scored the second in a 2-1 win, early in the second-half to put us in to the quarter finals. I grabbed the winner at Villa Park a month later in a 1-0 victory, meaning I scored four goals in four games against them. It's not for me to say, but I personally felt I answered any critics at that time and maybe showed Aston Villa and David O'Leary I was fit and still a threat on my day. It was very strange scoring at Villa Park against them, but I still had the frustration towards O'Leary and that acted as a motivation for me. I understood he had a job to do, but the fact is he's no longer at Villa, yet the club will always be in my heart.

Only David James made more starts in that first season for me at City, and in terms of my return that was probably my best season for the club. Cole finished on ten goals with me, so we were joint top scorers, but he'd obviously missed the end of the season through injury and was suffering a little prior to that. Claudio Reyna was a real talent in that side and I enjoyed playing with him. To be honest, the dressing room was packed full of big characters, a little like my earlier days at Villa, with no one bigger than Ben Thatcher. He had all the practical jokes, most of which I wouldn't be able to repeat in this book. He never played one of his jokes on me though, at least I don't think so although most of the squad experienced excrement in their shoes at some point and he'd just be laughing his socks off with Joey Barton never too far away. On one occasion, Ben was sat in the canteen and as the manager, Stuart Pearce, walked in wearing a pair of Timberland boots, Ben shouted 'what the f**k are those?' I was thinking, this is the manager, what are you doing? People were sniggering and laughing and Pearce gave him a look as if to say 'who do you think you are, son?' that look just made the joke feel more awkward. Then there was Richard Dunne who would keep people sensible and they would listen to him, and Sylvain Distin was one of the leaders of the group too. Sun Jihai was a good character as well and we were all learning how to say 'Ni Hao', which is hello in Chinese, and a few other words in his native language. There was quite a lot of expectation for Georgios Samaras too and there were certainly times when you would see him pick up the ball and show his skills, but he'd probably admit that he didn't quite do it often enough for City.

I can remember an occasion after one of our matches I was asked to do the TV interviews at the end of the game. I was all suited up ready to go but bumped into Graham Taylor who was being interviewed on another camera. He was invited to the game as a special guest and I made sure I remembered to come and find him once we were both finished. I approached him and shook his hand and asked how he was. I'll never forget his face. It was as though he was proud of me; his expression said well done. I think he knew that I had found a way to be a footballer that worked for me and was getting on with it. He was aware of how much attachment I had to Villa and probably had a better idea than me of the circumstances that lead to my departure. He also knew that I didn't like doing interviews but we were both out there after everyone else had left, each fulfilling our responsibilities, but this was at my new club. I was so proud to be at city in this moment.

At the start of the 2006/2007 season, my second with the club, Stuart Pearce added Ousmane Dabo, Dietmar Hamann, Bernardo Corradi, Paul Dickov and probably one of the club's most influential and best value signings, Joe Hart, whilst letting David James and Andrew Cole leave. Andrew's fitness meant it was a short spell with the club, but he still left his mark in that season. I had heard there was something physically niggling him but I was nowhere near comfortable enough to ask anyone for facts. I just crossed my fingers that he would stay and then I could further continue and develop S.K.A.T. F.C. while trying to improve my goal return.

It was another case of resetting for me, and playing up front with Samaras was different to Cole, but I was happy to do it as I'd had the experience of playing with a big man, through Peter Crouch with Villa. Pearce added the Belgian striker Émile Mpenza in February as extra competition for us too. We were knocked out early in the League Cup again to lower league opposition, this time to Chesterfield, but reached the FA Cup quarter-finals for the second season running, and improved on our league position by one place, finishing in 14th. I scored five goals in this season, three in the league and two in the FA Cup, and that return was partly due to me playing most of the season on the left or right wing and partly due to the team's own lack of a definitive goal threat, as we only managed to score 29 goals in 38 league games, with Joey Barton our top goalscorer in the Premier League with six. Samaras had some special moments together with Mpenza, but just not enough to certify a partnership.

Quite predictably, and in keeping with my time at City, my first goal of my second season came against Aston Villa, in a 3-1 away win at the end of November. I scored in front of the Villa fans but didn't celebrate on this occasion. Corradi and Samaras were up front, and I was drifting in off the left. It was strange how I kept scoring against Villa after leaving them and that made it five in five games. It was another example of how once again I felt like the finger of fate was pointing down at me. I scored a couple in our FA Cup run, both at home, firstly against Sheffield Wednesday in a third round replay 2-1 win, and then in the fourth round as we beat Southampton 3-1, before my final two of the season which both came away in April against Fulham in a 3-1 win and against Watford in a 1-1 draw. All in all, it was a pretty uneventful season on the field, apart from Ben Thatcher's well-documented elbow on Portsmouth's Pedro Mendes, for which Ben was booked but really should have been sent off. Ben was gutted with himself after the game, and despite being a competitive and aggressive player, he certainly would have regretted that. The aggression didn't stop there and maybe it was a sign of the frustrations at the time, but just a few days before the Manchester derby at the end of the season, Joey Barton and Ousmane Dabo were involved in a brawl at training. I didn't see it myself, but saw the aftermath of it and it's been well documented since. I got on well with both of them, and tried to find the logic in what happened. I really felt for the manager at this time as it showed the unrest and probably didn't reflect very well on him, but this was their responsibility and it came from tension and rivalry. Both players missed the game as they were suspended by the club, and we lost 1-0 and soon after Joey was arrested for the incident and was then sold to Newcastle United. Ousmane left the club a few months later. Off the field, there had been rumours of a takeover by Thaksin Shinawatra, which was eventually completed after the season had finished in June. There was some uncertainty in the dressing room at the time, and soon after we were informed that Stuart Pearce was leaving, and he was replaced by Sven-Göran Eriksson.

That summer I was at my old Villa youth teammate, Michael Blackwood's wedding; it was in the post-season break and although I wasn't feeling well at all, I had to be there. I met Michael accidently the night before his wedding at his stag do in Birmingham, with his ushers and friends. I was with my close friend, Kamaljit Singh, a very good friend of our family. I was attending the wedding anyway, but it was incredible to bump in to them all the night before. At the wedding I saw Dean Sturridge, Daniel's uncle, and he came over for a chat. I knew him through football, and obviously I got to know Daniel at Manchester City. I was at the wedding on my own and we started to talk about football. He spoke about goals, and how good he felt I was and could be, but that without getting prolific levels of goals I wouldn't be recognised. He was telling me not to make my runs outside of the box, but to focus on getting in to the box, to increase my chances of scoring and to be a lot more selfish. It was advice that I tried to take on board, and I respected Dean as he had been there and done it himself. Little did I know that the opposite would be happening, as I would be moving wide right with Sven coming in as manager.

As I've said, I really enjoyed playing for Pearce, and felt comfortable playing for him particularly that first season where I felt I hit some of the better form of my career. I think we underperformed as a team under Stuart, but in fairness we were never considered as even European contenders, let alone title challengers back then; it was a very different Manchester City than that of the club we see today, but there was still a huge relationship between the players and the supporters, and we all felt that strongly. Once again, I found myself in an uncertain situation. If we thought that Pearce's departure was the end of the change, then we were mistaken, as the takeover and Sven's arrival resulted in a number of big-name players coming in to the club including: Rolando Bianchi for £8.8million, Gelson Fernandes (£4.2m), Geovanni (free), Martin Petrov (£4.7m), Vedran Corluka (£8m), Elano (£8m), Javier Garrido (£1.5m) and Valeri Bojinov (£5.75m). I knew that Sven would always be fair and give me a chance to impress, and at least we knew each other from our time together with England, but that was three years ago, and now he was bringing talented and expensive players in, and players were leaving too including Sylvain Distin, Joey Barton, Trevor Sinclair, Stephen Jordan and Nicky Weaver. Despite those guys departing, you couldn't even get a seat in the dressing room at the training ground! It was that crowded and every Monday there seemed to be a new player sat in your place. As it happens, despite people thinking that I was close to Sven, I was actually meant to leave to make room for the new signings, who turned out to be very good players on the whole, but the existing squad didn't really know who some of them were. In some ways, and this can easily happen at a football club, it created a 'them' and 'us' situation. Sven clearly had contacts all over the world from his managerial career and players were coming in from everywhere.

We started the 2007/2008 season like a train, winning matches but I had to wait for my chance from the sidelines, with the very real risk of being let go by the club. Sven, in fairness to him, called me in to his office for a face-to-face chat, which he always did when he wanted to get his message across, and he listed clubs who were interested in me. He said all of the right things, but it didn't feel right to me as I wanted to stay. It was really awkward. I stuck it out and around this time, to deal with my football issues, I would come back home to Birmingham for a day or two and this is around the time I met my wife, Amani. I can remember talking to her and trying to work out what I would do next. I would turn up for training and there would be a session planned for the players who Sven was going to build his team from and then, on the sidelines, wearing bibs and waiting to be subbed on were those he was looking to sell, which included me. As a professional, I'd never seen anything like it, I mean, Paul Dickov and I were making jokes about how we couldn't even get on to the subs' bench at training, let alone the games, just to keep spirits up.

It wasn't just me struggling to get in to the side; there were so many players at City that it was impossible to train everyone at once. I remember Paul and I, when we got our chance, would both force defenders into mistakes by running around and tackling like the whole world depended on it. It was only training but I learnt how to be an annoying competitor from the master himself. Come to think of it, we were probably being left out because we were too good at tackling and they were working on attack especially. Yeah, that's a better excuse!

I decided I had to do something direct, and I worked out that the only way I could get back in to Sven's thoughts was to outdo the players he had signed, in training. I had to single those players out and show him that I was just as good. I trusted in the fact that Sven would pick people on merit, even if he was likely to favour his new signings, as any manager would do. No one will really know this, but I singled out Elano and had some real tussles with him on the training pitch, battling for the ball and giving everything I had to show that I could equal him, or do better. He was so good though. I'd rarely come across someone in the game who was a similar height to me and could match me in terms of strength and skill. Joe Cole was very similar and had proven himself a tough opponent when we were younger. Elano could move the ball well and had all the tricks too. He'd joined from Shakhtar Donetsk and apparently he liked the number eleven shirt, which was the one I had been wearing for the club. Now, I'm not superstitious as such, but I am proud and I didn't really want to just let this new guy take the shirt off my back. Sven called me in to the office and explained that the number was important to Elano, and asked me how important it was to me. I thought, I can't be a brat here, I need to show Sven that I'm a team player and I wanted to be on his right side, so I told him to take the number. The number I always liked was thirteen, but we'll come to that later. I've always felt, throughout my playing days, that good players want to be recognised by other good players. I didn't want Elano thinking that he could just take my shirt and not even know who I was. I had to show what I could do in training, and step things up, otherwise I'd never get a place in this new look side and I'd be out of the club in the blink of an eye. As it turns out we got on well and I think there was a decent respect between Elano and myself.

Slowly, but surely, I had worked my way back in to the reckoning, and I was coming on as a sub and then I had a spell where I was starting again for City. I think it was another example of application, when it looked likely that competition for places would force me out, just as it had for Villa and England, I was able to retain my place. As I've said, the season started really promisingly for the club and there was even talk of a title challenge at one stage, but we were still a work in progress and that was always premature talk. We finished ninth in the Premier League, our first top-half finish during my time at the club, reached the League Cup quarter-finals before losing to eventual winners, Tottenham Hotspur, and qualified for the UEFA Cup through the fair play league. I made 32 appearances that season, including coming off the bench, and scored six goals in total, and it wasn't easy, given that I was playing as a wing back for most of those games, and to add to that, in January, Sven signed another two attackers, Benjani for £3.87 million and Felipe Caicedo for £5.2 million, as if we didn't have enough competition already. My six goals came across six games; against Bolton Wanderers in a 4-2 home win, in a 2-2 home draw with Blackburn Rovers, in a 1-1 home draw against West Ham United, and two at the end of the season at Sunderland in a 2-1 win and in a 3-1 home win over Portsmouth. The goal I'll remember most though was at Old Trafford in the Manchester derby, a game we won 2-1. It also happened to be the fiftieth anniversary of the Munich Air Disaster, so it was a particularly emotional and poignant day. Both sides wore kits without sponsors on, so it seems almost timeless to look back on the footage. I opened the scoring on 25 minutes, after a long and tiring run to keep up with Stephen Ireland, who had received the ball from Martin Petrov. I had to run past Sven and Sir Alex Ferguson on the touchline, who were both cheering on their players in the foot race and my first shot was saved by Edwin Van Der Sar. I followed up and despite being knackered I managed to force the ball home. Benjani doubled our lead on half-time and Michael Carrick grabbed a consolation for United in the final minute. We'd completed the double over them; something I know that many City fans still talk about now, as they'd had so many years in their shadow. It's moments like that game, and that goal against United which inspired me to write this book, but it was hard at the time to put in to words as we were so focused on the job.

Watching my goals back now, I noticed that Martin Petrov set up almost all of them under Sven; he was part of the new regime of players coming in and I'd had to work my way back in to favour. When I scored my goals, I didn't know who had set them up as I was in the moment of elation. Watching back on TV it looks as if I had custard pied him off on each occasion and it was awful to watch. I've noticed that he played an important part, and that should be acknowledged and recognised as he was a great player. If I ever see him again I will thank him properly.

That period in time was a taste of things to come for City. We weren't consistent enough, proven by the fact that we picked up just one point from our next three games against Everton, Wigan Athletic and Reading. Sven had reignited something in the club though, and that's why he's still held in high regard by many City fans. Sadly, we only won three, drew two and lost seven of our last twelve games of that season, and the owner Thaksin Shinawatra lost patience and made it clear privately, without confirming it formally, ahead of the final game at Middlesbrough that Sven would be leaving at the end of the season. It was a very strange situation and we lost the game 8-1. Middlesbrough deserved the win, but everything they hit that day, whether it was long-range screamers or deflected shots, flew in to our net. We also lost our captain Richard Dunne, who was sent-off early in the game. There was definitely a cloud hanging over us and Sven's sacking still wasn't announced as the season concluded and he was in charge for a post-season tour to Thailand where we lost 3-1 to a Thai All Star XI, and then travelled to lose 3-1 to a Hong Kong Invitational XI in boiling hot conditions. It was a great tour for us in terms of enjoying the travel and the experience, but it was weird to say the least, that we had a manager in charge who had already privately been sacked. I went to do some Thai boxing with teammates and shopping and sightseeing while we were out there. There was a massive welcome show put on for us by the sea, with lots of amazing food. It was a hugely hospitable experience, and we were all saying that Sven was the man, and even though we knew he'd already been sacked Sven was professional throughout and completed the tour, and it gave us a chance to say a proper goodbye to him. I felt for him leaving, and the way it was handled, but I'm glad that I was able to explain through this book, the fact that he never did me any favours and always made me work for my place in his side. I am a better person having played under Sven, and that respect will always remain. Just two days after Sven left, Mark Hughes was appointed as the new City boss, and it was set to be all change again, in more ways than one.

Hughes was another hero of mine. Remember, my dad had claimed that he could have played with him when he was younger at Manchester United, so I'd always looked up to him. Sven's big spending during his year in charge continued until Hughes brought in Brazilian striker Jo for £18million, Tal Ben Haim for £5m and orchestrated the return of Shaun Wright-Phillips from Chelsea for £8.5m. His two signings which have truly stood the test of time though, were Pablo Zabaleta (£6.45m) and Vincent Kompany for just £6m. Right at the end of the summer transfer window came an even more influential change, when Shinawatra sold the club to the Abu Dhabi Group, who are still the club's owners, albeit under the name of the City Football Group. With that influx of spending power, City swooped to sign Robinho for £32.5million on the final day of the window. I felt like I'd gone through this process once too often, and with that calibre of player coming in, it looked likely I'd be on my way out. Having said that, just a few weeks earlier, I'd played in the UEFA Cup first qualifying round against EB Streymur, scoring in the last minute of a 2-0 win at Oakwell, Barnsley, as our pitch wasn't ready in July, securing a 4-0 aggregate win, and then started in the final pre-season game against AC Milan, a 1-0 win at home, a few days ahead of our first league game, away at Aston Villa. I badly sprained my ankle ligaments with 15 minutes to go in the game after a poor challenge, just when I felt as if I'd overcome this barrier of getting in to the side despite the extra competition for places and I didn't play again until November. Playing in the final games before a season starts would normally, as football fans understand, mean that you'd then be in the manager's starting XI, so after all that hard work to force my way in, to pick up an injury was devastating.

I was deflated as I'd put in so much hard work to be a part of things under Hughes, and made an impression on him having partnered Valeri Bojinov, who got the goal against Milan, I felt I had a chance of creating something with him, or with Jo when he was selected. We were a little inconsistent again throughout the season, and I was able to appear in eight Premier League games between November and the end of December, along with playing in a further four UEFA Cup matches on top of the two early qualifiers and one FA Cup game, a 3-0 defeat to Nottingham Forest, which turned out to be my last game for the club on Saturday 3rd January 2009. My return in November had come as a complete shock. The manager had grown impatient with Elano and just threw me into the starting line up when I was expecting to be in the stands again. I rated Elano highly and had broken that barrier and started to get on with him. I wanted him to play as I knew his ability and I wasn't ready yet. My instinct was to just get stripped and shut up and I remember playing my worst match for city and Robinho was also playing. I was heartbroken. I didn't get to solidify that place and I knew that the manager would be on the lookout for replacements. It was one game where I just really wasn't prepared to play. I had also wanted Robinho to see me as a player. Steven Ireland was getting a lot of recognition and had already proven that he can play the type of football that the Brazilians were bought for and this was evident in every training session. I wanted some of it too and I knew that there was some left somewhere. I just wasn't myself though and certainly wasn't mentally prepared to start so soon.

Just before the end of the year I was involved in an incident off the field which affected the way I approached my social life. I attended the club's Christmas party on Saturday 6th December 2008, which was white themed, so we all had to wear white clothes. I had a white jacket, white shoes, but not white trousers as that was a bit much. The whole squad did it, and it was an exclusive event so I didn't really mind although I wouldn't normally choose to wear white on a night out. I was told that everyone at the event was a friend of the club or member of our team. It helped as I didn't recognise everyone.

I had invited some of my Birmingham friends to come up, but unfortunately they couldn't make the night. I arrived late as I was waiting and hoping that my mates would make it, as some of my teammates had done the same and invited their friends. The party was already in full swing, we had a couple of days off and everyone was merry and letting their hair down. I had a few drinks and started dancing away, with Stephen Ireland laughing at my moves. Vincent Kompany lived opposite my flat on Barlow Moor Road and he asked me if I wanted to get a cab home with him, as he was and still is a professional guy. I wanted to stay as I'd arrived very late so Vincent left. People were slowly leaving and I was left at the bar with a couple of people I didn't recognise, we were chatting about the club and football all night. I assumed everyone was connected to the club and I got absolutely rat arsed. I somehow got myself a cab but was apparently followed home. I was stood on Barlow Moor Road and two guys got out of the car and started to approach me. I probably felt absolutely ridiculous as I was wearing all white. The two guys saw my watch and pounced. They were trying to pat me to see what else I had on me. I moved backwards to try and stop them, but one of them jumped on my back and the other one ripped my sleeves up. It's all a blur and Amani has better recollection of the incident as I was in shock that night but returned to my flat as it happened outside. I didn't hit any of them, but had tried to stop them. I was wearing a Cartier watch with diamonds on it. I know, what an idiot. As soon as they realised what the watch was, the guy facing me opened his jacket and revealed what looked like a gun, and I turned away and didn't look again; I just allowed them to take the watch, making them feel like they had what they wanted, whilst I'd kept my safety. I couldn't just stand there, I tussled with them both, but it was obvious they were going to mug me. I lost a chain I was wearing, so I presume they got that as well, unless it was just lost whilst we grappled. They sped off straight away and they were gone. As my flat was close by, I went home to Amani and she called the police. Amani handled the situation so well, and it just reinforced my mind that she was special. I was embarrassed by how it looked; I'm even embarrassed by how it sounds now as I write it. After the incident people were saying that I was setup. The police took my clothes that were ripped as evidence, and they offered them back but white was never my favourite clothing colour and it certainly wasn't now. They explained that there were similar incidents that had taken place in the area, and given that I was wearing white, and stood on the street at 3-4am, I was always going to be a target. The guys were never caught, but I was insured and more importantly no one was hurt.

I had to explain to Mark Hughes about the incident, given that it was in the press, and he asked if I was ok. We had a session in the gym on the bikes soon after, with the T.V. screens in front of us and it came up on Sky Sports News with the headline, 'England striker Darius Vassell mugged at gunpoint', so once people knew I was fine, there was plenty of banter from the rest of the team about the incident in a typical football fashion. Shaun Wright-Phillips had organised the party, so he was very sympathetic and was gutted that it had happened. I was next to Daniel Sturridge on the bikes, and someone changed the channel and the artist T.I.'s track 'Live Your Life', featuring Rihanna, was on the screen. The opening part of the video showed him beaten, with ripped clothes and blood running down his face, walking down a street. I turned to Daniel and said "Look, that was me the other day!" and Daniel burst out laughing, which wasn't easy as we were in the middle of a spinning session. I really loved having Daniel at the club, he is so down to earth.

Knowing that people are out there targeting you, and having experienced it, made me feel that I needed to have people around me. From then on, if I felt that I was likely to be on my own, in an unfamiliar environment, I would possibly opt out, or make another arrangement. It felt like another moment where I thought about my grandma and that she was watching over me. Looking back, I was happy with how I reacted, I put my life ahead of material things and realised that being safe and healthy is a bigger luxury than any item of jewellery. If I'd have tried to fight them more than I did, and kept my watch, who knows what lengths they would have gone to?

In the January window, Hughes signed Wayne Bridge for £10million, Craig Bellamy for £14m, Nigel de Jong for £16m and Shay Given for £5.9m. It was clear that he was looking to improve on what he already had and the turnover of players was unbelievable during my four years at the club. We reached the UEFA Cup quarter-finals that season and I played in all four of the group matches on both the right and left of midfield against Paris Saint-Germain, FC Twente, Racing Santander and Schalke, but despite us getting past those sides we were knocked out by Hamburg 4-3 on aggregate. I was so tired of fighting year after year for my place in the side, and tired of coming back from injuries, only to find that new players had been signed whilst I was out. The constant change was unsettling and I was running out of ways to reinvent myself the more I was left out. I was watching on from the sidelines and I was frustrated, more than anything else, but I was never a player who was a disruptive influence in the dressing room. Not once did I knock on Hughes' door to demand answers to go out on loan, or moan. He called me in and said that I was in his plans so a loan wasn't necessary, and he told me not to worry. He wanted to have a look at one of the youngsters at the club first, Kelvin Etuhu, as the club had to make a decision on his contract. I was calm and believed that I would be given another chance to impress at some point, but that opportunity never materialised and my time at City just faded out. I tried to look at it from Hughes' perspective; he had to keep such a list of players happy and he had to clear the room, like Sven tried to do too. It's often the case that a new manager can bring players in, but finds it difficult to get rid of those who are still under contract for over a year or two. For me, I just wanted to play, I wanted to earn my salary. I didn't want to feel that the only thing left was money. My contract was running out at the end of the season, and I knew that if I sat on my arse for six months, no one would want me and I felt I still had a lot to offer as a player, whether at City or somewhere else. I wasn't ready to give up on my body but I was now starting to consider my future realistically.

I found that by the time I was talking to other clubs in the summer about joining them, they were looking at when I had last played regularly. Those final six months at City made it very difficult for me to find a club who wanted to sign me. I didn't want to turn my back on City whilst they were on the way up, so any brief rumours or mentions of joining a lower league club on loan just didn't appeal to me.

The team for the majority of my final season was: Hart, Zabaleta, Richards, Dunne and Bridge in defence and then a midfield four of Wright-Phillips, Kompany, Ireland and Elano, with Robinho and Daniel Sturridge up front. Daniel won the Young Player of the Year award that season, something I achieved at Villa, and he has gone on from there to become an England player and one of the best strikers in the country. I got to know him quite well and he recalled a memory from his childhood, of playing football at Villa Park with me and Gareth Barry, when we were both young professionals. Daniel was one of several kids there at a five-a-side event, and

I remember we had a friendly match against each other. After the event and photographs a young boy approached me and said, 'you're the one that scored them goals for Villa, right?' It was Daniel. They were a very talented young side and this recollection of ours was just perfect. From then on, and with the Birmingham connection, we sat together on the coach, but I wasn't his Dion Dublin, in the way that Dion had been a mentor to me; it was more of an even relationship. I would listen to Daniel, and I trusted him. The way he plays makes us laugh and we both understand why. We would often get a bag of balls and go out and just practice 'Schlazers', different skills and tricks, he honestly has it all and there was nothing he couldn't do. I believed in him so much as a player and still do, so I would just support him and we would talk about things we both wanted to try on the pitch. I think we could have been a decent partnership together if we'd had the chance to earlier on. He's a very funny lad, which people can tell from his character on the pitch and through his social media. He's very good at relating to and interacting with people and I really do predict big things for him. Off the field, he's grounded and he knows where he's come from. He's set up his own record company called Dudley Road Studios, showing that he's more than just a footballer with a vision to help others achieve their dreams. I wish him every success.

I hate mentioning injuries as I feel they can be a curse, but I know that on his day Daniel is one of the best we have in this country and probably the world. We arrange to meet up off the field, when we can, and having seen his talent develop from those early days, I really feel he has become something really special. He has more than just ability though, he has the temperament, which I remember him showing during a 3-0 win for City over Arsenal, where he came on as an 88th minute substitute, won a penalty and stepped up to take it himself, despite Elano demanding the ball as a more senior player. There was never any doubt that he was going to score. He plays with a smile, and I think he is the right kind of player for the way the game is today.

Around that time, another young player had made a mark at the club, Michael Johnson. He was being tipped as the next Bobby Charlton and the likes of Sven and Dietmar Hamann sang his praises. He was even lauded to be a future England captain, but he suffered some devastating injuries and had publicised personal issues, and sadly drifted out of the game. It just underlines how delicate the line is between what we perceive as success and failure in football. I joined up with him again at Leicester City a couple of years later, and I was happy to see him there. I really hope that he's ok now, and that his life moves in a positive direction. I found him to be very humble and down to earth. It was clear that he genuinely wanted to help people in the future, he has a great footballing brain.

Looking back at my time at City, we finished around mid-table, between 15th and 9th in the four seasons, with a few quarter-finals and I scored a few goals, mainly against Villa and a couple against Manchester United. I take some great memories from those four seasons; it was the start of something amazing, and you only have to look at the club now to see the journey it has enjoyed. I think the fans remember those years fondly, even though the club is so much more successful now. I am proud of my time there, and to have played for such a fantastic club for four years is something that can never be taken away from me. I always gave my best, even if it wasn't always necessarily good enough. Every time I've been back to visit the club, or watch games, I am given great respect from the fans and that means such a huge amount to me. The club has been hugely supportive of this book as well, inviting me back to speak to fans and watch games; they are a real class act and I think very fondly of them. In terms of regrets, I just wish we had won something and perhaps done more for Sven in that season where we got off to a great start, but it wasn't to be. I'm grateful to Stuart Pearce for signing me, and I wish we could have saved his job, but I loved playing for him. With Mark Hughes, I guess that looking at my record on paper, it would have been difficult for him to keep me. I think that in my final couple of months I had one last bit of hope of being given a chance and staying, but it soon became clear that I would be leaving the club and with Robinho, Jo, Sturridge and Bellamy, you could understand what happened.

My agent at the time, Neil Fewings, went through a small list of Premier League clubs I could consider, and we crossed off anything that wasn't realistic. I knew in my heart, that having left Villa, I didn't want to play for another Premier League club after City. I wanted something different; a new culture, new language, a new me perhaps. I was still ambitious. I left City on 1 July to start another chapter of my adventure; but if Manchester didn't feel like home at first, then my next challenge was another world away...

DANIEL
STURRIDGE

The first time I met Darius was when I was around ten years old, when I was playing for my school in Birmingham, St. George's, Newtown. We had competed in a five-a-side football competition and the reward for the winning team was to play against a select Aston Villa five-a-side team. Our tournament victory meant that I, along with five or six other lads, was able to play against the likes of Gareth Barry, David James, Jlloyd Samuel and Darius.

It was an amazing time for a lad of my age, to play at the venue next to Villa Park, against professional players.

I was obviously aware of Darius as I'd played for Villa's academy from the age of eight or nine, and he was playing in the first-team at the time. It was a real privilege of mine to watch him play.

Years later, I moved on to Manchester City, which is where I had personal experience of working with Darius. I'd seen him play for England, so when I moved to City, aged 13, and was then invited to train with the first-team aged 15, it wasn't long until I began to speak with him and became closer. There was a group of us moving through at City, like Nedum Onuoha, Micah Richards, Stephen Ireland and myself, and Darius was one of maybe just a few people who were supportive and helped me to settle in at the club's old training ground, Carrington, which had been promoted from Platt Lane as it was at the time. We shared the Birmingham link and it helped me out a lot having a senior player there who I respected, like a figurehead. Having him there was like a blessing for me as it allowed me to improve, gain confidence and become a better footballer.

There were a few occasions during our time playing together where we would practice free-kicks or skills, and we would often laugh and joke in training. It was a great time to have someone like him around to help me.

In Darius' last season with the club, we all went out for the Christmas do, and it was a really funny occasion, maybe not for him, but for me it was. Vass was a bit tipsy and when he left the nightclub he was mugged and had his stuff stolen. It might have been a couple of days later, back in training, when he was explaining what had happened, and I can remember it like it was yesterday. I remember the artist T.I.'s video being on T.V. and the song re-enacted pretty much what had happened with Vass, which made for a really funny vibe.

We had a bit in common, as I can remember him always having his guitar with him at City, and I have my record label now, and I think people probably felt it was a bit strange that he would bring all of his equipment around with him. He was the first footballer I'd been around who was really seriously in to his music. I think it was something that allowed him to keep his mind clear away from football, almost in a therapeutic manner. You spend a lot of time in hotels as a footballer and music is a way to make your life easier, something that allows you to express yourself in another way.

Vass was also in to his cars; he had a couple of Porsches, a Turbo and a Cayenne. He was also someone who dressed his own type of way, did his own thing, wore his jewellery, which unfortunately was stolen on that occasion after the Christmas party.

Overall, Darius is a very good person, and who throughout his career, was well respected playing for his clubs and for his country. I feel that he paved the way for people like myself, as a black footballer, showing me as a kid that I was able to reach the heights that I've got to. I was just a young lad playing football around Birmingham and I saw him representing England, and then when I moved to City he took me under his wing. There was never any competition there between us. I think a lot of the time when you move to a new club, and you play with senior players, they may feel threatened by a young player and may not want them to excel or improve. Instead, I called him 'Unc as a nickname and looked up to him. There was an almost brotherly relationship between us.

I remember one year, we travelled down to London for New Years', and we drank a lot and had a great night out. Vass turned up for training the next day, smelling of vodka and trying to sweat it out of his system. I was only young so there wasn't as much pressure on me, but it was funny as I was sure he was still tipsy during the session!

One of the goals he scored at City which always sticks out in my mind, was away at Sunderland, his first goal for the club in August 2005. It was a toe-poke, the kind of goal that Romario used to score. It was very technical as a goal, as to run at full speed and do that is very difficult. It opened my eyes to what you can take from street football and bring to the game as a professional. It rarely happens in modern-day football and coaches will often discourage you from doing it as a kid, but it proved to me that you can always do things like this, on instinct, and it was beautiful.

I will always respect Darius and have admiration for him; not just because of what he has done for me but because of his achievements in the game and because he is a good person. He's someone who keeps himself to himself, and people probably felt that he was a bit different, but I understood why he was like that and why you needed to be on your own at times as a footballer.

Having someone like Darius around me has been good for me, I'm grateful for our friendship and I'm sure we'll continue to keep in touch in to the future.

8

WELCOME TO ANKARA
(ANKARA'YA HOŞGELDIN)

I didn't want to become a journeyman footballer. Aston Villa was the only club I'd ever wanted to play for and I'd grown to love Manchester City, but I just didn't want to go through all of that again in England; I wanted something new, something completely different. I knew that there was nothing right for me in England and I told my agent that a move abroad was the only option. I was capable of living abroad, learning a new language and adapting to a new culture, so I felt like it was a great opportunity. I had been learning French and I wanted to play there, but we just weren't able to find the right club, and there were too many offers of trials, rather than real concrete deals.

My agent, Neil, came to me with the option of joining a club in Turkey. He said that a Süper Lig club called Ankaraspor were interested in me. I asked if he was sure it was them and he corrected himself and said it was actually Ankaragücü who wanted me. They were even more obscure! Their club website didn't seem to be official and I felt I must have been looking at the wrong page, but no matter how much I searched for something else, it was their site alright. I got my head around everything and decided that it was worth flying out to meet them and take a look. Neil discussed what he felt they could offer in terms of a contract and we felt that they could be a good fit for me – not just for the money – but to have a real impact out there, a new lifestyle and perhaps to learn Turkish and to help improve a smaller club. There was the chance to make a mark and I was really excited about the prospect of achieving something really special.

I travelled on the 1st July, but I simply wasn't ready for the welcome I received at Ankara Esenboğa Airport. There were thousands of supporters there to greet me, with flags, shirts and they made such a noise; I was totally taken aback, I'd never experienced anything like this before. There were people holding up welcome banners, flares were set off and every television camera available seemed to be pointed at me. I must have looked like a rabbit in headlights when I walked out of the airport doors and in to the madness. People were bouncing up and down, chanting 'Dar-ee-us Varr-sell, Dar-ee-us Varr-sell, Olé, Olé, Olé!' As I made my way through the crowds, I was given an Ankaragücü club scarf to wear and then another couple of scarves and a shirt was draped over me. A young woman handed me a blue and yellow bouquet of flowers, the club's colours, and it soon became a real scrum to get to the waiting cars, with people pushing their way through to get close to me. It was the kind of reception you would have expected for a world leader, someone like Nelson Mandela, or a rock star, not an English footballer visiting a Turkish football club. The air was full of fumes from the flares and as this was all under a roof it made for quite a surreal atmosphere.

We eventually made it to the sanctuary of our cars, although many fans then jumped in to their cars and followed us out of the airport. I said to Neil and to the other agents that this unbelievable reaction seemed very strange to me. I reminded Neil that I wasn't signing, I was just there to look at the club and Neil said all the right things to put me at ease. Another of the agents, Lassani, embraced the reaction and put his arm around me and said, "Look, if you have a good season here Darius, I'll take you to Galatasaray, don't worry son, you'll be ok," but even they were shocked by this reception.

I left Ankara Esenboğa Airport to head for the hotel and away from the overwhelming noise and energy of my arrival. I had travelled with an open mind and just with the idea of looking at the club and the place to see if I'd like to join them. I felt like I was in a nice position as they were looking to impress me and boy, did they do that! There were blacked-out windows, everyone was suited and booted and the Turkish people couldn't do enough for me. I'm not saying that's what I had wanted, but they were leaving nothing to chance in terms of persuading me to sign.

I was later told that the fans and the club couldn't believe that I was coming to see them and that my welcome, both at the airport and over the next day or so as I toured the facilities, was an orchestrated show and that once the people saw me arrive they began to believe I would join. I was shocked by the reaction, but Ankaragücü were a mid-table side, so their fans were simply not expecting to see someone who had played for Aston Villa, Manchester City and England to potentially play for them.

I arrived at the Crowne Plaza, Ankara where I was staying, and was then taken for a tour of the club's facilities. There were around twelve of us in the entourage, just travelling around, meeting people and looking at the buildings that the club owned, whilst getting a feel for the place itself and possible areas that could be nice to live. I met Volkan Demir for the first time on that day, just a quick hello, but he became a good friend from my return visit onwards and we are still in touch today. I was taken to the training facilities, the club's stadium, and many restaurants. My representatives then met with Cengiz Topel Yildirim, the club's President, but before I knew it I was flying home to England. It was a whirlwind visit and I'd barely had time to stop and think.

Neil and I had an honest conversation back home and we both spoke along the same lines about trying to make this work. My biggest concern was the thought that they were just giving it all 'talk' and were not capable of organising what they were promising. We'd been won over by the reaction of the club's supporters, and by the reception I'd had. They offered me a great life out there and spoke about me in a good way. I gave them every reason I could think of not joining just so I had some space to think but they nullified it completely. We were enthused by the trip and I asked myself, 'how can I not go back to Turkey and see this out until the end?' There was nothing else out there from other clubs and time was running out. I was being asked to get myself back in training, go for a trial and see how I got on, and none of that really appealed to me. I was already training myself at the gym and I wanted to play for a club that wanted me first and foremost. I guess I needed that initial connection and I was now starting to feel something.

By that time in my life I was living in my current house, not far from Birmingham, with Amani, who was then my girlfriend and is now my wife and mother of our child. We worked out within the contract that Ankaragücü would arrange for flights home for me when I needed, and the route from Ankara to Istanbul and then to Birmingham wasn't too bad for us only living 15 minutes from the airport. I wanted my best friend to come with me, my dog at the time, Germaine, as I knew I'd be happy if I had him to come home to especially if I got lonely. I've had Germaine since I lived in Shrubbery Close, Sutton Coldfield, and then once I was settled and I had worked everything out we planned for Amani to follow me out there. Germaine was a Bullmastiff, so we began the enquiries and ordered his passport. The club told us this was all going to be fine, could be easily arranged and would be no problem. I was 29 years old and I didn't want to be out on the town or at the centre of all social activities or events. Just to play my football, score my goals and come home. This was all discussed and agreed prior to my signing. The club were offering me a great life and there was talk of a lot of bonuses but I just needed my living arrangements to be a priority. I fell in love with Bilkent, a small suburb on the outskirts of Ankara, overlooking the city. It was one of the areas Osman suggested and I agreed as soon as I saw it. It was now up to the club to arrange my move in date or alternative. They never did, and for the first six months I was just living in a hotel, waiting for the club to begin organising everything. I was being rushed by Osman, the club's sport secretary, to choose as quickly as possible before it was too late and he could no longer support me. I did this and it felt very strange to say the least, I started to ask myself questions the longer I stayed in that hotel.

Arranging the contract and getting the deal over the line was so difficult. You expect some differences as I was moving from England to Turkey, but this was a story in itself. I knew I wasn't going to earn as much as I was used to earning, but I didn't mind that. I hadn't played for a while and my agent had explained to me my current value. All that needed to happen was for the finer details to be ironed out. I was content with the contract but the Turkish translation needed to match the English and certain points needed to be clarified so there was no doubt. I knew I wouldn't give the club an off the field reason to sack me, so despite all the various protective clauses the club added, I knew that I was going there to play. I returned to Ankara to sign the agreement on the 21st July and then there was the most thorough of medical tests I've ever been through. I had my whole body tested, my eyes, even my hair was inspected. I knew my signing was big for them, but it really hit home at this point how serious this was for them. They also knew that I had been injured during my last season with Manchester City and that even when I was fit and available to play, I wasn't selected by Mark Hughes, so perhaps they had a few question marks over my fitness. Put it this way, I felt like I was in a film being prepped to go to space. The problem came when the club told me that I was injured and shouldn't be signed. Someone at the hospital had identified a problem with my knee, so after all the efforts to get my contract arranged, we were stalled. There were big meetings after this at the Crowne Plaza between my agent and the club President, and then another medical opinion was sought. The second doctor said I was fine to play and could be signed. I hadn't played in six months, so I knew there was no injury problem. I just wanted to get started but that nagging doubt was in my mind that something would go wrong. Throughout all of this, I was just sat in my hotel room, waiting for a call.

It must have seemed strange that there were four agents in these meetings representing me, and whilst I wasn't always comfortable having other people I didn't know involved, it did show to the club that they were dealing with someone who was serious about me signing. Neil knew exactly what we agreed, and he assured me that the club were serious about getting it over the line but the other guys wouldn't have come along without something being agreed also. We were all getting tired and whatever was said in the meetings eventually lead to no change in plan, despite me thinking it was all over it was pen to paper.

Once everything was signed, I stayed at the Crowne Plaza, a nice hotel which was attached to ANKAmall, a large shopping mall. It was only 15 minutes away from the training ground and the same time away from the stadium, with a nice view from the higher floors of the building across the city of Ankara. It wasn't too difficult for me to be there, at least in the short-term, but it wasn't great when the room had to be a physio, bed, storage, meeting and dining room all in one, or when you're completely bored of the hotel menu but too tired from training to go and wander. I wasn't greedy or desperate for something else; I was convinced that the club would make the arrangements as per our contract agreement so I remained patient. They kept telling me that it would only take a few more days and I couldn't put Amani and Germaine through the process of moving just to be in a hotel. I tried to make some sense out of things. This was a chance for a fresh start for me and a chance to grow up again. I didn't know anyone yet, so I had to go downstairs to the lobby and speak to staff. I was in Ankara and I wanted to know things related to the club. Making sure I was polite to everyone, I wanted to make a good impression as I was excited and optimistic too.

Unfortunately, there was no real time to settle. I had to fly to Austria for the club's pre-season training camp. The team were already there, five days before me, so I travelled to meet them. I was given the opportunity to meet the team on my first visit, a few weeks earlier at the training ground and I said no as I didn't want them to see me, a new potential signing in my suit, watching them train. I wasn't sure I was signing at that point. I hated pre-season training at the best of times, so knowing how painful it could be, I didn't want to be in the way making it feel worse for anyone. I was later told by Volkan that the team recognised amongst themselves why I'd done that and were very appreciative. I'd remembered how it was at Manchester City, with the endless stream of players coming through the door and I didn't want to parade myself as something special in front of them all before I'd even signed.

I flew from Ankara to Munich with Volkan and one other staff member, and then we drove from Munich to the training camp as we were based near to the German border. I'd made a small request to room on my own while I got myself together. I hate the way that sounds, as if I was being awkward, but it was important to me and I felt that I should be able to decide how I roomed. Sleep, silence and just being able to have some privacy to speak to people at home without others listening is important to me. It was even more important given that I didn't know the language or the culture that I was walking in to yet. I wouldn't have minded rooming with someone once I had got to know them, but not at the start. I could have ended up with the Turkish Ben Thatcher. All I wanted was to worry about the football and not anything trivial off the field. Volkan explained my wishes clearly on my behalf, but the club had still placed me in a room with someone. I felt like it would be perceived as if I wanted something different and I didn't want people to think worse of me before I'd even got to know them so I left it.

At my first dinner with my new teammates, I was immediately made to feel comfortable by Barbaros, a midfielder who could speak English and had come through the ranks at Bayern Munich before playing in Turkey. He asked me if I was ok and we spoke about Owen Hargreaves, as he knew Owen from his younger days and I obviously knew him from England duty. Barbaros pointed out the club captain to me, Ceyhun Eriş, and he looked like a captain, with long hair, a headband and stubble. He was a big, imposing player and was well respected by everyone having played for Galatasaray and Fenerbahçe. He looked like a centre-back to me, but surprisingly from the way he looked, he was an attacking midfielder. I noticed that no one could eat until the captain arrived, and no one could leave the table until the captain said so. There was huge importance placed on respect and I loved that. I shook everyone's hand and I was nervous of the reaction I would receive. We went to sleep and the next day was the first training session for me, but I just did some light work at the side of the pitch to get me up to speed. After dinner in the evening we all went to a little bar at the camp with some music on. Our coach Hikmet Karaman was there with us too. Obviously there was no alcohol given the culture and religions, but everyone was up dancing to Turkish music and then suddenly I can hear the group clapping together to the beat of the music, and one by one people are going in to the middle and dancing. I could see it coming round to me, exactly the kind of attention that I didn't want. I was dreading it. Sh*t, sh*t, sh*t! I just took a deep breath and jumped in, danced and suddenly they all welcomed me and were patting me on the back. I was one of them now. Hikmet was quite a thinker and I felt as if he'd set this up as a small test and was watching for my reaction. He needed me to show that I was comfortable as there was pressure on him as he was responsible for bringing me to the club. I hated that feeling of having eyes on me, but it was something I'd had to get used to over the years. Hikmet got that awkwardness out of the way in the space of a few minutes and I thank him here for that.

The club had signed another English player, Ian Henderson before me, after a successful trial in the summer. He'd played for Norwich City for a few years and had then left and spent time at a few other clubs in England before coming over to Turkey. He was an attacking player and had featured as a striker and also in midfield. I watched him and he was sharp and was very fit. It hit home to me that I needed to catch up after not really playing regularly for six months at the end of my spell at Manchester City, whereas the squad was overall ahead of me in match fitness. Ian was the only other English player there, and he was an upbeat and confident guy, who was already familiar with how things worked so he helped me to feel more comfortable in those new surroundings. He had a Turkish to English dictionary and all the CDs, so he was trying to learn the language and was really in to it.

The trainer had given me a bike to ride, but it had brakes on the opposite sides. I didn't release until I was forced to emergency brake going downhill on a mountain passage; I went flying over the handlebars and into the bushes. The trainer was mortified. He had a look like 'how am I going to explain this?' It was just the two of us sent to do some light fitness work in the mountains, while the rest of the team trained at the stadium. He certainly didn't want to be the man responsible for my absence through injury after the almighty effort it had taken to get me signed, and I hadn't even kicked a ball yet. Luckily, I was fine. I brushed the bushes out of my hair and carried on with a lot of caution afterwards. Apart from that incident, preseason in Austria was going well for me. I was easing myself back in after my summer break and I only played in one of the three tour matches as a substitute.

When I came back to Ankara after the tour, Hikmet didn't feel as if it was right to play me so early, ahead of the others that had been training weeks before my arrival and were obviously fitter. I was treated carefully in this regard, to build up my match fitness and show over the weeks what I could do in training. Things were starting to click again and I was becoming more integrated into the starting eleven. The club hadn't provided the personal translator or driver that was agreed, neither a house but I remained patient as I was adjusting to a new way of life. I became more accustomed to new circadian rhythms and found a peace to the music played from the mosques, as my teammates would leave to pray often between sessions. Osman was always close and I did have Volkan to help me, although he was very busy with other duties for the club in a player liaison role, as well as helping with administration. As I didn't speak the language, I decided at the very least that I needed to learn three phrases to be able to communicate with the players on the pitch; man on, hold and turn. I asked Hassan Ayvat at the club, an assistant who would help interpret, what the phrases were for those terms, or at least something similar and he explained that hold was kalsin, man on was geldi and turn was dön. I knew I needed that as the bare minimum to get by with the squad. Hassan was another good guy, he would always ask me how I was and make an effort to help the team. The manager, Hikmet, then ran a session in training for me to ensure that everyone said these terms, he too felt it important that we communicated. We started to sense an ongoing vibe around the club, something was happening behind the scenes. Schedules would change last minute and staff members and players started to appear aggravated. No matter how hard the team acted professionally, something would make us look like a shambles. Electricity cuts, players leaving suddenly with no explanations and stories of supporter group unrest but through it all, I was adamant that they would keep the promise to have my circumstances arranged and things organised.

I wouldn't say that I felt homesick as such, but I was family-sick; I missed Amani, and my dog Germaine too, but that's what happens when you move abroad. Although I didn't know it at the time, when I look back there were real problems. I wasn't paid my signing-on fee and there were many organisational aspects which didn't make sense and things weren't anywhere near as efficient as I'd been used to in England. For example, on one occasion early in my time there, I was told that after we had finished training, the bus would drop me into town and I would be picked up by a driver to take me home, but no driver came and I rang Volkan who confirmed that no one was scheduled to pick me up. Staff had gone home by then and the team bus had already left and I was stranded, sweating, with nothing but my boots slung over my shoulder and my mobile phone in my bag. The training facility was locked up so I was outside in the middle of town totally alone but fully kitted out.

I contacted Neil and explained what was going on and that nothing had been organised contract wise yet. I was supposed to have a driver 'at all times' and they said I would always have someone with me until I knew my way around. I was quite agitated, tired from training too and I was taking it out on Neil I guess. He got back to me and was clearly frustrated as he remembered that the club assured us what wouldn't happen just as much as what would. Neil said that I should expect teething problems and he couldn't do much given that he was in the UK at the time. I was so angry by now and that was my last interaction with my agent. All I had in my mind was to sort it myself, I just didn't know how. I think it was just the culmination of everything that had gone wrong so far and I was starting to question my patience. It was clear Neil could do nothing, if he could then I'm sure that he would have already. I was months into my contract and they hadn't yet arranged a thing. The fact we spent hours negotiating seemed to hold no importance. Neil emailed me many months later to apologise for how things ended up in Turkey, but I had no response. I was still trying to work through it all at the time. After that initial response from Neil I knew I was on my own in Ankara. This was the very thing we tried to rule out within the contract but there was nothing he could do. The season was in its busiest period and I knew I had to improve my situation; I knew I had to do something about it. These off-field issues were increasing each week and obviously affecting me and the team, but I realised that only I could solve my own problems. I had to start reading into my contract and taking note of the local news. I had to start asking the right people the right questions and stay up to date with the club's off field situations. I needed to know where to go and what do in any emergency and who to call. This wasn't normal but I had to do it. I started to keep record of what I was spending, and I kept my receipts. I couldn't have been further away in mindset than how I felt when I first arrived at the airport.

I made my debut for the club on the 8th August 2009 as a substitute against Diyarbakirspor in a 2-2 away draw. I can't remember much from the game, but I can remember a lot from the place and the atmosphere. My colleague, Barbaros had warned me that Diyarbakir was a very different place. It is on the south-east side of the country towards Syria and Iraq. It was culturally far removed from Ankara, with the city and stadium both very old too. I had a stomach ache all that day and let's just say that when I needed to go to the toilet in the dressing rooms it was just a hole in the ground, and I was concerned that I might fall in. There was no flush or anything. It was another world, but one I had to get used to. The last thing I wanted to do was to complain about Turkey as this was now my home. On a previous visit, the Ankaragücü players were warned by locals at their hotel door that there would be trouble if they won; they had even had bottles of p*ss thrown at them when they'd come out on to the pitch, but Barbaros had just told me to ignore any intimidation. I was a little nervous and wary of it all to say the least.

If I thought that was different, it was nothing compared to a home game later in the season. We travelled to the ground on the team coach and stopped outside our stadium for a goat to be sacrificed before the game. It was just the staff and players around. I felt like the goat looked at me just before and as I'd said at the time, via my blog, it was the point in time when I realised that I was most definitely an animal lover. I know I'm being dramatic but I've seen a lot from the seat of a coach during the years but this was certainly new. Some players then smeared the blood on their boots and head for good luck. You can picture me then, chilled and with my headphones on, just trying to prepare for the game. I didn't want to disrespect them at all, as it was part of their culture so I just watched. I wasn't asked to join in but the players made sure I was ok after, which was very respectful and not needed. They had no idea that my family back home in Jamaica would find this quite normal too. I changed iPod album from Tupac to Bob Marley, and got myself ready.

Back to my first game, and Hikmet was pleased with my contribution and had vocalised that to the rest of the group, which gave me the belief that I would be starting the next match. He didn't speak much English, but he understood what I was trying to do, and I think he was the first manager in my career who set out the team to play to my strengths. He would highlight my movement and runs off the ball and demand the team makes good use of the ball which was a real sign of respect.

My second game for the club, and my home debut, was against Manisaspor a week later, where I managed to grab a last-minute equaliser to seal a 1-1 draw. I'd realised by this stage that we were a decent side, but not good enough to be in the top six, so every game was going to be difficult. I received an incredible reception from the supporters when I came out on to the pitch, so when I scored I tried to return the favour by going crazy, running over to them and climbing the fence with Ian

Henderson. The other Turkish players didn't follow us and probably thought we'd overreacted. As it turned out, I ran over to a small supporter group, rather than the main and vocal one, but at least I was showing recognition for my amazing reception.

A week later and I was at it again, scoring my second goal for the club in a 2-2 home draw against Istanbul Başakşehir. That was three draws in three games and I'd scored twice. Barbaros was telling everyone who would listen that I was going to be the top scorer and there was a real buzz in the dressing room about the impact I'd had not just by scoring but by work rate also. I was labelled the 'Black Bull' by supporter groups and my confidence was sky high. Despite that, we didn't win our first game until 26th September, 3-1 away at Gaziantepspor, so we were nearly two months without that win. As you can imagine we found ourselves stuck in mid table due to the competition below the top clubs. I missed out on that game and the next, an incredible 3-0 home win over Galatasaray, as I was injured, and having arrived slightly late to the stadium that day I wasn't allowed to enter and there wasn't anyone from the club who could let me in. I was told that there were no tickets available, so I had to go back to my hotel. At this time, the press were reporting that there was a problem between me and the captain, Ceyhun Eris, which wasn't true at all. This was out of the blue and it seemed like it was linked to me being denied access to the stadium. I don't believe he had a problem with me and we'd always got on well on and off the field. He would organise a lot for the team as captain and kept us as a close unit. If ever he had a problem he told you, so I wasn't worried. Having said that, there did seem to be a few issues arising behind the scenes at the club, and I think that Ceyhun tried to publicly show to people that we were fine, so before a game we would warm up together, away from the rest of the team. I'd never really experienced anything like this before. I was told that Ceyhun didn't get on with the new president, Ahmet, who had taken over. Ahmet then held a meeting with me and Amani when she came over to visit, and asked me what my problems were and what I wanted. It was three months in and I hadn't even been paid at this point, so that was a problem for starters. I hadn't got a place to live and it was clear that organisation was poor and the speed at which things were processed was either very slow or totally non-existent. All they spoke about was their incredible 'power' and vision for the club which was both exciting and scary. I would often look around, at the room they put us in and feel like I've seen this scene in a film somewhere. My concern was the destiny of my character.

When Ahmet arrived he began to try and settle all the club's cases including mine and there were big changes such as a new team bus and stadium; with brand new villas promised, training facilities and a cinema complex in development. It felt as though there was a divide though, and that those of the prior regime preferred things how they were before. It would emerge that this was the battle going on inside the club, a battle for power. No side wanted to spend for fear the other would win the next election and leave the other out of pocket.

In September, Volkan was sacked from his role at the club, which was one of many warning signs that things weren't right at Ankaragücü. At the end of August there was a huge problem as there was a conflict of interest between my club and another club in the capital, Ankaraspor, now known as Osmanlispor. The Turkish Football Federation judged that the clubs had an 'unsportsmanlike relationship, which was deemed contrary to sporting competitiveness' as Ahmet was our new president, but was also associated with Ankaraspor, and they were demoted and all of their results were awarded to the opposition in the league as 3-0 walkovers. Volkan was a big supporter of Kemal Atatürk, who was the first President of Turkey and the founder of the country as it is today, and as I was told the new owners of Ankaragücü were allegedly not supporters of Atatürk, and as such Volkan's time at the club was up. After Volkan was sacked, he spent every day supporting me as my driver, a translator and we became good friends and trusted each other. The owners brought all their own staff in at this stage and there was a lot of confusion as there were two people for every role. They informed me that I had to work with a guy called Cenk, who was an employee of the club. They told me that I shouldn't contact Volkan and that he was a bad person, which was clearly not the case in my eyes. They also seemed to have a problem with Hikmet, and there was suddenly a very bad vibe around the training ground. Barbaros and Ian squared up to each other in training and Ian took a punch, but everything was eventually calmed down. There was a lot of tension amongst the group and I felt awkward as I got on well with both of them. I thought that I got on with everyone.

WELCOME TO ANKARA (ANKARA'YA HOŞGELDIN)

My frustration boiled over as I was injured in training and then the club officials didn't believe me. Here they were, looking at me in the face and calling me a liar, and nothing had been honoured in my contract yet. I was still gutted that I was refused entry to the stadium and now I'd taken a heavy kick on the ankle and I could feel it going numb. Walking to the side I was confronted by the coach and President and like I said, they didn't believe me. It would have been a great time to have my translator.

Hikmet was under huge pressure from the club to finish in the top eight and the less than impressive start didn't help with the mood, so he knew that he wouldn't last the season with the uncertainty above him and changes at ownership and management level off the field. He was sacked on the 12th November, which didn't come as a surprise to us as he was leaving training sessions early for around a month or so, just to meet with the owners. Everyone was in the same situation; frustrated at the uncertainty, but also trying to look after their own interests and get the wages they were contractually obliged to receive. I would have liked him to stay, but it wasn't to be, and I would say that a lot of that was due to the off-field issues. Hikmet was quite a big and loud character. He demanded respect, but I knew where I stood with him. If he didn't like the way you were sitting, he would tell you, with his big bald head pointed towards you. He was big on discipline and it was clear that he was becoming an angrier man as the weeks went past, up until his sacking.

It was a crazy couple of days around the time of Hikmet's departure, as the new regime were trying to clear the decks of anything from the previous management. They were trying to start from scratch. The team secretary, Osman, who I'd met on my initial visits to the club when the club officials were all suited and booted, had become a good friend. He would keep me informed on what was going on at the club, a little heads up here and there, but I felt that he probably shouldn't have been telling me some of it, as players aren't meant to know everything that's going on at the club. This meant that I knew the same or more than others in the squad, and Volkan and I could go to the notary, and make a record of all the contractual breaches, just to try and provide me with a better chance of being paid. I met Osman's family and went to where he lived, he would help me too with translations and sightseeing. We visited army barracks, had breakfast on occasion at the local nature reserve and now I look back,

I feel like he was just trying to keep my spirits up. I trusted Osman, and he was part of the regime that got me in to the club and told me that my signing was because the regime was trying to win the next election and they needed to show their ambitions, even if they didn't have the funds to compete against their opposition. I felt more comfortable having him close, and he was a great link to club supporters. Being club secretary, he was already starting to get very busy by this point.

I was staying at the Crowne Plaza at the time and just a day after Hikmet Karaman was fired I was sat in my room, when I received a call from the hotel manager. He was a nice guy and he had looked after me well during my stay, always trying to help if I needed anything. The tone of this call was different though. He spoke English well and was suddenly very blunt and explained that I had to leave the hotel by the end of the day. It was around 7pm, and he informed me that he'd met with the club and said that I needed to speak to them about the situation. I was thinking, 'surely the club should come to me and tell me what's going on? I mean, it's the evening and I'm being kicked out of my hotel,' it just didn't make any sense. I should have been given some notice or something. I didn't know who to ring at the club as there were new people in charge and I didn't feel comfortable with it all, so I rang Osman who had heard about it already. He told me not to worry and said he would come to the hotel and speak with me. When he arrived, he turned to me and said, "It's starting now," a reference to everything he had been telling me over the previous weeks about changes in management and the structure of the club. He felt that they were trying to create an issue for me and portray me in a bad light. They needed the hardcore supporters on their side not mine. I couldn't comprehend how bad this was especially when the hotel and staff became very familiar to me over the months prior. Osman told me to ask for a written and signed explanation from the hotel manager as to why I've been evicted. I spoke to the hotel manager and they refused to provide this. I needed something to take to the notary. I knew there was foul play.

Representatives of the club's new regime were apparently spreading rumours about me having an active nightlife, with people in my room and wild late-night parties. My problem with this is that the hotel was the best judge of this surely? The new regime had also tried to influence Hikmet in this way. He knew it was rubbish. All this just to get rid of me?

WELCOME TO ANKARA (ANKARA'YA HOŞGELDIN)

It felt like I was being tainted as part of the previous management and they were going to try and clear me out of the club, along with Hikmet but with the backing of the hardcore fans. I'm not quite sure how I was meant to have parties in my room, when it was full of medical equipment, with suitcases everywhere as remember, I was expecting to be living in a house by now. Either way, it felt good to be aware of what was going on and paying for my own translator felt worth it. I was so tired of this and really didn't need the hassle, I just wanted my club sandwich, lemonade and an early night.

Osman turned to me and said let me make a call. I was packing frantically and getting everything together. He was trying to find another hotel for me to stay in, and he knew someone at the Rixos Grand Hotel in Ankara. I hadn't spoken to anyone other than Osman and managed to haul all my possessions down to the lobby, where I was greeted by reporters and photographers. I thought to myself, 'how do they know I'm being evicted already?' Someone had leaked this story to them. I had a 3D picture of Atatürk, which was a gift I'd been given by the supporters, and I held this under my arm to not ruin it as I struggled with my already full suitcases. Little did I know at the time that if it was true that the new owners were not fans of Atatürk, then this could be bad for me. I calmly explained to the cameras what was happening whilst loading my stuff in to a large taxi, and at the same time another player, Bebe, was being evicted too. I made it over to the Rixos, where I had to pay my own bill to stay there, otherwise I'd have been out on the street for the night. The Crowne Plaza had asked me to pay, but that bill was the club's so there was no way I was going to settle it for them. Not one person from the club called me that night to explain it all, Osman had predicted it and maybe went against orders to come and help me out of there.

One of the problems that the club had at this time was that I'd built up a strong rapport with the supporters, and we were engaging through my blog I'd set up through my website. The responses to my posts were frequent, and the fans were given the opportunity to interact with me, rather than simply being given the club's view through the media. By this stage, I'd had enough of everything; I hadn't been paid, I was missing my family and I was being treated as badly as I'd ever experienced in my career, but I chose this time to speak very positively about the supporters and my bond with them. I explained about how much I wanted to stay at the club and do well for them, which was true, but it certainly wasn't what the club would have wanted me to say. I knew I had to stick this out. If I'd have left the club and gone home I would have achieved nothing. I hoped that by staying in Ankara, everything would be resolved eventually. I can only imagine if I'd have gone home to England, what else would have been said about me? All the allegations about parties and a wild nightlife never made the press, but the intentions seemed there and I knew, once again and more than ever, that I was on my own.

The club didn't like that I was still in touch with Volkan, and although I got on ok with Cenk, he was fine, I wanted to deal with Volkan, who they wouldn't even allow in to the club's facilities. On one occasion, they said they had sorted an apartment for me to live in and just threw some keys over. I didn't know where this place was, and I was meant to be involved in the process of choosing a house. It just wasn't acceptable to me and wasn't what we had agreed. It was like I was being provoked and at times I wanted to just go crazy, West Indian style and really curse some bad words. I just wasn't used to being treated that way.

The confusion was rife. Osman had already told me to never deal with certain members of management. We had Ender come in, with differing managers claiming the same role when asked. There were that many people at the club, fighting for power and trying to tell you that they could sort out your problems, that it was hard to know who to turn to and who to trust. The manager's job was the organisational side, like a sporting director I guess, so I'd be speaking with them, and then I'd go to the coach, previously Hikmet, for the playing side. Osman told me to never go to see Erk, or spend time with him. He was adamant that he couldn't be trusted. At times I didn't feel I could go to any of them to be honest, it was crazy. I thought Erk was a cool character, a bit smooth but probably in a position to help me as he had previously offered. We arranged to have dinner at some point since Erk spoke great English, I had asked him what his job was, and he explained that he was the manager of the club, later I asked Ender and he said the same, and told me that anyone who says otherwise is a liar. Erk took me into the manager's office to discuss the situation. He showed me some paperwork and said there will be a decision soon and that would sort the confusion out. He said not to worry and that he will be there to help me. I was wary of Ender as the first time we had met, it was a meeting at his request and someone must have told him to read me the riot act. I kept my cool and let him speak. He boasted of the great professionalism he was bringing to the club and all the great players he worked with. All of his players got paid on time and they were 'good' people. There was anger in his voice and it was clear from his tone that he was hoping for a reaction. He was loyal to the Ankaraspor owners, but I didn't like the way he dealt with me on our first encounter. For our first meeting, regardless of what he had heard, I felt he should have given me a chance and I deserved the opportunity to prove my character and personality to him. It left an awkward feeling between us both because I wasn't used to being spoken to in such a way and my instinct was to have a go back but I said nothing this time. He probably realised through talking to me, that intimidation wasn't going to work any more than it made him tired. We had later heard that it was Ender who had the meeting with the Crowne Plaza Hotel and arranged on behalf of the club for me and others to be evicted from our rooms. Something regarding the club refusing to pay the bills of all the players. Either way, there was something very wrong about the whole situation. I tried to think of how my ex-teammates in England would have reacted. When was it right to kick off? We needed someone to focus the blame and I was in a difficult position. The thought of playing football was fading, I was searching for a logical reason and found only confusion. Where did the mention of late night parties originate? It was beyond ridiculous.

Once I'd moved in to the Rixos, the club weren't prepared to pay the bill. Ender came to meet with me and Volkan at the Rixos and refused to apologise for lying about me. He said that they owned a different hotel and I can go and stay there if I want and there will be no more concern for the matter. We both knew right then he had messed up and was trying desperately to save the appalling situation from his side. Surely this was the moment to tell us what this was all about? Without telling me the truth, I was only ever going to assume the worse at this point. 'Let's make it Darius' fault, then we can sack him or fine him,' I thought. They said that me choosing to stay in the Rixos was none of their business, so I would have to pay for that. Ender explained that they had shown me the place that they had chosen and I didn't like it, which wasn't the case at all; it was just that a one bedroom apartment was never offered or agreed in the contract and I wanted to enjoy the process of choosing what was. Signing was a life decision not just a football one. The plan was to move for two seasons at least and one of the club's main promises prior to us stepping on a plane to visit Ankara, was a complete focus on getting us set up and in a house as early as possible. Neil spent hours organising this as an important part of any deal I would eventually sign. There was really no need to be throwing keys towards anyone. We had chosen under budget to speed things up but Ender and the new regime blocked this when they arrived at the club and I'd been waiting since; only for them to end up purchasing it anyway six months later which to me meant that all the hotel nonsense was completely unnecessary.

They were trying to make me look like I was being difficult because they didn't want to fulfil a contract that they didn't offer in the first place. I shouldn't have been surprised, as the new President, Ahmet, organised for me to meet with Cenk and asked me to secretly rip up my contract and sign a new 'better' one. They said they were asking everyone to do this starting with me. It was always at the back of their mind that they were trying to cut any expenses they could and any connection to the old regime. This was awkward, I barely knew these guys and the way they explained it all made me feel on edge. My gut instinct was to continue keeping records and allow the TFF and FIFA to decide. So I didn't even contemplate tearing my contract as the owners requested, as they weren't paying people anyway, there was no way they were going to sign a new deal, for less money and pay me. The club weren't even paying the administration staff or club suppliers, let alone the players. According to constant discussion and reports, no one was ever paid. People were scared to leave their jobs, as they stayed with the hope of getting something. These people had family to provide for. It was awful to hear. When I think back, I could only imagine how people must have felt when I arrived with all the fanfare at the airport, driving around in the car Osman had finally managed to get hold of for me, right before he left the club. They must have looked at me and thought I'd been paid the money they were owed, in order to join the club. It was absolutely scandalous and I really felt for the staff. We all still had to get along while regimes fought for power within the club. It soon emerged that we were all in a similar position so we stuck together. After a match, if we'd triggered any team bonus, led by our captain Ceyhun Eriş, the players would all give half so we could collect something for them. It got to the stage where if we didn't win, score or draw a game, the staff wouldn't get anything and it felt good to be a part of rectifying that. It kept the team closer through times like when our team bus got repossessed or whenever the power was cut. At mealtimes before and after training the staff would fill our dinner plates. I was growing closer to my team in the background of everything and slowly our frustrations would be shared and their English response was, 'this is Ankaragücü, it's normal.' We all laughed together. They really were so humble.

I scored on 12th December in a 3-2 away defeat to Fenerbahçe, a game which we were expected to lose and we were without a manager, with Umit Ozat our coach, filling in as a caretaker boss. This was the first time in my career that I'd scored in a league game and finished on the losing side. I hadn't had that feeling before and I was absolutely gutted. It was a strange game as we were playing the match behind closed doors, like a training match, after previous crowd trouble at Fenerbahçe. As such, there was a supporter mural behind one of the goals, similar to the one they had at Arsenal's Highbury Stadium in the early 1990s; it was surreal to play in front of that, but despite the lack of atmosphere it was a cracking game and we had a real go at them. They had very talented players such as Roberto Carlos, Diego Lugano, Daniel Guiza and Alex de Souza and were clearly a better side than us, packed full of internationals. I enjoyed the team camaraderie that day and I remember we were gutted together not to have got the draw at least. The goal I scored was a great team move showing that we could produce quality against the best, despite what was happening off the field.

It seemed to me that the new president Ahmet spent a lot on Ankaraspor, who were a small team with not a great deal of support. Once that plan had failed, they tried to do the same with us, and we moved to their training facility, which was much better, but the hardcore supporters seemed to be against all of the changes. They promised that they would fix all problems at the club, and the next thing I knew we had a new manager, Roger Lemerre, who had won Euro 2000 with France, and we were signing the likes of Geremi, who had played for Real Madrid and Chelsea, and

Jerome Rothen who came in on loan from Paris Saint-Germain. Vittek, an international striker from Slovakia was promptly signed too. A few players just left and disappeared as their contracts were terminated and there was a lot of change around this time. Lemerre was brought in on a six-month deal just before Christmas in 2009, with the aim of lifting us away from the lower reaches of the Super Lig. Ian Henderson was one of those let go to make international clearance for the others to join.

I went home to England for Christmas just after Lemerre had joined and I was a day late coming back. I was still in disagreement with the club over everything. My return flights were not organised and communication about when and where to meet was non-existent. So I waited a day to be sure and I got another night at home with Amani of course. I was told that the Turkish media portrayed it as me not coming back unless I was paid, but I was just trying to threaten to not come back to force the club's hand to start organising everything. They would always say promise after promise and I just wished they would stop as I was losing faith in that word by now. I was late to the winter training camp in Antalya. I was looking forward to meeting Roger Lemerre, although I was getting a little sick of having to meet new managers, having played for plenty in my career to-date. I arranged my arrival with Ender and explained that I wanted to room on my own again, as I'd explained in the past to Erk. I wasn't in the best of moods at this time and I didn't want to bring anyone else down. I had been told by the new owners to be wary of Barbaros, but I had found him to be a good guy and we got on well. By this time I was fed up of all the cat and mouse and who to believe. I took little notice and stuck to my mission of getting through this season while events of the club's disagreement with the TFF unfold. I finally arrived at the hotel after hours of travelling alone and got to my room, absolutely shattered after travelling, to find Barbaros sat in the room, chilling in his boxer shorts. This was after they had apparently just booked me a single room as promised. It was this scenario I wanted to avoid, I had not met the manager yet and I couldn't discuss anything over the phone if it was going to disrupt my teammates evening. Also this was the player who had punched our ex-teammate Ian square in the face weeks earlier. I needed sleep and we were probably going to run for training the next day. I was fuming that I'd been put in this position, and embarrassed that I'd walked in on Barbaros, who probably thought that I was angry with him. I believed that Ender had put us in the room together, just to f**k me about and wind me up. Either way I wasn't having good thoughts and I just wanted to lie down and talk to Amani as I had been travelling all day. When I think back, it was probably just another of their chaotic errors which I had become accustomed to. I went to meet Roger Lemerre and the coaches, and we made the decision that I would go back home after I explained everything that had and hadn't happened since I signed. Lemerre seemed like an honest and respectable man, he sensed my agitation and we shared a few words in French together. It was just basics but it was nice to have the management staff wonder what on earth was being said, for a change. I left the hotel and rang Amani and said I was leaving and coming home to her. I got a flight back and stayed at home in Birmingham for a few days, but then Ender called and promised that everything would be sorted and arranged. My expenses would be paid, translator and driver sorted, wages paid on time and I would get to move into the house in Bilkent. I came back on the 4th January and my head was all over the place, and I can only imagine what Roger Lemerre thought of me. Am I going or staying? It was another hurdle I would have to get over and I just wanted to show him what I could do. I apologised to Barbaros and explained that I wasn't upset with him and he was fine with me, but there was coverage all over the newspapers and television, including rumours being generated that I was in talks with Trabzonspor, which was completely untrue. The club confirmed that I wouldn't be leaving, but I felt everyone knew that there was a problem and that someone was taking the p*ss out of me.

I decided to get my head down and work as hard as I could; not just to impress the new manager and retain a place in the side, but also to show the new ownership that I was going to stick this out until the end of the season. As I've mentioned, I could see things moving in the right direction and I felt like if they got to know me properly, they would like me as a person. I wasn't the kind who would cause trouble within a club. I'd even managed to put the distraction of not being paid on time to the back of my mind, as a deadline was set for the club to pay me by the end of the season, which was confirmed by the TFF in writing at the notary, so it was official, and I felt like I could resume my focus on playing.

Amani and her sister, Amira, flew out to Turkey and went shopping on my behalf with club representatives for a house in Bilkent that the club were finally going to move me in to, which was completely empty. In a day, the place was full of some of the best furniture I'd ever seen. Ender orchestrated all of this on behalf of Ahmet, which I was really grateful for as it all happened without me there. This was the 'power' that they were on about in all those promises and meetings then? Bilkent was a nice area, which meant that I didn't need to travel in to Ankara all the time, in the same way that here in England I don't need to travel in to Birmingham every day. I really believed that they had the best intentions and there finally seemed to be some positive action. This was an attempt to keep me happy and keep me at the club I hoped. Every time a pay deadline came, it would pass without payment by the old ownership, but now at least some things were happening and I was receiving something, even if not a monthly salary. I really loved that house, I could feel more comfortable there than the city. It still felt like there was a divide in the club though. That those from the former regime preferred the club to be left as it was. Like there was something beyond football now that wasn't quite right. I also believe that the new president was not aware of the scale of the debt until much later and was possibly angered by this. I'll probably never know though. There were rumours that some Turkish players hadn't been paid for up to six months, in some cases dating back to before I joined. Slowly but surely players started to leave and others were coming in. I didn't fully understand this as I wanted Ian to stay but he was taking up one of the limited international places in the side just like me. There was always a third party around asking for a signature for a small bonus, not the club themselves. The stories I'd heard, and witnessed myself, were so alien to what I'd been used to during my time in England. Even the contracts were strange; if you were due to be paid at the end of a month, the contract would say that if payment was missed, you'd have to wait another two months until you could go to the notary to confirm this in writing, which would then be three months since you'd started working for the club. This cycle would be repeated month after month. Thankfully, I had Osman's advice and Volkan with me, so I knew where to go, what was being said and what to do. It appeared that if I had got this process wrong then it would void the following months report for non-payment. It was all made so difficult for me, but others were in similar trouble, as

Geremi, who I spoke to a lot, also had many problems. He said himself that he couldn't believe it was taking longer than six months to get sorted. I had told Geremi about the strange people that would knock my front door in Bilkent demanding money shortly after I moved in. We would joke about the organisation compared to Manchester City and Chelsea. We giggled at the list we made of all the possible reasons that guy was knocking on my door before realising how serious this could actually be. It was all enough to make me want to go home; the mood and the way we looked and spoke to each other as a team was becoming negative. I didn't want to return to England without anything, branded as a failure. I'd been through so much to get here and I wanted to at least say that I had played a season in Turkey. That experience would surely be valuable to me for any possible future employment.

I scored my final goal for the club away to Gençlerbirliği in a 1-0 win on 28th February 2010. They were huge rivals of ours and it meant a lot to everyone at the club to beat them. My memories of this game were focused around the fact that we had a series of big meetings in the build-up to the match; we met with the manager, the coach, the technical director, the president and his people, it was endless. I hadn't got a clue what was being said, but people were whispering in my ear in English to translate. We were being told, 'you have to win, it's a local derby, and if you win we have PlayStations for you.' I could see everyone's faces and no one cared about bloody PlayStations. We were professionals who wanted to win anyway, but being paid our salary would have been a start. Then the Mayor, who was our President Ahmet's father, turned up with his entourage, and promised us plasma screen televisions. I think they were making a big point that we needed to win this game more than any other. A lot of emphasis was placed on this and it didn't feel right to me, but at least we got the result. With all of the hype surrounding the game, I was so stressed and felt more pressure to deliver for the club, and given that I'd finally had some help, there was a chance for me to help them in return. I latched onto a short through ball and put it under the keeper and ran towards the fans. I celebrated in front of the Gecekondu supporter group and the other supporter groups and it was such a release for me. I was in bits and all my emotions came out. I had to fight back the tears, and it took me five minutes or so to compose myself. It may have seemed strange for me to cry after something so joyous as scoring, but scoring was what I wanted to do every week for them. All of those meetings at the notary that took hours to process, all the missed payments, the travelling back and forth from England, the sackings and sad faces, the accusations, the disappointments and above all the loneliness; it all came out and the tears streamed down my face. I can picture this day like it was yesterday, and it was so symbolic of a lot of my time in Ankara. Football shouldn't feel like this. I really didn't like it.

My last appearance for the club was in the final home game of the season, a 3-0 defeat to Fenerbahçe on the 9th May and then a week later I was asked to travel for the final game of the season, a near 600-mile round trip to Sivasspor, for a meaningless game given that nothing was at stake. All of the other foreign players were allowed to return home for the summer, but I had to travel and then having got all the way there I was named as a substitute. I had to sit and watch from the bench, no use to anyone. I knew I was one of the better players in the squad and knew I could contribute, but for some reason I was left out. It was so strange and given everything that we'd been through that season, all the battles and uncertainty, I couldn't understand the reasoning. If they had decided to allow a young Turkish player to play to gain experience and told me I wasn't needed, I would have understood, but this just seemed like a way to punish me and waste my time to make me travel just to sit there and watch. The management did not really acknowledge me the whole trip so I lay my head back on the bus and thought of how close I was to getting to the end of the season and back home.

I still had the deadline for payments to be made, and given that I had another year on my contract, I still would have returned despite everything. All the club had to do was pay what I was owed and I would have come back to work. We finished the season in twelfth place on 41 points, comfortably clear of relegation, but a long way from qualifying for European football, or even finishing in the top half of the table. It wasn't good enough for us and the fans and media were all disappointed and treated it as a disaster, with a difficult future ahead predicted.

Roger Lemerre left the club as his contract was up and I returned to Bilkent and had everything packed and ready to return to England. Ender constantly called me to get me to return the car, as I think he was

WELCOME TO ANKARA (ANKARA'YA HOŞGELDİN)

convinced that I would give it back to the previous club secretary Osman, but things had obviously got serious for him as he'd run away following the arrival of the new ownership. He told me he was in big trouble and asked if he could borrow some money from me. I had around €2500 in a safe at the hotel and told him to take that so he could sort out his problems. He said, "They are after me," and given that he was a friend who had helped me, I wanted to be there for him when he needed me; but I never saw Osman again.

I said goodbye to my home in Bilkent and returned the car to Ender at the new training ground and got a taxi to the airport to return home. It was quite an anti-climax to my time in the country, as I left without anyone really knowing I was leaving. It certainly wasn't the same as my arrival anyway. I now knew that there was one last deadline left for the club to pay, and it had appeared that there was money at the club now, as things were starting to happen for me, in terms of the house and furniture, and for the club in terms of the deluxe new training facility. There were also players being signed. I wanted to go home now as it was the end of the season, and I did everything that was asked of me, but I still held out hope that I would return next season under better circumstances.

Looking back on the season, there were some very talented players in Turkey, such as Harry Kewell, Milan Baros, Elano and Roberto Carlos, so the standard was good. There were some amazing Turkish players such as Alper Potuk, Canir Erkin, Arda Turan, Emre and our very own Ceyhun Eris and I felt like I could do well in Turkish football, it wasn't such a difference in standard than what I had been used to in England. I look back feeling that I made all the right decisions and committed myself to the club, showing great patience throughout my time there, but it just didn't work out. I honestly did my best but it wasn't just about what I was doing, it was about the whole ethos of the club, and I was just one man. I couldn't win every game and I certainly couldn't affect everything off the field. The mind is just as important as the body in football. My pride is important and that was dented heavily. It made me so appreciative of the organisation of the game in England. Just getting paid on time was a novelty. In hindsight, despite all the issues, I was glad that I went to Turkey as I gained more life experience; I made a great friend in Volkan and experienced another culture, which may have made me stronger as a person. Now I know that the contract that I signed wasn't even possible for the club to fulfil, which I didn't realise at the time. The new owners would have walked in and realised this, so whilst I was upset at not being paid, I can almost understand why as the money probably just wasn't there and the old owners that originally signed me probably knew they weren't going to be there much longer after. Managing a group of players is difficult, but managing a group of foreigners whom you can't pay on time must have been a nightmare for Ender. You need a strong head for his job and a compassionate one.

I loved my off the field time in the country though, experiencing the great food, like mouth-watering kebabs and lovely fresh fish and wine, and the people were fantastic to me. I had to leave the money on the table to pay, as they didn't want to take it. They couldn't have been more welcoming. I often spent meal times with supporters or my lawyer Cem Papila, Volkan or Osman. It was great to see the look on supporters' faces when we arranged to meet up and enjoy the fine food Ankara had to offer. It felt good to know that I had people at the club who were grateful that I was still there during those turbulent times.

I had Turkish cutthroat shaves, that rivalled those of my English barbers, George and Theo. I received gifts from supporters, got to know hotel staff by their first name, learned a little about Ataturk and slowly started to familiarise myself with roads and shortcuts to some tranquil places to dine out. Even when I returned to Ankara in 2015, people stopped me in the street and would recognise me, shake my hand and make me feel like I was returning home. Who knows, if things had worked out differently, perhaps I would have stayed there?

It was strange though to see in Ankara that a lot of the players seemed to smoke. My own teammates would take me out on occasions to welcome me to their favourite restaurants. As mentioned I was even invited out by fans, and the relationship with them was so strong through my blog, and also through Osman. They were turning up to protest in my favour, with banners at the training ground reading 'Vassell we are with you.'

I think that my experience would have been better if I'd had my agent there with me all the time, which I realise wasn't possible, but I needed to have the support to push for everything to be organised for me as originally promised. Instead I spent so much time battling for everything myself. I think the club probably took advantage of this situation and all processes were slowed down. I think they were pleased that I had no representatives; I may have arrived with four agents, but I didn't really have one during my playing days there. My close relationship with Volkan was probably another reason why they removed him from the club. I felt so lost and helpless at times that I actually wrote a letter to the President of Turkey asking for guidance. I didn't feel safe enough especially when the politics of Ataturk were mentioned to me. I didn't fully understand what I was involved in. Osman said this was the only way to guarantee safety, and the fear had us writing away. I was just a footballer, I wasn't trying to change the world. I went to the British Embassy with Ian Henderson, as he wanted help on owed payments and also to deal with the intimidation he was receiving at times in training, and it was helpful to be able to talk to someone about our frustrations. I don't know what I expected the authorities to do, but I just wanted someone to say that they would sort the situation out, instead of us worrying about everything all the time. Or at least tell me what was best to do. There wasn't a PFA organisation there so I relied on Osman, Volkan and Cem so much. They were all from Ankara and I knew that they were having their own difficulties off the back of me. The various legal processes involved made it hard for me to focus. I was turning up to training knowing I had to go to the notary after, which was always at rush hour and the queues in those buildings were so long. I would wonder what all those other people were reporting or claiming for, it all seemed so normal. If I was wrong in terminating my contract, then it would count as a breach and I could then owe the club an awful lot of money if they chose to sue me. Therefore I was there, to make sure I was doing everything correctly. I was told nothing can be proved unless I report there.

I can remember my lawyer, Cem Papila calling me at just before yet another midnight deadline to tell me that the club were finally transferring money into my account but they were having problems doing it, it was going to take a few more days. I was warned many times about these exact stalling tactics by people who worked at the club and that it was just to make me believe them so I didn't terminate my contract successfully. That was it, the final deadline had been officially missed and it was up to me. I knew my time in Ankara was officially over. Cem had liaised with the club, going back and forth with them, but he insisted they were just stalling and running down the notice, using every tactic they could. Cem wrote down everything from his conversation with Ender, and we had a concrete record of the whole shambles. I asked Cem for advice and he said they had no intention of fulfilling the contract. Cem told them that if they didn't, I'd be legally entitled to leave my contract and they replied by saying that they definitely wouldn't pay anything if I left. It was unbelievable. We successfully terminated my contract after informing the TFF and they judged that I was in the right. I was now in the position to pursue compensation but more importantly, go home feeling that I had done the right thing and managed the debacle accordingly. Cem advised me that it was unlikely that I would receive all that was owed due to the time it would take, the club's current position/status and I might have signed for someone else by then too and that would factor but that still didn't sit right with me; they were in the wrong. I was looking objectively at everything that had happened, trying to be the judge, but life doesn't work like that. Cem took that battle on for me, via the Turkish Football Federation and things work differently. I loved football, but this wasn't football. I had gone to Turkey to experience something new, but I knew I couldn't just return to football in England as I was used to. I didn't want to come back and be a failed journeyman with nothing positive to say, I wanted to bring back my new experience and contribute to a new club. I hadn't fallen out of love with football, but I almost had the feeling of wanting to go abroad again somewhere, and to prove that I could play outside of England. A sanction was placed on to the club, saying that they couldn't make transfers until their debts to all players and staff were settled. The club held the necessary elections that would determine who was responsible for the running of the club.

It took something like three or four years to begin claiming back what I was owed from my contract in Ankara and the battle is ongoing. FIFA have stated to me that the TFF ruling stands, and they will keep hold of my file should I wish to pursue anything different. I went with Volkan and Cem, to the Turkish Football Federation for a final time, and whilst they found in my favour, Ankaragücü were currently paying a backlog of similar cases.

I had to kiss goodbye to everything that was agreed in my contract and the life I dreamed of in Ankara. The ban was eventually lifted by all those with cases against the club including myself. We wait with hope that Ankaragücü return to the Super Lig in a better situation than when they left and with an administration that can look after the club and protect it.

I want to make it clear though that despite everything I've recalled in this chapter, I would consider going back to work in Ankara if given the right opportunity. There are many people there that I would love to see again and everyone mentioned helped me at some point in some way. There was Dr. Ates, who left the club very early but I remained in contact with him and he would always welcome me to his surgery. There were the staff at both hotels and the restaurant workers and owners. The barbers Huso at ANKAmall's M.O.S. outlet and those at the British Embassy who sat and spoke to myself and Ian for hours and pointed us in the right direction with regards to using the Notary and general safety. Despite all the drama, I am still grateful for everything that got done to help me. I only wish I could have focused on the football and been part of a team and club that could also do the same. Who knows what we could have achieved.

I was happy to be back home with Amani, and back with my dog, Germaine, who whilst I was out in Turkey was diagnosed with cancer. I was gutted that I wasn't with him. My sister was looking after him and I'm very grateful to her for that, but I wanted to be next to him to make his final days more enjoyable. We were gutted that we didn't get to experience family life as we imagined in Turkey, with Germaine by our side, and sadly I had to say goodbye to him for good shortly after returning to England.

It had been a difficult year for me; one which had challenged me on and off the field, but not long from now I was about to be reunited with an important character from my career for a third time, as I made my return to English football...

9

A GOOD PLACE TO STOP

I was waiting to find out whether the termination of my contract with Ankaragücü had been accepted and confirmed, whilst adjusting to life back in England, and once that came through I was allowed to sign for another club, without any issue coming back on me from Turkey. It was a relief that I could move on and draw a line under the past year, but I knew that I would still be waiting for my player registration to be handed over.

I'd been away from home for a long time, considering the four years in Manchester and then my year in Turkey, so there was a lot of going back and forth. I hadn't been at home to run my house properly, so Amani was here and my sister was helping out, but I felt like I had a lot to sort out. I was happy to be home and back in a familiar environment, but obviously I had the sadness of coping with my dog, Germaine, passing away. He was my best mate and I'd already missed him for the majority of a year whilst in Turkey. I'd set up a webcam in the room where he was sleeping, so I could see him whilst I was in Turkey as I really missed him. He meant such a lot to me. I mean, looking back a few years to my time in Shrubbery Close, I had Germaine, my girlfriend of the time and my cleaner, Jo, who still helps me out occasionally and she also used to be Peter Schmeichel's cleaner; that was my little family for five years. Germaine was loved, well looked after and was such a lively puppy. Without me realising it, Germaine had been a real constant in my life. We had grown up together.

Amani was a basketball player, who was offered a scholarship in America, which I'll talk about later, but we didn't have the time together that we would have liked, so it was nice to be back home. Amani loved Germaine, despite the fact that she wasn't in to dogs, but she knew what he meant to me. After he passed away, we decided to see if there were any more dogs from the same blood line, so we could get a puppy, as the house hadn't been the same without him. So that's when Denzel came in to our life; not as a replacement for Germaine, but just so there is a little part of him still with us.

I wasn't actively speaking to any agents at this time, but it did get a little ridiculous with the number of similar enquiries I was getting. It was public knowledge that I was back in England, so agents knew that I was prepared to travel, or alternatively they were looking at a move for me in the UK. I really wanted to play in France, as I was learning the language and I wanted to experience life there. I received enquiries from Dubai, but the longer I was at home, the happier I became. To be honest, I did begin to contemplate retirement then, as I had become pretty tired of it all. I just wanted to enjoy time with her for a while and have some normality. We had a summer together and life was settling down, and then my phone rings and it's Sven-Göran Eriksson. I could tell by the tone of his voice that he was serious and after a quick hello he wanted to know what I was doing and how I was. He got straight to the point; he'd just become the manager of Leicester City, who were struggling towards the bottom of the Championship. I told him my situation and I explained that I was free to play, so the club's administration staff looked in to this and I drove over to the Belvoir Drive training ground to meet him again. The opportunity came out of the blue and once I weighed up just how near Leicester was and that I already knew and trusted Sven, I felt very comfortable, especially after all the uncertainty of Turkey.

I can remember Googling Leicester to check the players who were in the squad. I knew of them but hadn't played with many. Chris Powell and I had played for England together and he was on the coaching staff, and I knew Sven, and of course his assistant Derek Fazackerley. Chris took me under his wing a little for England and looked out for me, so it was nice to see familiar faces again. Sven took a day to make his decision and around two weeks to sign me, which was a real endorsement. He'd brought Curtis Davies and Kyle Naughton in on loan, and then I was his first permanent signing. I knew of Lloyd Dyer and Richie Wellens from the past, but I quickly got to know the rest of the guys and they were a great bunch. Sven took a look at me and wanted to check that I was in decent shape, which I was but I wasn't match fit, so I would need to do a mini preseason. I had discussed it with Amani and we both agreed that it would be a great opportunity to play again with minimal disruption. Having not played since May though, I knew that I would have to train and work hard, like never before, to get up to speed with the rest of the guys. It wasn't like an interview, it was just two people who knew each other and I trusted and respected him, so I was honest with him, as I didn't want to let Sven down. We had a brief chat and catch-up and I was eager to get going. He then asked me how much money I wanted, but I found it very uncomfortable to answer and I was used to having an agent do all of that for me and negotiate so I said nothing. Sven went back to Andrew Neville, the Football Director at the club, and they sorted everything out for me and I signed a two-year contract. It was so refreshing to deal this way after what I had previously experienced. Having said that, months later when I heard what other players were being paid, I probably could have spoken up and asked for a little more! It wasn't about that though, I was more than happy with what they put together for me. Leicester made it clear that they wanted me, so I was happy to accept as soon as they made an offer. My medical was interesting to say the least. Remember, I hadn't played since May, so I was doing inclined interval running on the treadmill as part of my medical. Afterwards my urine test showed traces of blood, which the physio, Dave Rennie, explained either means you have a kidney problem or you've over-exerted yourself. He sent a sample for testing, the results indicated that I was fine. I knew I'd pushed it to prove I was fit, but didn't expect to be passing blood! At least it showed Dave I had the right attitude and I was serious about playing for Leicester.

I started training with a group of players who weren't in the team at the time. I looked around and got to know them and I was surprised by how good the guys were and how competitive it was for places. Steve

Howard was huge; this big, strong striker who could score from anywhere and Martyn Waghorn a strong but tidy player, with a lot of confidence, taking incredible shots at goal, whilst I was a bit rusty. These guys were very sharp, but they weren't guaranteed a starting place, so I was thinking ' how am I going to get myself into this side?' Matty Fryatt was starting, with Howard and Waghorn on the bench, and Sven would load the midfield, but eventually as the side became more confident, with new signings coming in, we would play a more positive and attacking style.

I made my debut on 6th November 2010 in a 2-0 away win at Barnsley, with Waggy playing up front, and me out wide, I was shattered and was replaced by Lloyd Dyer after an hour. I'd had two weeks of training and worked really closely with Dave Rennie, who was a good guy, someone I really got on well with and who helped me a great deal, which I'll come to later. It was clear that there was a lack of confidence or winning habit at the club, but Sven added a lot of optimism to the place, and the new signings added a bit of class too. I remember thinking that Andy King was a real talent; you can make preconceptions sometimes in football, as I had done in the past, and when I saw how good he was it really shocked me. He's gone on to play in, and win, the Premier League and represent Wales at Euro 2016 where they reached the semi-finals, so he's fulfilling his potential, and he's a reliable guy, even if I haven't spoken to him in a while, we always pick up where we left off. Paul Gallagher had some real talent, and Richie Wellens was quality. I'd played with him at England under-18s level, and back then during an England training session, I was asked who my favourite player was in the team, in front of everyone. It was a bit embarrassing for an 18 year old, as I didn't know everyone's names, I've always been shocking with names, so I shouted out, "Richie Wellens," but I'd meant Steven Gerrard, who was his midfield partner. I couldn't exactly take it back! Steven Gerrard had already said that I was his favourite player, which meant a lot to me, and then I'd had the chance to return the favour and got it wrong. I had to give the reason for it, and said it was because he tackled well, had great passing ability and would score goals, and all the time I was talking about Gerrard, but Wellens got all the glory. He was a good player anyway, so it didn't really matter.

I scored my first goal for Leicester against Doncaster Rovers at home in a 5-1 win in December, where everything clicked for us and instead of looking at relegation, pundits were beginning to tip us as an outside bet for promotion. There were some really good players in the group, like Yuki Abe who was a Japanese international and a Bulgarian international called Aleksander Tunchev, who sadly was always injured whilst I was there, but he was a nice guy. The skipper was Matt Oakley who was sound and I'm still in touch with him now, and he has gone on to play for many more years. I think one of the issues that developed though was that no one felt comfortable as the squad was getting bigger. Sven was bringing in new players, but not as many were leaving.

We won 1-0 at Hull City on New Year's Day, with my second goal for the club, when Greg Cunningham sadly broke his leg, and then the signings continued as Sol Bamba joined, along with new strikers Roman Bednar and Yakubu, so there was real competition, as they joined a group which included Fryatt, Howard, Waghorn, Gallagher, Dany N'Guessan and myself. I scored again, in a 2-1 home win over Swansea City in the next game and we were on a roll, climbing the league and beginning to dream about promotion. The result at Hull was the first win in a run of seven league wins and a draw. We won five games on the bounce, the fifth of which was a 2-1 home win over Bristol City thanks to a last-gasp volley on his supposedly weaker right-foot from Martyn Waghorn; we were seventh in the league, just a point outside the play-offs and four points behind second-placed Cardiff City in the automatic promotion spots. I was in the stands for that Waghorn strike and got to celebrate that win with the crowd, the stadium erupted and I was so happy for him.

The addition of Yakubu reminded me of when I was at Manchester City. The signing of a talented striker who'd scored everywhere he'd played, and now he was scoring for fun in training, ready to play and there was no way he was going to be left out if he was available. Looking at him, he was the kind of guy that you felt you could just be sat next to at the cinema, not necessarily a footballer at first glance, but give him a ball and you'd soon realise you were wrong and appreciate his gift. He was a natural goalscorer and finished with 11 goals in 20 games for us. He was pretty special. Similar to my previous two clubs I was eventually employed in a wide midfield role again, with more defensive duties and to use my pace and support the attack. This is something that Sven had done with me in the past and I was willing to do now, so I could play my part.

Sandwiched in between that league run, the finger of fate was pointing towards me once more. The FA Cup third round draw took place live on terrestrial television and Leicester band Kasabian's Serge Pizzorno drew us out, followed unbelievably by Noel Gallagher drawing out his team and both mine and Sven's former club, Manchester City. In front of a full house at home, Sol Bamba put us ahead after a minute, before City fought back through James Milner and Carlos Tevez, but Andy King earned us a deserved replay. I got to enjoy the presence of both sets of supporters on the same day and I believe they witnessed a decent game. We really gave City a scare and it showed how far we had come since Sven had taken over. We lost 4-2 in the replay and I didn't play in that, so didn't have the chance to return to City, but it was great to experience playing against them again. I was proud of Leicester and how we performed against City and I was determined to show to my old club that since leaving them, I had found another great club.

Our league run came to an end at Cardiff with a 2-0 defeat, which kicked off a run of four games without a win and all but ended our promotion hopes. Added to the players already signed, Sven brought in Ben Mee and Patrick Van Aanholt and then Jeffrey Bruma, followed in March by Diomansy Kamara. Perhaps the most notable signing of that season, certainly in relation to me, was the Portuguese international goalkeeper Ricardo, who had of course saved my penalty in Euro 2004. I honestly didn't know who he was when he first showed up for training. As I've said, I've always been terrible with names and I'd tried to put that incident out of my mind, and it had been nearly six years anyway. Often, I'd be chatting to someone without knowing who they were, as I'm sure many people do and I'd be hoping that their name would come to me. I think one of the other lads told me who he was and I couldn't believe it. Around that time, a group of us used to go off and play golf when we had the spare time; Matt Oakley, Steve Howard, Andy King, Martyn Waghorn and I would play on a Wednesday at the Belfry. I was starting to get in to golf, and I had all the gear but no idea as they say. Steve was a really good player, probably the best out of us all, and it was a good challenge for me and a nice break from football. There was a good atmosphere at the time, despite the squad size growing, and we decided to invite Ricardo along to join us and help him to integrate. It worked out that some of the guys had left the course early one day and it was just me and Ricardo on the back nine at the Belfry. We got chatting and it was the first time I'd probably thought properly about the penalty. I opened up to him about it and told him that I hadn't even realised it was him. He explained that he knew what each of the takers were going to do in that game, apart from me. He didn't have a clue who I was. As I've said earlier in this book, they had analysed all the takers, but there wasn't really any footage of me, so he just guessed and judged it on the day. We shared a nice afternoon together, in the sunshine and I guess what gave me most pleasure about the day was that I'd been to Turkey where I was the outsider, but here I had the opportunity to help another outsider to feel comfortable in another country. Who would have thought that the two of us would have ended up on a golf course together, playing at the same club after that night in Lisbon? Football has a funny way of throwing up surprises like that.

I think that from Sven's perspective, the new players he had brought in were an attempt to keep us all on our toes and prevent any risk of complacency. I have to say that at different stages during that season, I didn't know whether someone had signed, was on loan or was on trial, but in his defence he needed to see how good these guys were in person, as he was always on the training ground with us. It did sometimes feel like less of a team ethic, the bigger the squad became though, which was a shame. I don't think there is a ready way to avoid this and it's part of any selection and deselection process within a team.

We ran out of steam at the end of the season, but just kept our hopes alive mathematically, despite a few defeats and draws. With four games to go we travelled to Nottingham Forest knowing that a win would put us within touching distance of the play-offs. It was an end-to-end local derby. Our skipper Matt Oakley drew us level after Marcus Tudgay had given them the lead and despite us looking on top, we were 2-1 down late in the game, when I managed to grab an equaliser. As we pushed for the win, Paul McKenna scuffed one underneath our keeper Chris Weale and our promotion hopes were all but over. The game also ended my run of never having lost an English league match when I'd scored. I still hold the record for Premier League matches, although at the time of writing James Milner is closing in on me. It was a weird feeling to lose on that day, at Forest, as I used to take it for granted that when I scored, we wouldn't lose. We got another seven points from the last three games and finished tenth. Having been in the bottom three when Sven joined it should have been seen as a decent season, but we were all disappointed as we really should have made the play-offs and only had ourselves to blame.

In summer 2011, we travelled to Sweden and Austria for our preseason, playing some local sides and also Bursaspor, Valencia and Real Mallorca. The summer was busy for the club in terms of transfer activity and Sven used his contacts and reputation to attract a number of big-name and talented players to the club, whilst letting go of many of the loanees from the previous season. The likes of David Nugent, Matt Mills, Kasper Schmeichel, Sean St. Ledger and Paul Konchesky were signed and we were installed as favourites to win the division and reach the Premier League. There was a great deal of fanfare around this time and our Thai owners had managed to attract the mighty Real Madrid to play at our stadium as part of pre-season, a game which we lost 2-1, but an experience that those playing will never forget. Lloyd Dyer scored our goal towards the end of the game and we certainly didn't embarrass ourselves. To be honest, the owners had set out to reach the Premier League and all of the thinking at that time was Premier League, not Championship. When you look at what the club has gone on to achieve, you have to say that Vichai and Top deserve the success.

We were confident of doing well, but I felt personally that it was likely that I would be playing out wide if at all. It was a position I had worked out by now, especially defensively and having an attacking threat to go with it always provided the balance managers require. We didn't have a settled team as such at that time, as it was a very experimental time for Sven during the summer, as he tried to work out his starting XI. Along with Mills and Schmeichel, others who'd joined from my old club Manchester City were Michael Ball and then Gelson Fernandes and Michael Johnson. We had some really good guys and I felt like on paper we were very strong. I fought for my place and I started in the first game of the season at local rivals, Coventry City. It was clear that just knowing Sven wasn't going to be enough for me and I'd have to work my balls off to stay in his team. Perhaps that enthusiasm cost me against Coventry as I was given a straight red card after just 11 minutes of the new season. I wasn't a dirty player, but I was putting extra effort in and having lost the ball I went in too hard on a 50/50 with Richard Keogh with my studs showing. It wasn't deliberate, it happens sometimes and it was the first red card of the Championship season. Carl Baker was sent off for them around 20 minutes later and thankfully we won 1-0 with a header from another new signing, Lee Peltier, on his debut.

My first goal of the season came in a 3-2 home win over Southampton on Saturday 27th August, followed by my last goal for the club and what turned out to be my last in professional football against Derby County in a 4-0 home win on Saturday 1st October. Our form was inconsistent though and we were sat just outside of the play-offs before a home game with Millwall on Saturday 22nd October; we lost 3-0 and we were absolutely awful that day and on the following Monday afternoon Sven was sacked by the club. The manner of that defeat wasn't something I was used to and we all knew we'd let Sven and ourselves down that day.

I was absolutely gutted when Sven was sacked; I knew he was genuinely trying to get us to the Premier League, and that feeling of having to go through getting to know a new manager again, which I'd experienced at Aston Villa, Manchester City and in Turkey came back to me. The players felt responsible and remember, he'd brought a lot of them in to the club, so we all owed him. You could tell that Sven was hurt after the game and it was unacceptable for us to lose in that manner. After he left, Sven and Derek Fazackerley both took the time to call me and to wish me the best in my career. I spoke to Sven and told him I hoped he would go on to be successful, but I felt terrible. I looked at myself and wondered whether I could have done any more? We knew that it was our fault, as we were a good group of players and we were expected to get promotion. It should never have come to this really and the crowd were unhappy too, so the raised expectations meant that we had to deliver, which we simply didn't. Sven wasn't replaced straight away and for the next three games Jon Rudkin who was the club's academy director at the time and Mike Stowell, the goalkeeper coach, were placed in temporary charge.

Our first game after Sven's departure was away to West Ham United, which we lost 3-2, but for me the game will always be memorable for the wrong reasons. I wanted to do well to yet again show everyone that I was prepared to work for the club and that I wasn't just there for Sven. I was playing on the left-wing, which I often did throughout my career. I didn't find that position a problem really as I was comfortable with both feet and I wanted to do what was best for the team, so I didn't have to be an out-and-out striker as such. I jumped to control a goal kick out of the air but in performing the skill, I landed on a straight leg. The knee joint was forced backwards into hyperextension. I was on the floor, holding my leg but I didn't want to come off. I had to get up to show that I was up for the fight. I tried to jog a bit, but it didn't feel right and my leg was loose. The adrenaline was keeping me going and I felt I could run the injury off. Dave Rennie, the club's physio came running on to see what I'd done. He took a look and put his hands on the area and took an immediate look over to the bench to let them know that I would be coming off. I thought, 'you've not even asked me there,' so I knew it must have been bad. Dave is a real professional and I was in pain but I felt like I would just come off and be back in training later that week. He organised for us to go and see a specialist, in order to rule out the possibility of a serious injury, which was a nice way of dealing with a bad situation for me.

Dave and I went to London and he was adamant that he would show me the severity of the injury, whilst I was still convinced that I would be ok and back in training. The specialist's test confirmed Dave's fears and I had ruptured my anterior cruciate ligaments and would probably be out for the rest of the season. I was put in a cast and the test on my knee proved that my ligaments were just hanging on by a thread. The pain I was put through in the test was something else; I walked into the surgery but had to have a wheelchair brought in as there was no way I was walking out or driving back; I couldn't even move. It was pure agony. Shereen, a friend of mine based in London, who introduced me to Amani, had to come and pick me up and I stayed with her as I had the operation down in London. I was very disappointed and started to wonder whether it was time to hang my boots up, as I wasn't sure whether I'd be able to come back from this. The surgery went well and I was set to be out for between six to twelve months, which would take me up to the end of the season at minimum. The timing was awful, as I wouldn't have a chance to train with the new manager and my contract was up for renewal in the summer. All I could do was get fit again and hope for the best, but it was confusing as I wasn't sure what I was getting fit for. Dave showed me some evidence of players who had returned to fitness early and that gave me a focus and a target to set my eyes on. This was the point where my relationship with Dave developed and I regarded him as a good friend, not only for his advice and expertise but for the way he dealt with me throughout. I began to get to know Aleksander Tunchev at this time, who had been out with a knee injury and spent a long time on the treatment table. I was desperate to get back in to training, just to show that I could get back fit in time and maybe have an outside chance of playing again to earn myself a new contract. Dave advised me on the right equipment to use, and I got a lot of stuff in at home and worked around the clock to get fit. Amani looked after me whilst I was on crutches and both of us would go and see Dave in Leicester late in the day, when it was a bit quieter and he would trust me to work on my own, and then set tests, which would show the day-on-day improvement I was experiencing. I was ringing and emailing him around the clock, and he was such a support. I wouldn't say that I got back to how I wanted to be at the end of the season, I still needed longer to get back to 100% fitness, but I was so grateful to Dave for everything he did for me and being so approachable at a time when I had so many questions.

The permanent replacement for Sven was Nigel Pearson, who was returning for a second spell at Leicester City, following some time with Hull City. Nigel and I never really had that big conversation when he joined, regarding my future. He had to focus on the fit players who could help him and he had a lot of work to do, so I was not really any use to him. He made that clear to me when I asked him for a chat, so I used this refusal to talk as motivation to heal quicker. It didn't matter what I thought of him at that stage and to be honest, I knew nothing about him. Our physio would sing his praises as he knew him well but none of it mattered if I wasn't fit and I had to stay focused. He seemed more likely to favour those that he knew well and whilst my only concern was to recover and do the talking on the pitch, he said we would speak nearer the time when I was fit, as there's nothing much to talk about now. I just wanted him to know that I was committed and had every intention of fighting for my place, for this I had so much practice. There was occasional unrest as I think that the changing of roles and team selection throws a lot up in the air, especially when players would have been used to following instructions and being rewarded by the old management team.

I had always made every manager find it difficult to leave me out and it's a challenge that I never shirked during my career. I was a player that you could bet on in big matches, that would understand the role of substitute completely; support the team, and be ready to cause havoc when introduced while not neglecting my defensive responsibilities and full knowledge of my set piece positioning whatever player I replace. Win everything that is a 50/50 challenge and use my pace to be first to any ball being cleared or bouncing around and waiting to be controlled. It's what I do and have been doing for years now.

The months passed and I only really crossed paths with Nigel because I was asked to train a few times before the season end, but it was still difficult as I was having to ease my way back in. There were a further few months of rehab to get through even if I did start first team training. We were in mid-table and I was named as a substitute in the final game of the season, away to Leeds United without a full week's pain free training under my belt. I remember being so shocked at the call up as it was out of the blue. Dave had got me cutting and turning in training but I didn't feel deep down that I had the same explosive power, but we both believed I was getting there. I was doing well in my recovery but months away from the surgeon's recommended one year full recovery period. I kept my mouth shut and fingers crossed. If I said nothing about pain and managed a goal or two, then I could sneakily get myself in the thinking again and manage the pain quietly with support from Dave. I was brought on for the second-half against Leeds and had 45 minutes to try and do something. I clearly wasn't match fit and I was chasing the ball, looking at Lloyd Dyer racing away with ease, which was a real challenge for me to see as I'd been used to running like that myself. We won the game 2-1 with a first career goal for a young lad called Harry Panayiotou and I was so pleased for him as I remembered that same feeling I'd experienced all those years ago at Aston Villa. It was great to get a run out and I thank the manager for that; the youth in me wanted the opportunity but the senior professional in me knew that I needed a few more months minimum just to get sharp. Match sharpness is so important and being sharp was originally a big part of my game. We finished in ninth place, and now it was time for players to sort their futures out. The likes of Matt Oakley and Steve Howard had spoken with Nigel and they were leaving the club, whereas I hadn't had that conversation yet, as I was worried that there was no way I was going to be taken on whilst the club didn't feel I was fit. I attended the end of season awards evening, despite many others who were leaving the club choosing not to come along, as I felt it was important to show my face and that the club could realise that I cared. I wanted to support the lads like Kasper, Kingy and Lloyd who had played all season. At that awards evening, I received a message passed to my table saying that Nigel wanted to see me the next evening, which was obviously going to be the conversation about my future as everyone had finished for the summer. I hoped that I might be offered six months, the time I was out of action. I had seen this done at other clubs and it made sense. Nigel explained that the club wouldn't be able to keep me on, on the money I was currently earning. That threw me as I wasn't even thinking about the financial side, so I asked what the offer would be and what they would drop my salary to so I could stay on. It took a little while but I realised what was happening. It was soon clear that he didn't want to keep me, as Nigel asked me to call him in two weeks' time and offered to help me out if I wanted. It sounded like he had just made that up on the spot. I could see that he was finding difficulty in telling me and I wasn't disappointed, I was just embarrassed that I was in that situation. I knew I'd conducted myself in the right way and I didn't want to put him through another awkward situation by calling him up. We shook hands and I left Nigel and Leicester City knowing that I never ever started playing football to feel like this. I thought of all the young players that had been let go while I was in the Villa youth system and how they would have felt, I thought of the time in Ankara and how it all affected me. Football just wasn't fun by this point. I quickly became eager to hang the boots up and let my injury naturally heal rather than try and find another club to assess the injury again and continue my rehabilitation. Literature given to me by Dave said that there were other related injuries or operations possible due to the nature of my original injury. As I have said in the past, if there was no connection between myself and the club then being there seemed wrong. I grew up playing for the club I loved; I used that love to perform well and control the disappointments. I'm glad that I never played football without respecting my club and those that support it.

There was a bunch of players leaving and I think, looking back at that time now, it allowed Nigel and the club to build with younger players and look to the future, which they have done brilliantly. I guess it would have been different if I'd have known the manager well, like Sven, and they knew what I could do or how to best utilise my strengths. A footballer has got to dream, right? The club went on to have a great balance and Nigel did a very good job, which Claudio Ranieri has built upon. I don't have any regrets about the decision to allow me to leave, or over my conduct, as I couldn't have worked harder to get fit and recover as quickly as I did over in Leicester or back at home.

Having so much free time was very strange, but I was determined to make the most of it, so during the end of my recovery at Leicester I played a lot more golf and improved, whilst also learning how to build a water cooled personal computer. I could still play guitar and Amani was my co-op partner on Gears of War 3 (Xbox 360). I still have that, somewhere. I can see how footballers can become depressed during these times. I wanted to show people that I wasn't just picking up a pay cheque every month whilst not contributing on the pitch to earn it but it wasn't possible. It's a useless feeling in every sense. For example, I would bump in to the owners during that six month period and I would feel guilt. Like they were thinking the same thing. I definitely felt that way in relation to Nigel Pearson, as I understand why he decided to let me go. He would have looked at my salary and then looked at my injury, as well as the lack of goals I'd scored, and that probably made his mind up.

When I look back on my time at Leicester, I feel like it was the right move for me at the right time. I hadn't expected a club like that to come in for me, and there was real ambition there, which clearly still exists given that they have sealed the Premier League title. I don't feel, when I look back on paper, that I did enough during my time at the club. I know that I gave all my effort, but when people look at my time there they will probably say that I didn't do much or achieve much. I'm proud to have played for the club and to have been there at the start of this journey they are going on. There are still many people there now, like in the backroom staff such as Dave Rennie, Mike Stowell, Craig Shakespeare and until 2016 Steve Walsh, who both offered to help me out in finding a new club abroad after Leicester, which they didn't have to do, and obviously at the time of writing, Andy King, Wes Morgan and Kasper Schmeichel are still there and Jeff Schlupp stayed until 2017. I got the feeling that Craig and Steve's offer to help would have maybe come from Nigel as well. I guess that Nigel was the one manager in my career who I didn't have the real opportunity to play for or get to work with. I felt after meeting him, that it was a good time to stop playing. He said that he is more likely to select players that he liked rather than those who were the 'best', if that meant anything other than me talking through my football then I knew my time was up. Nothing else made sense to me, I was certainly not wanting to discuss or make a new friend. Our careers were largely spent in different eras and leagues. Getting a manager to like me meant working hard in training and in matches, helping the team wherever possible and being honest. That's the best way I can put it all.

The future may have been uncertain in terms of my football career, but off the field, I was set to be busy by securing my own most important signing, Amani.

10

DECISIONS IN THE FINAL THIRD

I'd been planning my marriage to Amani during my final season at Leicester, so the injury I had there provided me with unexpected extra free time. I can remember talking to Dave Rennie at Leicester about my forthcoming wedding all the way through the rehab, and we'd talk about his memories of his own wedding day, so everything was building up towards that for me. I had to process the whole Leicester situation and I think that the wedding was a positive focus for me during that time. My knee was in a little pain, and I knew that there was more to go through in terms of rehab if I wanted to play again in the next season.

Any calls I received from agents or clubs after I'd left Leicester started almost word for word, with the questions, 'how's your knee?' and 'how are you feeling?' I knew that if I was going to play again, I'd have to prove my fitness, regardless of what I'd achieved in the past. As anyone who knows me will say, I'm not great with phones, or as I've said names for that matter, so I wasn't really on top of who was in contact at that time. I don't actually think people knew I was released until much later in the summer.

I said earlier that I was planning the wedding, but planning might be stretching things a little as Amani and her mom were doing all the work.

I want to say congratulations to them both here in writing, and give them all my thanks for everything they did. I was just the groom really, they relieved me of any real pressures and I'm so grateful. I did at least sort the suits out and a few other things. It was a nice period and a chance to just breathe and not think about football. I'd worked so hard on the rehab and all the hours in the gym, not just during the recovery, but throughout my whole career, so it was nice to just have a break and think of life outside of the beautiful game. I think I was just mentally tired at this point. It would be a big statement to say I'd fallen out of love with the game, but I just felt like I'd had enough; I wanted to be with Amani and I wanted to be at home. I'd been through quite a bit over the years and it was time for some stability. I'd had enough of hotels, motorways and airports; I was looking forward to some time with Amani and some time together on the golf course. I'm a homely person and home was finally where my heart was.

My uncle Steven was my Best Man on my wedding day, and for the stag do I had the male relatives from my family and from Amani's family with us, and it was a nice opportunity for everyone to get to know each other. I survived it and there was no silliness to it; I think people knew better than to do that with me.

We were married at The Ickworth Hotel, near to Bury St. Edmunds in Suffolk on Sunday 27th May 2012 on the Bank Holiday weekend. Amani and her mom had visited many places and then we all fell in love with the venue, and the day was like a dream, absolutely fantastic. It was scheduled for rain but it was beautiful sunshine, so Amani had the perfect day she had dreamed of, which meant I was happy too. My ushers were my relatives from my stag do, and there were around 100 people in attendance, including Dion Dublin, Michael Blackwood, Darren Byfield, Reuben Hazell and Jlloyd Samuel from my football days, and there was a great photo taken of us all together. We'd all been together at Aston Villa so that was pretty special to have them there on our big day. I feel like anyone would say that their wedding day was perfect, but that's exactly how I would describe it. Amani was late, as brides often are and she said she was nervous, whilst I spent a lot of time looking at my watch. We had musicians playing outside in the sunshine, so it really was idyllic.

Our first dance was to Robin Thicke's 'Lost Without U' and Amani kept laughing and whispering in my ear that she was going to fall over in her shoes. I'd had a bit to drink by then, so I was very happy and I dance a little anyway, so I didn't mind too much. We've got it all on video as a memory, so it's there forever.

We stayed a night at the wedding venue, before flying out on our honeymoon to the Zöetry Paraiso on the Riviera Maya in Mexico for nine days, which included some golf, before flying to Detroit in the USA and a 320 mile round road trip from the airport to Mount Pleasant, where I drove and Amani navigated, to see the comedian Kevin Hart live in concert on the 9th June, staying at the Soaring Eagle Casino and Resort, and playing golf again at the end of our trip. I was sh*tting myself at the comedy, as I was sat at the front and they do have a habit of picking out people and hammering them in jest. It was all good in the end and great to be there.

We flew home and celebrated my 32nd birthday on the 13th June with a big family barbeque at our house, which was lovely and was the perfect way to round off our two weeks of celebrations. It wasn't long before the phone started to ring and it was agent, after agent, after agent, offering this club and that club. There was always a condition though, 'give me permission to use your name, Darius,' or 'let me put you forward, Darius,' and I'd never know the full terms or what was being proposed. I didn't feel like this was an option. I felt that if I was going to sign for another club and play again it would either be with someone locally, or through a contact I had, in a similar way to how things developed at Leicester City with Sven. I didn't really want a third party, like an agent, involved at all and because of that I was almost playing games with these people, where I'd confront them and say, "Ok, what's the offer then?" and nothing would come back. During that period I did receive support and still do from The PFA, who I'm grateful to. Back then, Matthew Buck who is now their director of player management and has worked with James Milner, helped as an intermediary, filtering out the real options from the fake ones on my behalf.

I suppose if my experience in Turkey had been more reliable, I would have enjoyed trying a new country and culture, but it was out of the question completely. Unless people were clear about everything, I just wasn't interested. Being at Leicester, as I've said, had reminded me of how straightforward things were in English football. I didn't care about what

I earned in my career by this stage, I just wanted to know that everything was organised and people had my interests as a player in mind.

I would certainly need extra support given my continuing recovery from injury. Also, I didn't want to waste any more time with nothing materialising. There was some interest with Inverness Caledonian Thistle in Scotland apparently and then I met with Derek Fazackerley at Oxford United, who had moved on from Birmingham City where he'd worked after Leicester, to become assistant manager to Michael Appleton. I enjoyed speaking to them both and hearing their vision, but my inner fire for playing was fading and I couldn't lie to these people. I'd lost six months of my career and it probably cost me the opportunity of moving on to another club after Leicester. I'm not someone who would push for confrontation, but I was just sad that I didn't get those six months back that I'd been robbed of. I'm not complaining, as I earned during that time, but as I've said before I never felt comfortable just picking up money and not putting on the shirt to compete.

I do love football but it isn't everything to me anymore. I'd loved every minute of my time in the game, but I also needed to know that it might be time to step away from playing football and look at what else there was to do with my life. I have to mention as well that England changed things for me forever. There was an expectation, wherever I went after playing for England, that I should do better, be the best player on the pitch and show that I was worthy of being an England player. Even if it was years after I'd played for my country people would still refer to me as 'England's Darius Vassell', or 'Former England international, Darius Vassell', and that tag followed me everywhere I went. The lower down you drop in the game, the more that's noticeable and then the expectation is even higher. I wasn't thinking about football in the same way by this stage, perhaps influenced by injury, by my time in Ankara, by some of the other disappointments I'd experienced, and everything was pointing towards me staying at home and looking away from playing football. It probably wouldn't have been fair on my body either. If I'd have had the chance to stay on at Leicester then I would have, or maybe a local club near to Birmingham, I would have considered that. I did speak to Walsall at one stage, as Richie Wellens put me in touch with Richard O'Kelly who Richie knew from his time at Doncaster Rovers, with O'Kelly then at Walsall as assistant manager to Dean Smith. We spoke over the phone but I seem to remember that they wanted me on a trial basis, which was completely understandable from their perspective, but it just wasn't for me. The cruciate ligament injury was something everyone was wary of and it affected the way I was confronted by clubs.

I decided not to announce my retirement, as I wanted to keep any options open. It seemed like it was non-stop football since the age of nine, so now the feeling that I could sample what my life could be like outside of football was refreshing. I know that footballers can suffer from depression when they stop playing as they miss the game, but I didn't feel like that. I knew that I would always be known for football, so I started my coaching badges, which I would need to do if I wanted to work in the game at a later date. I think everyone automatically presumes that once you finish playing you want to become a coach or a manager, but I just wanted to explore this route. I must give the PFA credit for setting me up to do this at St. George's Park, and they have been a great support. I started with my level 2, which I could have done back when I was playing at Villa, before John Gregory took me out so I could focus on playing for the first-team, and I have also started the FA Youth Award. It's all about being up to date if you want to work in that area and at the time of writing, I'm currently taking the UEFA B Licence, with the certification due in summer 2017.

I went to visit Steve Burns, who was my schoolboy and school of excellence coach at Aston Villa at the age of 12 through to 16, and I spoke with him whilst he was still at Villa to get some advice on my next move and what I should be thinking about doing with my life. I didn't want to sit there, dry out and leave it too late to have an option of staying in the game. Steve spoke to me about the importance of sports science and how influential it has become in the game. Since then, Steve moved to Wolverhampton Wanderers, and my favourite player from my childhood, Tony Daley had gone in as the sports scientist at Wolves as well. Steve suggested that if I had time and was interested, I should look at qualifications in that area. I must value his opinion highly as I got myself on to a sports science degree course at Loughborough University with help from the PFA. I started in November 2014 and it's extremely hard and intense, but the course had already started so I was playing catch-up straight away. I do realise now that in some ways I've had it easy in life, having seen things from another perspective. In the world of football, everything is done for you and arranged, whereas now, it was all on me to perform and there was no one else to rely on. I'd have to revise, research and most of all listen, learn and write in an academic style, which I still feel like I'm getting my head around to be honest. My course will finish in 2018, depending upon my grades, but I realise that there is a lot of hard work ahead. I feel like this process has helped me to learn a lot about myself, as well as learning about sports science. I remember Andy Gray, the Villa legend and former Sky pundit speaking about me on television when I was playing at Aston Villa and he said that if I was given too much time to think, I'd probably miss, indicating that I almost acted within football purely on instinct. If I accepted that, then I knew that if I could study and learn the scientific side then I would be as close as I could to having two different understandings and perspectives of the game.

If I look back on my playing days, I don't really have any regrets other than not scoring more goals. I would have liked to have played again, in the right circumstances, but I can't complain about how my career went. Put it this way, I'm not sat here wishing that things had been different. Nowadays I'm not noticed too much and I don't crave the attention or need it as such. If people don't remember me, I guess that helps me. I don't go out or socialise that often, as I got used to not doing it too much as a footballer. The two just don't mix really. I guess I go out in the day quite a bit with my daughter, Persia, and she has helped to bring me out of my shell. Life for me is mainly studying or maintaining my home. Amani and I enjoy going to the cinema and everything I do is usually for my family now really, that's my priority. I think I'm known reasonably well locally and as I say, that's probably due to playing for England. I think that sometimes, because you are viewed as a footballer, there is an expectation of what you should say or do. Often, I'm probably not even thinking about what I should say, so you can bet your bottom dollar that I say the wrong thing!

I would have to say that the three best players I played against were Rio Ferdinand, Ledley King and Ronaldinho. Rio and Ledley were two footed playing defenders; they were strong and quick and I couldn't pick a weak side to attack them on. I had to be extra sharp against them.

Ronaldinho could do anything with a ball. It wasn't just the goal against David Seaman in the 2002 World Cup for Brazil, it was the dummy he threw Ashley Cole, who was probably our best left-back for many years, and they scored from it as he created the space for Rivaldo. It was like playing against a wizard.

I feel like I'm doing the right things at the moment, and if that leads me back to football or away from the game, then I'm easy with either. I met with Steve Burns again recently, at Wolves, and he has invited me to come in and take a look at the academy there and observe them and the way they work, which was very kind of him. Steve doesn't tell me what to do, he just tells me what he thinks. He was surprised to learn that I'd gone down the sports science degree route and that I'd listened to him, but for me it feels like there's a pathway I'm on at the moment and I'm working towards something. If I can get the degree, I'd have the tools that could be of use to someone, and I suppose that may lead me back to football, who knows? I just love sport, all sports, and that's why it feels right for me. I've got the experience of having had a career in professional sport, at the highest level and that, added to the academic side, should be a strong combination, which may open some doors for me. From everything I've learned so far, I feel it's even helped me with our nutrition for our family, let alone with my career. We've started to look at the energy we gain from food and Amani is ensuring that Persia's diet is better, as well as our own.

I officially announced my retirement in January 2016, at the same time that I announced that I was working on this book. It made sense for me to draw a line under that chapter of my life, and I felt like it allowed people to know what the book would be about too. I realise that I hadn't played for three-and-a-half-years, so it may seem strange for people who perhaps would think that I was desperate to be back on the pitch, to learn that I wasn't thinking in that way at all. By the time of the announcement I was knee-deep in my degree, playing the guitar, Persia was a year old, Amani and I were still playing golf, I was working on the book and our house was up for sale. It wasn't like I was just sitting around waiting for the glory days to return. I guess that's the beauty of this book and my career, the timing just seemed perfect. I mean look at my former clubs in England; Leicester City won the Premier League last season, their first ever top flight title, whilst Manchester City reached an historic UEFA

Champions League semi-final, and Aston Villa have been relegated and are at a real crossroads, and then England despite their early exit from the Euros, have exciting talent coming through to add to the likes of my good friend Daniel Sturridge. Hopefully this group of players will go on to achieve the success that we came close to doing in my time playing for England.

Everything happening in football has made me reflect on my time in the game. Perhaps this is Aston Villa's chance to regroup and start again, just in the same way that I feel like I am starting again.

11

REASON
TO SMILE

I met Amani through a friend who lived in London. I'd bought my current house just before I joined Manchester City in the summer of 2005 and had a couple of years playing under Stuart Pearce, before Sven joined City and at the same time I met Amani.

During the summer break, or on a Bank Holiday weekend, we would go to the Bel Air nightclub, which is within the Belfry Hotel and Golf Club, near to Sutton Coldfield as they used to put on a really good night. A group of friends came up from London on 27th May 2007 and Amani was one of the people who came along with my friend Shereen. We'd enjoyed a good night and soon after I was heading off for a holiday in America, but I wanted to keep in contact with Amani and wanted to get to know her. I thought she was nice and I simply couldn't take my eyes off her. I went down to London before meeting my friend Nathan as we were going away together and I stayed at Shereen's house. We were all going to go out together and when Amani turned up she looked amazing in a beautiful black dress, with red accessories and big curly hair. I was lost for words.

I went on holiday and all of this happened in the days of Myspace, so given that I didn't know Amani properly I needed to invent a way to keep in touch with her, without being too obvious, like asking Shereen a lot of questions. I didn't want to risk a knockback, or whispers within our group of friends, so, I sent out a message on Myspace to the group to say what a great night it was and that I hoped everyone had enjoyed it. That is really out of character for me, as I'm less than active on the social networks but everyone replied and said they had fun and hoped we could all get together again. Amani and I began communicating via Myspace. I was in Miami for a few days and with music being a big thing for me, I had arranged as part of the trip to travel over to California on my own to see one of my favourite artists of the time, Germaine Williams, at a show. My friends may have thought that was strange, but I really wanted to see him live. I had even named my dog after him. I returned to the guys in Miami, but the whole time I'd been messaging Amani back and forth on Myspace, getting to know her a little better and I'm sure that she would have known by then that I liked her. When I got back home to the UK, we arranged to go out together and it was a little different; you could sense an edge to us both as we knew more about each other. We shared our first kiss that night and I think I've spoken to her every day since.

Meeting Amani was the best thing that could have happened to me, at the perfect time in my life. I was feeling like things weren't quite set in stone at Manchester City and I really wanted a reason to smile and Amani was just that. The complication was that she lived in London, I had a home in Birmingham and I played football for Manchester City. As if that wasn't enough, Amani had a basketball scholarship in America. I liked her a lot, and hoped beyond hope that we could be together, but didn't really see how it would happen. I wanted to make the most of the little time we had together to ensure that she knew me more. I guess that the attraction and the fact that we got on so well, just kept us together and kept things going. She would drive up to Birmingham and meet me here during the season, and if I wasn't in Birmingham I'd be in Manchester or somewhere else playing football, but none of that mattered, as we just wanted to be with each other. It might seem hectic and unlikely looking back on it, but at the time, nothing was going to stop us from seeing each other; it was just easy. I was also very used to motorway driving.

Throughout our relationship, I always feel that Amani has had to show patience. Being with a professional footballer or ex-player as I am now

Follow up shots, goal chances never wasted!
Goal! I've done it. Come on everyone, make your way to the stage. Mayhem!

Friend or Foe? The great Alpay getting the better of me here.

Left foot strike and goal for England against Iceland.

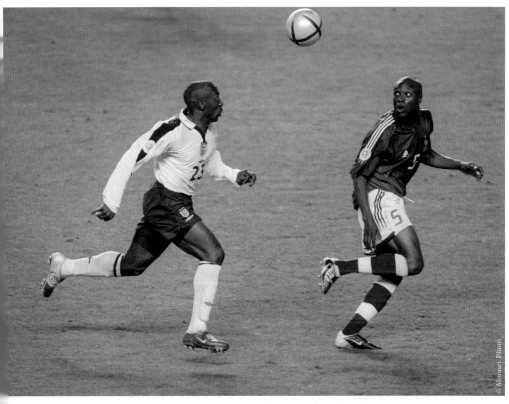

Extreme focus; myself and William Gallas going one-on-one in the 2004 European Championships, England vs France.

The space was out wide but I needed to be in the box. A frustrating quarter-final for one reason only...

My final penalty kick for England in sudden death after extra time.
From the moment I struck it, I felt something wasn't right.

Goalkeeper Ricardo makes the save to my dismay. Another tournament gone and was to blame. Ashley Cole and David Beckham consoling as my tears flow.

Felt so good to score twice against Villa and O'Leary at home for Manchester City. I had to prove to myself and everyone that I'd moved on.

Manchester derby, the biggest Premier League game I've played in by far.

The only way to silence the crowd.

Trevor Sinclair and I both on the scoresheet in the Manchester derby.

Stuart Pearce, a great motivator for me during my days in Manchester and the man who signed me from Aston Villa.

The arrival of Sven at Manchester City. The beginning of great changes.

Later on the arrival of Mark Hughes and more new players would follow.

Welcome to Ankara.

I still can't fathom this being all for me.

The appointing of a new president in Ahmet Gökçek (left).

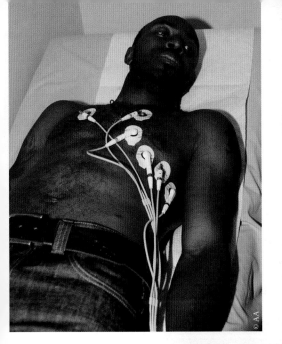

More tests in Ankara as our entourage get the deal done.

It was a pleasure to represent Ankaragücü and be revered by their fans.

Celebrating my first goal with Ian Henderson.

Captain Ceyhun Eriş taking our warm up.

Barbaros, Ceyhun and myself getting the team organised after a goal.

The appointment of Roger Lemerre and the dismissal of Hikmet Karaman. There was never a chance for anyone to settle it seemed.

Goal celebrations and a final kiss goodbye to Ankara.

Championship football at Leicester City; Andy King and I celebrating his winning goal against Nottingham Forest together. Another great friend off the field and fellow golf enthusiast.

Ex-teammate Joe Hart and I contesting a corner during an FA Cup third round match against Manchester City. Another great guy off the field too.

he end of my run. A goal celebration against Nottingham Forest, though it turned out to be the rst time I'd scored a goal and lost a game in English League football.

Sven and José Mourinho converse before our exhibition match against Real Madrid at King Power Stadium.

Nigel Pearson did a great job on his return to Leicester City, despite letting me leave the club.

Dave Rennie helped me come to terms with the realities of my ACL injury, whilst providing support and rehabilitation during my final six months at Leicester City. It's amazing to realise how much work the support staff at football clubs actually get through.

is not easy, but she has just taken it all in her stride. She's had to be very patient with me, perhaps when I was down about how things were going at a club, or particularly when I couldn't be at home and football took me away to Turkey and all the issues that came with that, Amani has always without fail been so supportive. I genuinely couldn't have done any of it without knowing she was there for me. The move to Turkey was always planned with Amani in mind as I've said, and we felt it would be nice for us both to go out there together, but it just didn't work out that way. I hadn't always coped very well in the past with relationships and football and those two mixing, but with Amani I have. In Turkey, I would go to sleep with my voice in my head saying, 'I miss my girlfriend, I love my girlfriend,' and I could hear it echoing in the room. That was such a difficult time in my life and even though she wasn't there with me, Amani helped me to get through everything. I think it's important to have that someone in your life you can turn to, and especially when things are not going so well at work, or there's upset in your life, you need someone there to help you. It was often a horrible state of affairs for me in football. I can remember being unhappy at times while I was at Aston Villa, and I can look back now and realise that I must have been pretty difficult to live with or be around.

The last thing that Amani would have wanted was to be with a footballer. Shereen had to lie to her at first and didn't mention that I was playing professionally. I think they had a few words afterwards, but obviously it all worked out for us in the end. Amani does love sport though, as I do, and as our relationship developed we would go and watch each other play football, netball or basketball. People say that you need a friendship for a relationship to be successful and I had that straight away. We could speak about football and we had shared interests. I'd changed over time as well, perhaps I'd matured, but it helped us to get on with life.

I can vividly remember Amani and I playing basketball together, one-on-one games in the yard. I didn't know the rules of the sport, but I loved playing and loved watching her play. She beat me 10-9, but wouldn't have beaten me at football that's for sure. We sit down and watch basketball and football together today, but she wrongly believes that basketball is the best sport ever, so I have to put her right. Amani still plays basketball and netball locally, so has played all of her life. She had the big decision to make over whether to continue her scholarship in America or not soon after we'd met, and she ended up staying here in England to continue her studies closer to her family. Result for me! When we were starting to date, it wasn't a case of 'are we going to be together?' it was more 'I have to see this person again.' We didn't feel like we had a choice. If she'd have gone out to the states it would have probably been very difficult for us to stay together, but who knows, it's all about timing. She doesn't like being considered as a footballer's wife, she's definitely her own person. I've lived on my own for a long time, which can make me a difficult person to live with now I would think. I was used to having things my own way, and I've had to adapt a lot over the years. I'm stubborn in my ways, which must be very frustrating for Amani at times. I'm an independent person, I say independent, but people have helped me a lot over the years too. When I first got the house at Shrubbery Close, my mom was back and forth helping me out, so I was never completely on my own. I'm a capable person, but I can remember when I was first working with my agent, Neil, who helped me with my contracts at Aston Villa and Manchester City, as well as the move to Turkey, he also helped me with off-field stuff like my house, cars, holidays, you name it. He was very keen to sign me and as part of that he promised to provide me with a PA. At that time, there were rumours of me being linked to Manchester United and there was a lot of interest in me in those early days, so agents were really pushing to work with me. As such, I was adamant that he would live up to all of his early promises and I made him deliver on providing me access to a PA. He allocated someone to me and they ran my life, so to speak. Over the years, Nicki Clarkson, Vicky Silverthorn, Alex Beard and Kate Stapleton were all so helpful and the only thing I ever had to be concerned with was how to have my house; the rest of my life was taken care of. I think that in my current house, it took me around two years to get the place how I wanted it, and Amani moved in to that environment, which must have been a challenge for her to adapt to. I've always wanted my own way, but then I don't want that to sound negative, so my reason for saying it is that when people come round to my house I hope they have a feeling of happiness and they enjoy the house as it is, in the way I'd always hoped. That is what I mean by 'my way'. I love that Amani is here, because she's made it all so much better. Like all couples, we fall out sometimes and each time we make up I just love her even more.

There are so many stories, too many in fact, from my time with Amani; we are as thick as thieves, laughing and joking and always together at home. We were abroad a few years back and we met a German couple in their 50s and we were set to play an 18-hole round of golf with them. I don't know what to say, but the fella just couldn't stop farting, no matter what he did, he was farting. I was so sorry that I laughed, and I'm laughing now as I write this, but he must have had a real problem. His wife was absolutely mortified with the whole thing, but me and Amani had four hours of this and we were in hysterics. At one point Amani was in front of a tree, whereas they were on the fairway. She was waiting to take her shot, and the chap just let rip again, and we couldn't hold the laughter back. Amani swung to hit the ball, which crashed in to the tree and came back and hit her in the stomach, leaving the dimple marks of the ball on her skin. Once they realised that she was ok, they were laughing with us, and that set us off again. I could reel off thousands of those kind of stories, where we just can't stop laughing and I guess when you strip everything back in a relationship, the friendship and the laughter is what really matters, and we have so much of that.

In 2014, I was travelling back from Loughborough and my car's engine failed on the motorway. At this time Amani was pregnant and it was taking me forever to get home. Amani was on her own and had to take our giant bullmastiff dog, Denzel out for a walk, and he ran off in excitement and slipped on the wet leaves and hurt his spine. He couldn't get up and was too heavy for Amani to lift on her own. I was stuck on the motorway 50 miles away and had to ring my friend Damian to come around, pick Denzel up in the pitch black and carry him in to his car and take him to the vets. I was awaiting recovery for hours at the service station. My phone battery was running out drastically. It was horrible not being there for them but Denzel has now recovered and is fine, thanks to Damian and sorry for not being there Amani.

I've always liked to try and learn new things. I really enjoy that challenge, like trying to learn a language, or when I was away with England for a tournament for six weeks, I would buy the books that taught me a skill such as building a computer, rather than fantasy or horror. I like being able to complete these tasks myself and I gain a certain satisfaction from not needing to ask someone else. It's like I'm testing my own competency at times. If Amani has a problem then I like to be able to fix it for her, if she needs, it's only right. Although I do need to start accepting her help too I suppose.

When I roomed with Jlloyd at Aston Villa, we would be showing off our gadgets, like iPods at the time, as we were both really in to our technology. I'd go to sleep with my music on. I've got an eclectic taste, but in my younger days I was really in to Tupac Shakur, and also Bob Marley and Germaine Williams. Now, with Persia here, I'm dancing along to Justin Bieber with her; my music taste now is basically whatever she listens to. Amani and I have always had a similar taste I would say, and we like all music, but now it's just a case of making sure Persia likes it. She's always up dancing to music now which is great to see. I love to be out in the garden and if the weather is right, I like to play tennis, and I've spoken of my love of golf, which goes back to my agent Neil, and when I was at Villa. He had various deals in golf, so I was sent all their gear, and my contact at Nike would send me everything too, but I had absolutely no clue what I was doing. I would head up to the Belfry with Amani and play on the Derby course, which is more for beginners, and until Amani showed me a video of me playing I didn't appreciate just how awful a golfer I was. I was a professional athlete, so there was obviously some sporting talent in me, so I had to fix that. I went through my whole analysis process and started to watch golf DVDs and read golf magazines and sort myself out, but it's such a difficult sport. One day, you can play well and the next you are terrible. I didn't like the difference in standard that happens with golf, which was leagues apart from how my days in football were. I didn't mind being bad at golf, but I didn't want to be awful, I couldn't accept that. I got my handicap down to eleven, but would love to reach single figures one day. I love the sport so much and I'm always up for playing. I've found that it's a release for any problems I may have, and it is incredible how easily you can forget about other things in your life while you are out on the course. Amani is very good and has won a couple of competitions at our local course, the Warwickshire Golf & Country Club, so her name is up on the board, Amani Vassell, which makes me very proud. I need to get my name up there now as well!

As for music, I don't just have an interest in it, I actually play a bit of ·

guitar, which I learned whilst I was at Manchester City as I've mentioned. I don't speak about it too much as people will just ask you to fetch it and start playing a tune, and that's not really why I learned; I think it's for myself, and it's a therapeutic process, where I can pick it up and play, especially with my eyes closed and it's something I really enjoy. I had a block of lessons with a great guitar instructor called Jason Brown while I lived and played football in Manchester and after that, with those lessons, it was enough for me to be able to play a little. Jason is an artist himself, and he played at our engagement party with his wife, who plays strings. I'm not a proper guitarist, but I can play. It's great that I can play golf with my wife, but also that we can go on holiday and have a game with others, whereas in the past I was way out of my depth. It's the same with cooking, which I enjoy, but I don't do a lot; Amani is the chef and she is amazing. She will cook for the whole family on Sundays, something we all look forward to. I think my tastes have changed since I met Amani too; one side of her family are from Yemen and the other from the Caribbean, and her mom is a fantastic cook, so there is always great variety in our cuisine. In fact both my mom and her mom are always baking us cakes, so I have to be careful with my waistline now I'm not playing football.

I really got in to motorbikes after I'd finished playing. I couldn't have had one whilst I was a footballer because of the injury risk, and I'd often look at people on them and wonder what the hell they were doing. I can remember my cousin Carl, in America, gave me my first real experience of motorcycles close up. I remember him taking my mom for a spin down a Brooklyn freeway and I was so scared for her and relieved when they both came back fine. Now though, the thrill of being on a bike is really something. I got rid of my Porsche a few years back and I was gutted, even though I never drove it, so I needed to balance missing the thrill of having one and that's when I went for the bike. I ride quite often these days. It took me three times to pass my test; I was turning up and the assessor was asking for my autograph and even that didn't ensure a pass! On one occasion, I rode to Scotland to meet my uncle and auntie, who both ride and that was an amazing experience. Riding through the Scottish countryside was something I'll never forget , life just felt so easy on those open winding roads. We went from Fife on the east coast, all the way across to the west coast and back; it was spectacular. It makes me realise that there is so much more to life, so much for us all to experience.

Having said all of that about trying and learning new things, I'm a very home-oriented person. A normal night in the Vassell household would be a home cooked meal by Amani, whilst we watch television, perhaps a film, and spend most of the evening and daytime entertaining Persia. Perhaps people will call that boring, maybe some of the friends I used to hang around with and go out to bars and clubs with will think that too, but that's my life now; I don't want anything more than that. Amani has a new partner in crime now and I love the way they are together and watching them laugh and joke. I miss Amani more than she realises when they're on their day-by-day activities, but hopefully I'm able to pass my exams and coaching badges, release this book and be the second person to hold a degree in my household.

I'm the same with holidays; I know why we go on them, but I feel like my home is my holiday. I've been fortunate to travel with England and my clubs; in fact I'm trying to think of places that I haven't visited. I've been to enough places to say that I don't feel the urge to travel at this time in my life. It's more about being prepared should I have to. I feel more of a desire to make my home as the place I really want to be, rather than desperately trying to experience somewhere else. I want that to be at home with my family. That is true happiness for me. There was a lot of promise associated with me in my early days in football, and that led to a lot of nights out and freebies and people wanted to be close to me and congratulate me. Now I look back, I can pinpoint when things changed; around the time Villa's results went wrong, I didn't feel as comfortable showing my face around Birmingham on a night out, it just didn't feel right. If I wasn't playing well I wanted to get home, and just the same as my time at Leicester, when I was injured, I didn't want to look as if a bad performance or a bad result didn't mean anything to me as it really did. I slowed down and matured a little when I spent time in Manchester. I was also affected by being mugged in Manchester, and that left me feeling a little withdrawn and vulnerable. I realised that I needed to be at home. Back in the day at Villa, if we'd won, me and Jlloyd would be out on the town dancing. We loved dancing, not as in being a professional, but it was something that we shared, and we would have moves to certain songs which we would have practised. We would even work on our moves in training! Amani says I've still got rhythm, but I think she's just being kind.

It's quite strange when I look back on my life so far, that most of my interests and the profession that I am known for, all involve people watching you and judging you, and yet that is something that I have always felt uncomfortable with and have shied away from. From joining new teams and the England penalty heartbreak, to being made to dance in front of everyone with Ankaragücü, to being watched when I tee off at golf, maybe I subconsciously just try and force myself to do these things and not allow myself to be held back by my nerves. I can remember Joey Barton smoking his drive down the fairway in front of everyone at a Manchester City golf day, and then my name was read out over the tannoy system and I just wanted the ground to swallow me up. Maybe I've just always tried to get over my fears, but it's still a challenge that I face today.

In terms of me as a person, I think that sometimes people can just find me a little difficult to work out; that they don't know whether I'm happy or sad. Perhaps it takes me a while to warm to people, or to trust them and eventually they find it easier to speak to me and get on with me. I don't try to be difficult deliberately. I'm notoriously bad at getting back to people on the phone, and Amani has had a word with me about that. If I'm at home, I like to just be at home and not on the phone or working, it's my time to relax and that's just me, perhaps spending time with Persia, or my dog Denzel, or maybe hitting a few golf balls. If I decide to dip my toe in to the water of the world of football again, then that would need to change for certain. I think the way I am has probably affected a few of the people I know, and they perhaps just feel that I want to be left alone. If I'm busy, I'm not the kind of person who would come out of that busyness to tell you; I'd just get back to you later. That's not me being rude, but perhaps people have felt that I am.

When I've bumped in to people on the street, I've often had the feeling that they expect me to be a certain way because I was a footballer and inside I would just absolutely hate to disappoint them, but I'm just me, Darius Vassell. When I go out of my house, I feel that there is always a chance of people recognising me, which is not a normal feeling to experience. I would say that most footballers don't care about it, but I always did to be honest. I still have that attitude of not wanting to let people down, whether it be my family and friends, or the general public. I always wanted to give a good impression of myself when possible. I think that nowadays, so much is said about footballers, that they almost have to not care or worry about what people think. I'm glad that I wasn't playing football during the days of social media and that immediate way of communicating with people. Now if a Premier League or international footballer goes out for a beer, it's all over the media; they can't have a normal life, because it's simply not a normal profession. I went to watch the England vs. Holland friendly match at Wembley Stadium, prior to Euro 2016, and I bumped in to Benito Carbone who I played with at Villa. I didn't even recognise him with his beard and different hairstyle. It was great to catch up with him and reminisce, but it showed how detached I'd become from the game, unlike others who live and breathe football way beyond the end of their playing career.

Looking back on my playing days, Graham Taylor tried so many times to get the best out of me. At one point he had two or three different psychologists in a room with me, trying to get to the bottom of what made me the person I am, and whether they could get more from me on the field. I was there for two hours and I didn't feel like we were getting anywhere. Graham said something about my subconscious and how I'm trying to protect myself from something, as I don't really want the limelight. I didn't respond at the time, but I knew that he was trying to help me. I think I understand him now but it's way too late and still may not be the actual case. Every footballer would love to be the best in the world, but not every player could handle that accolade and everything that comes with it. Take David Beckham, as I've said before, everything that he handled and coped with, I wouldn't have wanted any of that. I guess that Graham Taylor was looking for the goal selfish number nine in me, a stereotypical striker, and wanted to get that out of me. He believed that I would do things, without knowing I'd done them, to avoid being in the limelight. This was parallel to the way I scored my goals. That without me realising, I was protecting myself from having to take on that responsibility. I'll never know if he was right, but it must have been frustrating for him. He felt there was more in the tank and maybe he was on to something, we'll never know. Retiring from being a footballer has revealed many of my flaws as I look back on it all. Amani is usually first to witness these and I admit to my stubbornness being the worst. This may have cost me a few friendships in the past but I've realised through my career that we can all make mistakes. So, I'm working on this from now on Amani, ok?

If I hadn't been a footballer, I feel that I would have wanted to become a professional within sport in some way. If not the sports route then something creative would have attracted me, maybe music if I'd have stuck to that earlier in my life? I've always been determined and keen to learn how to perform a skill. Amani thinks I'm one of those annoying people who would have done well whatever I did. I think, like a lot of people, as long as you are interested in something then that helps in you becoming good at it. Football certainly affected me most as a child. It took me out of my shell, and placed me in to another one; a better one. As a youngster, I was very fragile and people were always worried as to whether I was alright. I was more of a follower than a leader, and football pulled me out of that and gave me the confidence I needed. When you strip away everything that football gave me, a certain level of fame, attention, and all of that, I was just a boy who loved to play the game a lot like everyone else. I would have played anywhere, at any time when I was younger. I couldn't get enough of it. It's sad that I can't do that so easily now, as there are many social or environmental expectations that I must deal with when trying to be normal.

I'd feel like I would rather not go to a park and have a kick around as people could be judging me as an England footballer, not as someone who wants to play and enjoy 'free' football just like them. That's if I was recognised of course. It was such a stupid thing to worry about when you just want a kick around. Now we've had Persia, she's bringing me out of that, and I'll go to the park with her and kick a ball around, and she's given me back a lot of the love of the game that I'd lost and of sport overall.

Mates would ask me to play in 5-a-side tournaments in their teams, but I didn't want to be someone being used to help them win trophies, I just wanted to play for fun like they were. I'm well capable of falling on my arse and having a good time trying new skills and tricks but I'm not sure they would appreciate the taunts of losing when they had me in their team.

Despite not playing in the Premier League for eight or nine years, I go to watch games and I'm treated as if I'm still a player and it means a lot to me. I've been going in to Wolverhampton Wanderers recently, thanks to my old youth coach Steve Burns and the young lads there had to Google my name to see who I was, which was funny, and I much preferred them not knowing straight away. It was nice that I could speak with them about football and remember what it was like for me when I was starting out at Villa. For everything that football gave me, and it gave me so much, I guess it also took something away, perhaps my freedom to walk around Birmingham without feeling expectation. I didn't want to let people down especially if they looked up to me. I wasn't special I was just normal and I've had similar problems to my family and friends in life but been very fortunate, that's all. Becoming a footballer also affected my family in so many ways but I just had to do it, I craved it, even if I didn't exactly crave everything that came with it. Football has made me smile and cry, taken me all around the world and has given me confidence in life. I was able to perform autonomously on the pitch at times, and there was nowhere I would rather be, but the moment I stopped to think about it all, to worry about what could happen, it all became so different again.

12

PERSIA

For this chapter, I felt that it was important to get the perspective of the woman who knows me best, Persia's mother and my best friend, Amani, in her own words...

We could have met a year or two before we did. Our mutual friend, Shereen, would often try and get me to go out with them to a night at The Belfry, but I didn't want to be one of the hangers-on. As soon as I moved back from America, Shereen told me she was going out in Solihull, and given how bad my geography was, I didn't even give the place a second thought and agreed to go out with her. We were around twenty minutes from arrival, when someone called Darius rang Shereen, and I knew the name but just couldn't think where from. I asked her whose house we were going to and she explained it was Darius' place, and that he was her friend who plays football. I was so angry and we had such a big argument that we actually crashed in to a roundabout. Shereen was driving, and our other friend Cassie was in the car with us. I was still tired from the jet lag of my journey back to the UK from America, and now I was in a bad mood. I'd decided that as soon as we got there I would call a cab and go home.

The car was damaged from the accident and a kind gentleman changed our tyre for us. We drove to Darius' house, but got lost as the satellite navigation stopped working. Darius came to meet us, so that was the first time I saw him. I felt like I was in the worst situation, my absolute worst nightmare; being at a stranger's house in the worst mood, when everyone else is happy and excited to go out. As we pulled up to the house, I couldn't get over what a beautiful place it was and how nice Darius was. I was pretty rude to him to be honest as I was so agitated. He gave me a drink and already I was thinking that he was trying to get me drunk. I was so negative. He was convincing me to come out with them all and promised me that if I wanted to leave early he would make sure that I got back safely.

I felt like everyone knew I was upset, especially Darius, and he must have thought that I was a very socially awkward person. Usually when I go in to Grinch mode nothing can cheer me up, but Darius kept making me get up and dance and making me laugh. Before I knew it, I was no longer the Grinch and I was having the time of my life. I remember Robin Thicke's song 'Lost Without U' which is still one of my favourite songs, coming on and feeling a little tipsy I ran on to the dance floor and started dancing to it. I realised maybe it wasn't a big hit in England at the time, as I was the only person dancing to it. Darius saved my shame of dancing by myself, and by the way, I can't dance as I have two left feet and two right hands; this guy had some serious moves that he even made me look like I had rhythm! We were doing this made-up salsa dance and then everyone in our group took over the dance floor for the rest of the song. I didn't realise that this song would play such an important part in our journey together. I remember being really ill a few months into our relationship and Darius was learning to play the guitar, which I found very attractive, and he called me and said I've learnt a song for you and then he played 'Lost Without U' down the phone. It was the best gift anyone had ever given to me and I remember thinking for the first time that this guy was special. This song was later our first dance song at our wedding.

I had been at East Durham Basketball Academy, before studying out in America at the University of West Florida, which was an amazing two years and probably would have gone back if it wasn't for meeting Darius.

I remember the first official family event I got invited to was his mom's 50th birthday party at The Belfry. I was so nervous and I can remember I had a basketball game before in London and felt so dehydrated. I accidentally got horribly drunk and can't remember much. The next morning my friend

Shereen, who was also there, told me I was a nightmare and threw up all over Darius's downstairs bathroom. I was so embarrassed, and because we had only been together for a few months, I thought Darius would run for the hills and you couldn't blame him if he'd done so either. He was so lovely the next morning and just kept making sure I was ok and giving me cuddles. Phew!

Still, to this day, I don't see him as a footballer though. I think it's because when I came in to his life he was near the end of his playing career, so in the ten years we've been together almost half of it he hasn't been playing. I didn't go to many of his games as I usually had a basketball game on the same day. This is why it's still so weird for me when we're out and people recognise him. Sometimes I'm so oblivious to how often it is but I notice Darius becoming a little uncomfortable and then realise. Sometimes I become a camera woman when I'm out, but I don't mind because usually the people who approach Darius are lovely. I can imagine it can get a bit much for Darius at times especially when he's got to have the same conversation 20 times. It must sometimes feel like Groundhog Day for him but he will always try and take the time to have a little chin wag with anyone who approaches him, probably the reason we are always late!

There have been a few incidents where I feel he's been targeted due to people knowing who he is. I'll never forget the night when he got mugged in Manchester. It was just horrible and Darius isn't arrogant, flashy or extravagant so I just didn't understand why someone would target him. I was at his apartment in Manchester and it was about four in the morning when I heard this really loud banging at the door. I didn't want to answer because I thought it was someone who probably had got the wrong apartment. The banging continued so I tried to call Darius but his phone was going straight to voicemail. Then I heard Darius shouting my name. I ran to the door and he burst in. I saw straight away his ear was bleeding. He was in shock and was disoriented. He kept saying, "They had a gun, they had a gun. Call the police!" Nothing made sense. I managed to calm him down and he told me he'd been mugged. I asked if he was hurt and he didn't know. I called the police as I was checking to make sure he was ok. He kept saying "They kept saying burn him, just burn him," and he thought that meant shoot him. It was so scary. They must have followed him from Manchester City's Christmas party as they jumped him as soon as he got out of the taxi. After this incident, Darius avoided going out unless it was a really special occasion.

He did become more comfortable going out until another incident where some guy decided to punch him in the face for no reason. I couldn't believe it when I saw his face. His lips were double in size and he has lovely full lips already. I couldn't understand what he was saying for days. He was so brave about it all but I knew it had really affected him. That was almost five years ago and since then I can probably count how many times he's been out on one hand. I didn't get why someone would want to hurt Darius. He's so chilled out and humble. It just didn't make sense to me. What made it worse was that it was the end of the night in Birmingham, where Darius felt comfortable and familiar.

On a happier note, Darius got me in to golf. It's not a sport I ever thought I'd play and I'm so grateful he introduced me to such an amazing game! It's weird but I associate golf more with Darius than football. I think it's because we took it up together. Darius and I are both very competitive but he is annoyingly good at every sport. I really believe no matter what sport he picked he would have been amazing at it and golf is a prime example. The way he applies himself, researches, and practices is unreal. His first handicap was 19 and within a year he was playing off 11. I was very proud but secretly jealous in a competitive way. He has really helped me with my golf. When I was eight months' pregnant he got me some new clubs which I went on to win the Warwickshire women's club knockouts with. He was so proud when he heard I had reached the final. He came to the golf club and when I'd finished my match and told him I won he was more chuffed than me.

Darius and I are both pranksters, constantly performing tricks, mainly by trying to scare each other. I'm quite a jumpy person, so he would wait until I least expected it and would jump out on me, which would then turn me in to a ninja; I've lost count of the number of times I've kung-fu kicked him, but he always seems to catch me unawares. Thankfully, he doesn't do it as much these days.

One thing I love about Darius is that he finds sentimental value in things that others wouldn't. I remember him showing me the step to his bathroom. He kept going on about the importance of the step, how he and his friend Jlloyd often spoke in their hotel rooms, when they were at YTS level, about stepping in to their bathrooms when they were older. When Darius first viewed the house, he noticed the step and it was almost a sign that this was the house for him. Hearing him talk about the significance of the step, sort of transported me back to him buying the house, even though I wasn't there, which was a nice moment to share with him. I know it sounds silly mentioning a step but for me it's more than a step and to Darius, who was a young boy talking about dreams to his friends all those years ago, made sure he succeeded and didn't forget about the little things that were important and inspired him to work hard. He achieved that step to his bathroom, and so much more, and his determination to do that with everything is one of the reasons I love him and am so proud of him.

Darius is one of the funniest people I know and that might shock a few people to hear who have met him as he can sometimes be a little introverted until he gets comfortable around a new crowd. We would have rap battles and be in fits of laughter all night. I've been described as a lyrical G, honestly I'm the worst rapper in the world, but Darius gives me a good run for my money!

There are pros and cons to everyone's character, and he is, at times, too serious, but that just shows that he cares. He sees the bigger picture a lot of the time, and I think he sees things before others do. I'm always in a rush and never have the time to stop and consider that, but the way he is isn't necessarily a bad thing. We both have the same objectives in life, but we often have a different way of going about achieving things. He won't always see that I'm on the same lines as him, but since we've had Persia, we are becoming a stronger team.

On my first birthday with Darius, he bought me boxing gloves and protective headwear along with loads of other sporty goodies, and we were filming each other sort of sparring; it was me, Shereen and Darius. After Shereen and I had finished, Darius and I were then play fighting and I was sure he wouldn't take it too seriously. He was hitting me on my arms, lightly, like a sharp jab, but then I made the mistake of walking in to one of his punches, after trying to dodge it and I fell to the ground. Immediately, Darius asked Shereen to stop filming, but she carried on anyway, and he had tears in his eyes and was heartbroken that he'd put me on the ground. He wanted us to go to the hospital, but I was fine and was laughing about it. I guess it does show just how competitive he is, that he even achieved a knockout win over his new girlfriend, on her birthday!

Something he used to struggle with, although this is both of us, is remembering people's names. We are both absolutely terrible. We'll bump in to people and I'll be praying that Darius will say their name, and he doesn't, and we'll just be saying hello, and trying to politely move on with the conversation, but it must be obvious that we don't know their name. Darius will say, for example, 'hello, Sue,' and later in the day 'Sue' will explain that she's called Sarah, and I'll be dying with laughter. It happens to us all of the time and has left us in such awkward situations. We are both getting better though, just from us both making that extra effort and from the time in Turkey.

Before we got engaged, Darius was in Turkey, and we started talking about having kids. We'd been together for 3 years and we had a solid foundation. I had never had a proper relationship prior to Darius so it was not anything I'd ever thought of. I wasn't sure if I was ready, and as I was five years younger than Darius I had other things I wanted to achieve first. Darius was very understanding and assured me that no matter what I wanted to do he would support me. After that conversation the thought of having kids with Darius excited me. He knew I wanted to be married before I had kids and he respected how I felt so much. My mom was married before she had kids, and to me it meant a lot to do it that way. The conversation was in October 2009 and we were engaged in December 2009.

Darius has always spoilt me. He would buy me my favourite chocolates or get me the most amazing basketball trainers and not because it was a special occasion, it was literally just to make me smile. Going back to when we had been together for about two years he gave me a ring; it was the most beautiful gold band, with five little diamonds in it as five is my lucky number. Nobody had ever bought me jewellery and I remember thinking at the time 'yep, you're in an adult relationship.' Big gulp. I wasn't used to wearing jewellery so I couldn't even sleep in it. I would put it on the side, or in my Xbox memory card case that was on my keys. One night I stayed at my Godchildren's mom's house, got up to take them to school and I lost the ring. I was devastated. I even bought metal detectors and put posters up around the area with a reward to try and find it. That's how gutted I was. How could I be so careless with something so precious? I called Darius up and explained what had happened and he was very calm, and just told me to try and find it, but if I didn't he said, "Just make sure you don't lose the one I give to you when I'm on one knee." It was such a lovely thing to say as I felt so ungrateful as I'd lost it within two weeks.

I didn't think anything more of his comment, but then two years later he bought me a ring, in Turkey, almost exactly the same as the one I'd lost. We went off to get it fitted but little did I know that this was a decoy ring to get my true ring size. The replacement ring would allow Darius to know my size, for the other ring, which was set to be my engagement ring. On Christmas Day, back at home in England, I knew something was wrong with him, as he seemed nervous and he would jump every time I walked in to the room. It was totally out of character for him. I was just wrapping presents in the bedroom and he came up, right next to me, got down on his knees, both knees as he was nervous, and handed me my Christmas present and looked at me and said, "Yeah, it's the one…I want you to be my wife!" and I just started crying, that horrible, ugly burst of tears, thank god I didn't have my mascara on. He had to check that I'd actually said yes, as all he could see was me crying, but of course it was yes. He said, "That's a relief", I've been sat here for twenty minutes waiting for a reply!"

The ring was the most beautiful I'd ever set eyes on, however, knowing what a klutz I am, I thought he would reconsider the huge gesture he'd made, given that I'd lost a ring he gave me before. So, literally two weeks later, I was flying to see Darius in Turkey, was leaving my flat in London and placed my ring on my finger. I can remember looking at it and playing with it in the taxi on the way to Heathrow Airport, and then as I arrived at the check-in desk I handed my passport over and there was a big gaping hole in my ring; the diamond had fallen out. I threw my passport, and the check-in girl must have thought I was crazy. I looked around on the floor, called the taxi, and it was raining outside, so my white shirt dress was now brown as I'd been searching on the floor. Luckily, I'm organised, so I was at the airport very early. I'd already secured my seat online, which had to have the number five within it, my lucky number, so that I would feel safe. I knew I had time to look for the diamond, and I must have searched for two hours and I got to the trolley bay, thinking that it could have come loose there. This member of staff from the airport came over to me to ask how I was. I was crying, with mascara everywhere, and at that stage I was also on the phone to Darius, explaining to him what had happened, and he was very calm and told me to carry on looking for the diamond and to miss my flight if necessary as the ring wasn't even insured yet.

I had around 45 minutes until my flight was leaving, so I called Darius to tell him that I was going to have to miss the flight, when all of a sudden a guy was shouting in my direction, from behind me, that he'd found it. I ignored him at first as I didn't allow my hopes to get up and just thought it might have been someone winding me up. He then grabbed hold of my hand, and placed the diamond in to my palm. I burst in to tears of relief and joy, and hugged him as hard as I could. I took his address down, and later we posted him a card and a hamper to express our gratitude. Then I made my flight, and couldn't get my hands on a glass of bubbly quick enough. When I called Darius to say I'd found the diamond he didn't believe me. He said, "Who finds a diamond at a busy airport, in the rain, it's impossible. You are the luckiest person I know!" As soon as I arrived in Turkey, he took me to the jewellers and we had two extra claws added in to make sure the diamond was going nowhere. He also got it insured that same day as I clearly couldn't be trusted. It felt like a sign that having found it, our wedding and our marriage together, wouldn't be jinxed.

As I've already said, we seemed destined to meet, not just through our mutual friend Shereen, but also the fact that one of my close friends is Sarah Crouch, who is Peter Crouch's sister. We all went to Drayton Manor School together, and Peter then ended up playing for Villa with Darius before we got together. Sarah and I lived in the same apartments as well. It was bizarre that there were so many links between us. It was Sarah who had asked me what I wanted for Christmas, and said, "What if he proposes?" I didn't imagine he would, but I was delighted when he did.

We booked our wedding day around two years in advance, and then the Queen decided to move the bank holiday weekend forward a week for the jubilee celebrations. We'd already booked Sunday 27th May 2012 for our big day and we wanted to give our guests the Monday to travel back as part of the bank holiday. I was going to change the date, but Darius stopped me and said that this was our day and we should stick to it. This was the day we had met on that bank holiday at his house and at the Bel-Air nightclub. On our big day it ended up being beautiful, whereas the next weekend was pouring rain. I was roasting in my dress as it was 27 degrees, and if we'd have moved it back the wedding would have been cancelled as the venue was under water. It was fate that it all worked out so well.

We'd had testing times in our relationship, as anyone does, particularly when Darius was injured at Manchester City and at Leicester City. He was pretty down and moody when he couldn't play, and he's quite a private person, with a close-knit group of friends around him, so the last thing he would want is for people to know that he was struggling and he certainly didn't want any sympathy. I can remember him having this device on his knee, which needed to be iced every three hours, and I would need to set an alarm through the night to do it. Talk about practice for when Persia came along! I think from those Manchester City days whilst injured it really set our foundation. If we could make it through that and with smiles, laughter and golf I knew we could make it through pretty much anything. I would want to give him a cuddle and he would be offended and just see it as a sympathy thing. It was like Déjà vu when it happened again at Leicester and it was so frustrating to see the thing that he loved taken away from him and the way it made him feel.

I was so proud of him for how determined he was to get fit. Both times he injured his knee was in the last year of his contracts at both Leicester City and Manchester City. He would do absolutely everything, and more, to get fit and was always back earlier than anticipated. When his contracts weren't renewed he saw it as a failure but I didn't see it that way. I saw how hard he was working. He'd come home from training and work out and would do all the exercises the physio gave him religiously. So he took it hard when he put blood and sweat in to getting fit but it wasn't enough. He really wanted to stay at both teams especially Manchester City as he'd already had to fight his way back in to the squad when Sven arrived. I can remember Sven saying to the press that Darius wasn't in his plans for the team. Darius could have accepted defeat and I remember a few teams wanted him but he wasn't going anywhere. He worked so hard in training and a few weeks later he proved everyone wrong and was back in the starting line-up. I think Sven really respected Darius' mindset on not giving up and I think it made him trust him.

I think that probably the incident in his playing career that had the biggest impact on him was his time in Ankara. It changed him; in fact it probably changed me too and made me more cautious of people. Darius was told by senior members who worked at the club, don't drink the team water as they may have it orchestrated that you are drug tested on the same day. He was also invited to the palatial home of those that were supposed to be plotting such things but found them really warm and welcoming. Darius didn't know how to think out there at times. I remember him calling me to tell me that he was on a 'drip' in his room as one of the medical staff insisted that they gave him nutrients before the game. I can only imagine how shocking he would have felt to allow them to do this, saying no would have come across as 'Big Time' potentially and Darius would avoid that if he could as it wasn't true. I'm used to being friendly at first with people, and I still am, but now with caution. The way they dealt with him really showed that he didn't trust people as much anymore, which was totally understandable given everything that happened out there. He would tell me to get everything signed and written down on paper or on email, rather than agreeing in person, even if I didn't need to. He was lied to in Turkey and some of the people around could not have been completely genuine with so many conflicting stories about the truth. Originally I didn't want him to go out there, but he didn't want to drop down the divisions in England and still wanted to play top flight football. He wanted something different to the usual story of a footballer ending up in the lower divisions due to getting old and slow. When they sold us the move, they made it clear that Darius would not have any problems out there and that his wages were certified by a large bank and this is why the agents were taking an awful long time to get the deal done. They were waiting for the eventually received confirmation.

Turkey was an amazing experience; the people are just so lovely and the food was out of this world. We would go to this amazing fish restaurant called Park Fora, and pick our fish from the see-through counter. The staff would look at us like we were crazy as we'd pick so much and I'd just say, "Don't worry, you're about to see something impressive as I'm known as the bottomless pit!" I loved how they adored Darius. He learned all their names and would always try and talk in Turkish to them. I think that's part of the reason they loved him as he made them feel like a friend.

The first game I went to was against Bursaspor away. I can remember the long drive and when we arrived I was starving. I was taken to this restaurant and they brought out this food. It was the most amazing kebab

I've ever had, and I don't like kebabs. They told me Bursa was famous for kebabs. Afterwards, we went to watch the game and Darius was amazing. I was so proud of him, even though they lost 1-0. We went back to the restaurant and they gave Darius a kebab double the size of mine. I was so jealous but knew he'd just worked his arse off, so didn't want to pinch his food. I knew he loved me when he shared it with me, as I knew he was starving, and it was amazing.

We had some struggles in Turkey; a lot of things that were promised to Darius in his contract didn't happen. He lived in a hotel room for months. Some might think that's luxury but I saw how he was living and it just didn't feel right. Darius would pretend that things were getting better but his room said it all.

After Darius got told he had to leave the hotel he was living in for the last five months I can remember him calling me when I was back in England, really confused, explaining what happened. He was humiliated that local media were there and felt like it had all been set up to make him look bad. He had to leave most of his stuff there as he couldn't physically pack it all up in time and he went to stay in another hotel. I remember him feeling like he couldn't trust anybody and he just wanted to come home. It was Christmas, and he was able to come home for about a week. He was under the impression that by the time he was due to fly back out to Ankara everything in his contract would be honoured, including his living situation. Unfortunately, that wasn't the case and when Darius returned three hours after he got off the plane he called me and asked me to book him the first flight home. I could hear in his deflated voice he'd had enough. When he got home I can remember asking if he was ok and he replied "I'm gutted, I really wanted this to work." He was so upset and he really didn't want to leave, but having nowhere to live and not being paid in a foreign country, around people he couldn't completely trust or understand, almost broke him.

I remember him saying he'd made such a connection with the fans and he was sad because their support meant the world to him, and he felt by leaving he was letting them down. I need to say here, the Ankara fans were just lovely. The support they gave my husband during some of his toughest times, I will be forever grateful for and I truly thank them. Some offered to let Darius stay in their homes which meant so much to him. They didn't realise that he wasn't actually 'homeless', the media made the most out of it as it was quite bizarre.

The club contacted Darius within a few days of him returning home. They promised on his return everything would be sorted, starting with his living arrangements. Darius decided to give Ankara another go and he still had faith that it could turn around. I flew out a few days later following a phone conversation with someone from the club. They said that Darius had somewhere to live and when I arrived they were going to take me to stores to furnish the place. When I arrived I was taken straight to the house and it was beautiful. I felt at that moment maybe Darius was right and things were going to work out. Maybe Neil was right and the last five months were just teething problems, but as soon as club representatives arrived I felt extremely suspicious. The mutterings between themselves in their language made it seem that there were shady things going on and it brought out paranoia in both of us. I felt like I could read body language well, so even if I didn't know what people were saying, I knew we were being manipulated. I would ask them to repeat in English and they would just laugh it off, so it was obvious something wasn't right. They promised money for me to help with the house out there, but I didn't receive a penny. Instead, we went to shops to get furniture and it was as if we were just taking items, with the staff looking scared. I didn't want to take anything, but if we didn't I had the feeling that the shop owner would be in trouble for not providing items to our liking. I was almost accepting stuff as the atmosphere changed whenever I said no.

The whole Turkey period in our life was just chaotic. I can remember speaking to Darius' agent, Neil, to explain that nothing was happening as promised for him. The chaos had clearly affected their relationship. Darius didn't give up though and stayed in Turkey to try and see things through. He did fly home occasionally, as he's explained, and no one can ever accuse him of not showing loyalty to the club. When you have a contract and the terms are agreed, then that should be honoured. This was Darius' way of living, his career, and all I kept thinking was I wouldn't accept this from any employer.

Darius is a boy at heart, I still see glimpses. There are scratches on our living room ceiling from where he's been practicing his golf swing. He has also broken a couple of windows playing football in the garden. I keep telling him to sort his first touch out so we'll stop needing repairs. He writes music but doesn't really share it, he does it to occupy and ease his mind and be creative. I leave him to it because I don't want him to lose that youth; it's where his humour stems from.

Our life together changed forever with the arrival of our beautiful daughter, Persia. She wasn't a planned arrival as such, and I didn't know I was pregnant until around two months in to it. I thought I had been poisoned as the pain I had in my kidneys was unbearable and I was throwing up day and night. I was convinced that some wine and cheese that Darius' auntie and uncle had brought back from France had made me ill. I decided to take a pregnancy test to just rule it out and it came up positive. I couldn't believe it. When I went in to the room, before I'd had the chance to tell him, he was already raging after an argument with his sister over the phone. I felt like I couldn't tell him, but had to. He went from being noticeably upset to the happiest man in the world. We went to the doctors straight away and they confirmed we were expecting a little person! They sent us to Solihull Hospital to have a scan as they were worried about the pains I was having. We saw this little cashew nut on the screen and we just stared at it in shock. Darius asked the doctor, "Is that it?" and we just burst out laughing as we both were expecting to see a tiny child swimming. It all became real for us at our twenty week scan. The change in six weeks blew our minds. There was this dancing and flipping, with baby going crazy in my belly. It was like she was showing off for us. Both our moms were with us and whilst Darius and I were in fits of laughter they were in floods of tears. We asked to know the sex and the lady said she wasn't sure because the baby wouldn't stop moving but she thought it was a girl. I just heard girl, and started celebrating I was sure we were having a girl so it just confirmed it. I heard Darius asking the woman how sure and she said 70/30.

When we left the room Darius said we need to get a second opinion. He wanted to be certain as he didn't want to start buying girls stuff just in case. We booked to have a 3D scan where they can tell you the sex with 99.9% accuracy. Darius had booked it on my birthday, which was a lovely surprise as it meant I got to see our baby again. I was a bit anxious as I imagined our little girl and I think I would have been a little upset if it was a boy, as it meant that all I imagined hadn't come true. About 30 seconds in to the scan, our daughter mooned us and the lady doing the scan confirmed it was a girl. We just looked at the screen and Darius said, "Hello Persia," and I just welled up.

We came up with her name whilst in the bath, on the night we found out we were pregnant. We discussed what our names stood for, with Amani meaning 'wishes' in Arabic, and he spoke about his name being in The Bible, as Darius was the King of Persia, and I just loved the name Persia straight away. In my family, all our names begin with the letter A, and we looked in to the name Athena, the goddess of wisdom and courage, amongst other things and so we came to Persia Athena Vassell. It was all set in stone before we even knew she was a girl, before she was even with us. We were calling her Persia through my stomach. It brought the two of us closer and on to the same page more than ever. Suddenly, everything that he was trying to put in place for us made sense. Nothing else mattered now. I became obsessed with researching the right foods to eat, the right exercise to do and I was committed to having a natural birth. We wanted to be as organised as possible, and we felt like parents, like a team together before she was even here.

I can't wish for a better dad for Persia than Darius. I look at Darius and Persia and I'm so grateful; it is more than I ever expected. I think we are good parents together and the product is Persia and how happy she is. She is such a character and so different; she isn't shy at all, she'll be dancing at classes and showing her independence. I dress her like me so she looks like me, but all I can see is Darius in her. They are very close; he will bring her in to our bedroom in the evening, claiming that she had woken up, when all along I've been watching her monitor, knowing that she was asleep the whole time. I'll be mad with him, but if I'm honest I do the exact same thing, as she gives the best cuddles.

I also played golf during the pregnancy and played some of my best stuff, as I couldn't hit it as hard as I normally did as I couldn't swing, so I became more accurate. I even got my name on my golf club's wall for winning the Biggerstaff trophy and the summer knockout competition whilst eight months pregnant! Persia was my lucky charm for sure. We don't play as much now as all of our time is spent with Persia, and at the time of writing she is not speaking fluently yet so I want to be with her as much as possible to ensure that she is ok as I know what she needs instinctively, which a carer or baby-sitter wouldn't necessarily pick up on. I'm sure that us both being sporty will play a part in Persia's life though. We've given Persia a stable start. Everything is organised around her and we don't eat until late as we ensure that she has eaten earlier and is happy.

Around a month before I was due we decided to get a cat. Since our last cats had passed away we had a few mice in the house. We live in the country so field mice, although cute, were becoming a pest. I told Darius we needed to get a cat. I was in pregnancy mode and was shouting at him, but it was Christmas, so we had to wait until Boxing Day to get our cat, Spartacus. I'm convinced he helped to start my labour. The night before my waters broke he fell asleep on my stomach purring, and my body felt very different all of a sudden, almost dreamlike. I felt blissful and at peace that evening, like Spartacus signalled that I was ready to give birth to Persia.

It was the night before New Year's Eve and I was completely swollen and Darius knew instinctively that Persia was coming. The next morning, around 8am, I went to the toilet, shouted 'uh oh' and Darius knew that my waters had broken, and this was two weeks early. I took a bath and some painkillers, and Darius came in to see if I was ok, but all I could think of was the fact that we had bought lots of 2015 baby stuff, but that she was going to be born in 2014. When I went in to see the doctor I had barely dilated. The contractions continued and I was panicking as water was gushing out of me. Sorry, I know that sounds awful, but it was true. We later found out that Persia was back-to-back with me, and almost blocking herself from coming out. I was in so much pain and I knew that something was wrong and started to regret planning for a natural birth. I got in to the bath at the birthing centre and threw up everywhere so had to get out without feeling the benefit of the pain relief. I was told I was only 1cm dilated and that I shouldn't push, but I felt like I needed to. Darius gave me the gas and air upside down and then broke it, so I swore at him. It's probably the only time I've ever really flipped out at him properly. I looked at his face and he was so shocked. I felt Persia drop inside me, and she was in my pelvis. As soon as the birthing centre realised there was an issue, I was blue-lighted to Birmingham Heartlands Hospital and given an epidural, and the pain was gone. I thought I was going to split in half before that. It took a matter of seconds for everything to kick in and I was exhausted. Everything was a blur at this point. I remember doctors and nurses coming in to wish us a Happy New Year at one point and I remember Darius telling me he was going home to check on Denzel and Spartacus, while my mother stayed with me until he returned. I can remember being checked again and hearing doctors saying I wasn't dilated and they gave me some hormones. I was so dazed everything seemed like a dream and then there were doctors running around everywhere and there was a mad rush to get her out. Darius calmed me down as I was so scared they were going to tell me she didn't make it. I could hear doctors discussing her low heart rate and telling me they were going to take good care of us both. That was all at 11.30am and by 11.45am she was with us by emergency C-Section. I can remember hearing her cry and asking if she was out yet. They said no and they'd never seen a baby cry whilst still in someone. It took them a while to wedge her out of my pelvis and although I didn't feel any pain I can remember feeling tugging and stretching around my stomach. I remember thinking she was so small, so I was disappointed that I hadn't managed to get her out; she was just 6lbs 15ozs and as I held her, I didn't care about anything else. She really did look like her dad though.

I want to say thank you to the staff at Heartlands; they supported us throughout, they were amazing and nothing was too much trouble for them. We checked out early, and everything just felt different in our lives. We just wanted to make everything safe for her, and the house was a completely different place for us. I can remember Darius cooking for me as I couldn't really do much in those first days, and it was the most amazing meal ever, so I got a bit emotional. I couldn't even empty the dishwasher without splitting my stitches. I felt so helpless but Darius made sure everything was ok.

We have a folder of photos for Persia, collated since she was born, and there are over 10,000 images in there now. We even do a collage picture of the week, every week, and share it with our families, as mine are in London. I guess that sums up how much we both love her and we just don't want to stop. Hopefully she'll enjoy that picture book, and this book one day, when she's older.

13

THIRTEEN

I can vividly remember a raffle taking place at Romulus Boys' Club and Carol, the manager's wife, called out her lucky number, nine. She paused between saying her number, and I started to wonder why someone would have a lucky number. What did it mean? I was only young myself, probably around nine or ten years old, and I'd never really thought of the importance of it. I didn't win and I thought at that point that I wanted a lucky number. The easiest to go with was the number of my date of birth, thirteen.

I went to school and started to look in to the number a little more; it's a weird number, thought of as unlucky and I considered whether it was a prime number, that kind of thing. I started to think about Friday 13th as being unlucky and my fascination with the number just grew. I was born on Friday 13th June 1980 and I started to wonder whether I could adopt the number as mine, maybe just to be different.

As I grew older, my association with the number thirteen just grew stronger; milestones such as when I first broke my leg I was aged 13, and that prevented me from visiting my grandma Ethline who was known as Etty and had moved back home to Jamaica. My grandma absolutely adored me and together with my Grandad, they had sold up and were enjoying their retirement out in the Caribbean. I was gutted that I couldn't see her out there, but as I grew older I learned more about her and learned that she was born on the 13th too, which just continued my intrigue.

At Aston Villa, when I scored my first goals for the club against Strømsgodset in the UEFA Cup, after my grandma had been out in Jamaica for around five years, she was ill with cancer and I was hoping to get some time off to go out and visit her. I wanted to see her before she died. I was so sad when she passed away, mixed with the professional delight of having scored my first goals. I wanted so much for her to have seen what I'd done, but I started to attach those goals to her and I felt it had to be her who was watching over me and who made it happen. I couldn't be so happy and sad at the same time without there being a connection.

From that day onwards, I would associate any goal I scored as being my attachment to my grandma; I would thank her for each goal and for the gift of that moment. I know that scientists will have a legitimate explanation for how I scored my goals, but as I've said previously I would attribute what happened with my actions on the pitch to my grandma as I didn't have a clue how I'd done it. In a spiritual sense, I still feel the same way. She died on the 13th too. Then years later, I made my England debut on the 13th February 2002 and scored against Holland. It felt like the number had a hold on me. One moment I would think that the number was lucky, the next minute it would feel as if it was the opposite.

I suppose you could say that when I went to Turkey, I only had myself to blame that it all went so wrong, as they gave me a choice of which number to wear on my shirt, and yes, you guessed it, I went for number thirteen. I love that shirt now though and I have it framed in my house and look at it with pride about that challenging year in my life. Through writing this book, I stumbled upon the fact that I took the thirteenth penalty in the Euro 2004 quarter-final shootout against Portugal, and obviously I missed. I was looking back at the footage and it just dawned on me that it would be number thirteen. It just had to be. If only I'd have known, perhaps I could have taken a different one!

I'd never worn the number thirteen shirt until I joined Ankaragücü. At Manchester City, when I gave my number to Elano, I asked for the number thirteen, but one of the goalkeepers had it, so I took twelve instead. I never wanted to take someone's shirt from them and I'd had the feeling of my number eleven being requested from me, so I didn't want to repeat it. At Leicester I was given the number 37 when I joined, but then in my last season I took the number thirteen, and I didn't think about the decision at the time, but it turned out that I suffered my final injury at West Ham wearing that number. My final game in football, away at Leeds United, was in the number thirteen shirt too.

Even my little brother Ezra, on my Dad's side, his second son, was born on the 13th. I guess some people are like this, and they look in to signs of the Zodiac and read a lot in to it. I don't. All I know is that the number thirteen always has, and probably always will, keep me on my toes at least.

It's not just numbers that I attach importance to though; my name has always meant a great deal to me. Darius is a unique name and when I was young I didn't really notice many people with the same name as me, so when I did I felt it was strange. My parents chose the name, from The Bible but I soon noticed how people would pronounce it as 'Dar-ee-uss' instead of the correct way for me, 'Dar-eye-uss'. It's just something that I had to get used to, and have had to explain throughout my life, but it's never been a big deal for me. My mom is adamant that her pronunciation is the right one of course.

My dad always wanted me to have a biblical name; I think they were toying with the name Ezekiel and it was important that the name had a link to religion, not so much for my parents, but more for the generation above them. I never met my grandma on my mom's side as she passed away when my mom was young, but they were all religious. As I've mentioned I went to church when I was younger and I enjoyed the experience, but it wasn't something that I was in to as such. I admired the amount of depth to religion and you could look in to it and discover more, but I'm yet to take things further. When my grandma gave me a copy of The Bible, I didn't necessarily read it properly, I was so young. I would just turn to the chapter that mentioned my name, King Darius of Persia. I started to get a bit deep on it as a kid, and started to imagine that I could be that person. I was too young and without a developed intellect to understand it, but I would always turn to the Book of Haggai and I would be reading intently. I can remember the following line verbatim:

'In the second year of King Darius of Persia, on the first day of the sixth month, the word of the lord came through the prophet Haggai to Zerubbabel son of Shealtiel...'

I didn't find out who the others were, but I knew that my name was in The Bible and therefore I had a meaningful name, with history attached to it. I don't necessarily attach myself to religion, but I guess the attachment is there regardless.

When Amani and I came to naming our daughter, it just seemed like the obvious name as we liked it, and there was the association to my name. Amani picked it out really, and as we both agreed, our daughter would be named Persia.

I think that the process of writing this book has helped me to appreciate the role of religion in my life, and how much more I'm yet to discover in that regard. It's amazing how a name can be so inspiring if you dig deeper.

I had some shocking jokes made about me at school around my name. At primary school I was known as 'Dry Arse Vaseline' instead of Darius Vassell. No one wants that, trust me. When I moved to senior school, I had to tell my good friend Adam Colvin, not to breathe a word of that nickname as I didn't want another five years of it. I think this is the first time I've mentioned it in writing since then.

I wanted my final words in this book to be about its title character, our gorgeous daughter, Persia. Being honest here, she wasn't a planned arrival as Amani has said, but we couldn't be happier to have her in our lives and we are grateful every day for her being with us. As soon as I knew Amani was pregnant, my mindset was changed, and will be changed forever. I wasn't playing football by then, in the period that can be very difficult for many footballers, where we are unsure of our next move and our attitude can be greatly changed as a result. I'll never know whether or not that would have happened to me, as Persia was already on her way in to our lives and as such, nothing would ever be the same again. I didn't have the chance to evaluate, reflect on my career and find another path. Immediately, our joint view was how we could make life as good as possible for Persia. I guess it settled us as a married couple too. I felt that everything happened in the right sequence.

I'm certain that knowing Persia was on the way meant that I started to think about the kind of person I was. I knew straight away that I had to study and that I needed to be able to teach her things, so it's no coincidence that I then enrolled on the sports science degree in late 2014, ahead of Persia's birth in January 2015. I'd always been thinking about studying and putting my house up for sale, but now all of a sudden these things were getting done. The thought of becoming a father and the responsibility that comes with it, was so much bigger and more important than, for example, being a professional footballer, so it put everything in to perspective.

For me, there were two crucial periods; being told that you are going to be a father and all the panic and preparation that comes with that, and then the moment that she is here and the big exhale you take, when you realise that all that matters in the world is that Amani and Persia are healthy. It wasn't the easiest pregnancy as Amani has explained, so you put that in to your mind and everything else, any other worries you've ever had, just disappear. We'd had a private hospital suite booked and our route all confirmed, and then as things didn't entail as planned we had to go to Birmingham Heartlands Hospital and I, like Amani, will always be grateful to the fantastic staff there for all they did. All that mattered to me was that the number on the monitor was stable and I didn't care about anything else.

I was in hospital with Amani and her mom, and she was a great support. It allowed me to travel back and forth to check that our dog Denzel and our cat Spartacus were fine and fed whilst preparing the house and bedroom for the new arrival. Between us we stayed with Amani and Persia until they were both home and Amani could sleep. Whilst Persia slept in my arms, I couldn't have been happier. All I did was stare at her. I couldn't take my eyes off my beautiful daughter and I can't do that feeling justice in words here. All fathers would say the same I'm sure. I just wanted to protect her from the world; suddenly everything felt like a threat, even the drive home from hospital was totally different. I couldn't wait to have Amani awake and for us to share the experience together, but she needed to rest now more than ever.

I think that seeing the way that Amani reacted to Persia's arrival, and then witnessing just what an incredible mother she is, has been amazing; one of the great feelings of my life. I see something special, and I know that people see it when they see Amani and Persia together. She is an awesome mom, simply awesome and there's a very close bond between them; one which I'm not going to mess around with.

Whilst Persia has changed my habits and my activities, more important than that she has helped me to come to terms with my own childhood. I feel like I've had some negative things to say about my childhood as I felt like I was the one, out of my family and friends, who always had the finger of blame or fate pointing at me. I realise that we all have felt this way and now and I understand why things have to be the way they are. My mom and I would have strained interactions and I would be so angry, but now I see that she just wanted peace and an equilibrium and that has given me such a strong appreciation of everything that my mom did to give me the best chance in life; the sacrifice and the love she gave is everything I aim to give to Persia. She was on her own, with two jobs and three kids at one stage and that elevates her, if that's possible, beyond what she already is and what she means to me. I see that bond now forming between Amani and my mom and that makes me so proud. Being a parent is so difficult but I see that if you have love, you'll stop at nothing to make something good happen for your children.

From now and in to the future, I want to be the person who supports and encourages Persia as much as possible. I'm so excited about her making her own decisions in life about what she wants to be. I played with a football and that was my choice, so I feel she can find something, excel and maybe even become a professional in her own field. At the very young age she is, 18 months at the time of writing, she is in to dancing, music, singing, playing sport, particularly putting in golf, and just generally being active. She has a lot of interests and I'm so proud to be able to show her things and introduce her to the world of opportunities she has out there. I am fortunate to be able to spend so much time with her and I'm thankful for that every day. I'm learning on the job, but there is no better job than being a father.

I'm proud that Persia is now fully potty trained. I was worried she'd have the occasional midnight accident like I used to as a kid and that wasn't the gift I was looking to pass down to her. We would run the tap for her, something which I learned from my auntie Marion, who would run the tap before I went to bed, as she was babysitting for my mom when she was working nights. Marion and my uncle Steven didn't want me weeing all over their nicely ironed bedsheets. Either way, the toilet got used before bedtime and everyone was happy.

Whilst this book is about my career, and probably wouldn't have been

Working on the golf game in La Manga.

Caddie in training and long-time friend Damian supporting my efforts

Trackdays at Silverstone testing out the bike.

Thai Boxing training away with Manchester City, whilst saying goodbye to Sven on our end-of-season tour in Thailand.

Daniel Sturridge scores the winning goal for England against Wales at Euro 2016; a real talent and good friend who will go on to achieve even more in the future.

Checked into my new hotel room at the Rixos after the night of my eviction from Crowne Plaza. Working out my next move.

With my Ankaragücü teammates out for dinner at a fish restaurant in Ankara.

Nice swing, ideal vacation.

A Darius Vassell coaching session in the Tobago heat with some of the local young players. Huge thanks to Dwight Yorke and the PFA for the opportunity.

Germaine Vassell, forever missed.

Practicing guitar in Bilkent, Turkey.

Madame Tussauds, Japan, during some of our free time on international duty.

Volkan Demir and myself travelling both to and from Turkey during my time at Ankaragücü.

Support from the boys at my engagement party.

The family and Groomsmen on my Wedding Day.

Bride and bridesmaids taking all the time they need.

My Beautiful wife, on the most beautiful day
of our lives.

Many reasons to smile
and a big thank you to
our wedding guests.

The Mother of Persia.

For all the guests at our wedding including Shereen Shabana, Lorna McClelland, Jlloyd Samuel, George Boateng and Dion Dublin to name but a few. These photos are for you all. Also a big thanks to Amani's mother Mary for organising the day. We danced and partied into the early hours. I really hope you enjoyed the highs and lows of my football career.

Wedding photos courtesy of TRS Wedding Photography.

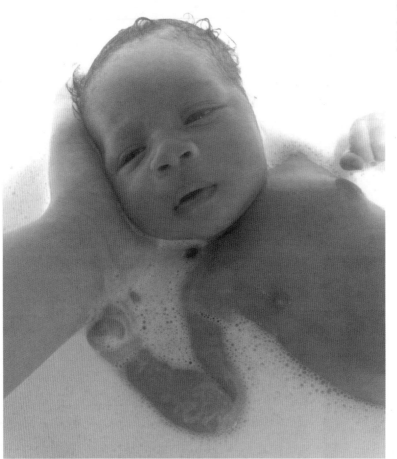

Getting to know
our baby daughter,
Persia Athena
Vassell.

Travelling with
Persia

Taking a power nap

"Practice, Practice, Practice"

Mummy doing Persia's hair

Spending time
with Daddy

"Smiles"
And
"Kisses"

Persia

THIRTEEN

written if I hadn't been a footballer, it almost feels like a love letter to Persia. I wanted her to know about my life before she arrived in the world and I want to be there to support her as her own life develops. There will be a day when she reads this and I want her to know what I've been through, good and bad. I used to spend so much time imagining the lives of my mom and dad when they were young. My dad would describe life outside barefoot, in Jamaica with his brothers, outside in the sun, trying to steer clear of trouble whilst chewing on sugar cane. Mom would talk about school life and her and uncle Steven going back and forth with Grandad trying to get each other in and sometimes out of trouble. I want Persia to enjoy her life but listen to her mom and dad when we say slow down!

My advice for Persia now would be; remain close to mom, she is very important and loves you so much. You have two lovely grandmothers who have many funny stories to share with you, and a family to enjoy and learn from. Make sure you continue to return their love and make us all happy by being you. There are certain things I can't teach, but you should always ask whenever possible. Daddy will find a way and if not, mom probably already has or is working on it.

I am no longer a footballer, I am not rich and famous and I am not a superstar. This statement makes me content because what I am is your father and I will aim to be your hero. You must work for everything you want to achieve and try to be kind to those around you. Life is not one big rainbow ride; you must learn to communicate and take part in creating the rainbow rather than sitting back and expecting everything to happen. You have a gift of making people comfortable and making them smile when they are down. To me this is the greatest gift and I want you to treasure it forever.

Do not worry about people saying you can't do something, or you're not good enough; you can always work out your own way to do things, like I've had to at times. I feel positive that music, dancing and sport is in your life. I believe all three are linked and I hope that continues. I'll do whatever I can to ensure it does.

Everyone has their own background and a story to their lives; a way of perceiving things that's unique to them. Learning to respect this can be very difficult at times but you should always make the effort by listening.

There is so much out there to learn from others. Be grateful for your blessings and be aware of when people are trying to help you. It is a big list but we can work on it together, as I need to start doing more of these things too.

I could never have imagined, or even dreamt that I would one day be writing a book about my footballing life and that book would be for my daughter to read. It is beyond anything I'd ever hoped for. I feel like I don't deserve it sometimes, then I smile and I think of Persia. I want her to know that anything is possible; that I went from inner-city Birmingham and the terraces of Villa Park, to playing football for my country and now to my greatest role, being a father. There are highs and lows in life but if you want to achieve something, you must believe in yourself and be willing to work for it.

My gift to you is, 'The Road to Persia'.

FROM THE
AUTHOR

Darius Vassell is not your stereotypical former footballer; that much is clear. As he pulled up outside Leicester City Football Club's stadium on Wednesday 27th October 2010, it was also clear that he was a man looking to get back to what he did best, playing football, after a more than challenging 12 months in Turkey.

I'd love to say that as we shook hands for the first time, in the car park, and I briefed him on the media interviews and school half-term signing session he had arrived for, that I could picture us writing his life story together, but nothing could be further from the truth. In fact, I can remember that he wasn't actually that keen on doing the interviews that day, but knew they came with the territory. He knew he was going to be asked about Turkey, when all he wanted to do was to get back on the pitch.

Years later, after we'd both left our respective roles at Leicester City, we met at The Nottinghamshire Golf & Country Club, at a charity event organised by his former Aston Villa teammate Ian Taylor and ex-Birmingham City man Michael Johnson. Darius and I chatted and arranged to stay in touch; since that day my company has worked with him, we still do today, and in 2015 we tentatively discussed writing his autobiography. I didn't really get to know Darius properly until we penned this book together though. That's when I learned about his life away from football, with nothing off-limits for him as he strived to produce a book that represented all aspects of his life. He has shown that he is thorough, thoughtful and dedicated. Journalists from his playing days may be surprised to learn of his openness, as he was the guy who would give a one-word answer, when ten were required, but he never craved the limelight; it just found him.

We've sat for hours in his beautiful home, surrounded by acres of West Midlands countryside, with his lovely wife and daughter, Amani and Persia, popping in to say hello from time-to-time, and we've drank endless cups of green tea and eaten boxes of shortbread biscuits, and I think and feel it's been worth it.

Darius wanted *The Road to Persia* to be a vehicle to thank his friends and family for all their support, but also to clarify how and why certain things happened to him. Trials, broken legs, penalty heartbreak and toe drills, plus all those managers he played for and the men he played alongside, it's all in here; stories you'll have heard and stories he's told for the first time.

He was the unsung, super-sub and occasional hero of England's golden generation; a Villa fan who lived the dream of thousands of Birmingham boys, and whose light flickered brightly, but in all honesty probably not often enough for his explosive natural talent.

Darius may have been a man of few words as a player, yet there's over 100,000 of them here to make up for that. I'd like to thank you for reading the book and hope you've enjoyed it as much as I've enjoyed writing it.

Dean Eldredge
Co-author

TO THE
READER

A special thank you for making it this far with me on my journey; I am very appreciative of the time taken to read this book in its entirety and I welcome the positives and negatives that arise from its release. To have my entire footballing career relived, scrutinised and recorded within a book is an achievement within itself and I'm very proud to have this story to tell.

I would like to briefly describe the process that led to *The Road to Persia* from my own perspective.

I decided to write the book in order to remember and share the amazing experiences I have had over the 13 years spent as a professional in the sport. Once Dean and I had agreed to get the ball rolling, we quickly worked out our most efficient way of working and then quite frankly... got on with it. Utilising the many tools available in this era of technology we have remained connected and have navigated my career to the point where we have little left to cover. Exactly the feeling required for a comprehensive review of my footballing experiences.

Dean has spent hour upon hour on the motorway and on his computer, all for the book. During recording sessions at my home we have steadily covered the majority of my life and I now find him reminding me of some of the talking points I managed to forget and places I have visited. Reminiscing often made me very nervous for myself as I was in the zone, replaying an event from my memory. With Dean sitting opposite with the recorder, I would look up after realising that I may be going off on one, only to see Dean just as into it as I was, telling me to 'keep going!'

To say Dean was committed to the process would be an understatement; it really has been an enjoyable experience and I encourage current players to make the most out of their careers and make provisions to write their own stories for when they retire. It has been a great tool for me to understand where I went wrong and to consider how close I got to greatness. At the same time, it's always good to bring back those 'football feelings' and share them with those that speak our universal language and more importantly to those that are learning it.

I look forward to the day that my children get to read this together and argue, like I used to with Vanessa, about who's the best and who's quicker, and who can jump the farthest.

I hope this book and or elements of it are able to inspire those that read it. I hope it answers those questions you may have had about me or my career and I hope that it serves as a fitting end to my life as a professional footballer.

"My time, my moment…I've been here before
I possess everything needed to shoot and score
Clockwork, footwork become the same
The dream becomes real when I hear my name."

APPEARANCES & GOALS

Brackets indicate substitute appearances

CLUB CAREER

Aston Villa
124 (77) appearances
45 goals

Manchester City
110 (14) appearances
22 goals

Ankaragücü
25 appearances
4 goals

Leicester City
37 (8) appearances
6 goals

Total club career appearances 296 (99)
Total club career goals 77

INTERNATIONAL CAREER

England U18s
5 caps
5 goals

England U21s
11 caps
2 goals

England
22 caps (6 starts and 16 as a substitute)
6 goals

Goals for the England senior team came as follows:
13 February 2002 vs Netherlands at the Amsterdam Arena in a 1-1 draw
17 April 2002 vs Paraguay at Anfield, Liverpool in a 4-0 win
26 May 2002 vs Cameroon in Kobe, Japan in a 2-2 draw
2 April 2003 vs Turkey at the Stadium of Light, Sunderland in a 2-0 win
5 June 2004 vs Iceland at the City of Manchester Stadium, two goals in a
6-1 win

HONOURS

2001 Intertoto Cup
2004 FA Summer Tournament

ACHIEVEMENTS & NOTABLE LANDMARKS

1998 Senior debut for Aston Villa
2002 Played in the World Cup for England in Japan and South Korea,
reaching the quarter-finals
2004 Played in the European Championship for England in Portugal,
reaching the quarter-finals
2005 Manchester City paid £2million to sign Darius Vassell from Aston
Villa
2009 Joined Turkish Super Lig side Ankaragücü
2010 Returned to English football with Leicester City
2016 Retired from professional football aged 35

Holds the record for scoring in 46 Premier League matches without
losing between 2001-2008

BIBLIOGRAPHY

Books
Aston Villa The England Story

Newspapers
Birmingham Evening Mail
Sunday Mercury
The Guardian
Manchester Evening News
Leicester Mercury

Websites
BBC
The FA
Aston Villa Football Club
Soccerbase
Soccerway
England Football Online